THE ANCIENT GLASS OF
CANTERBURY CATHEDRAL

CHRIST APPEARING TO ST. MARY MAGDALENE. The pictorial medallion has in recent times been enclosed within borders and ornament contemporaneous with it to fill Window I in the Water Tower. About 1210–1220. P. 113.

The Ancient Glass
of
Canterbury Cathedral

BY BERNARD RACKHAM

C.B., F.S.A., FORMERLY KEEPER OF THE DEPARTMENT
OF CERAMICS, VICTORIA AND ALBERT MUSEUM

WITH A FOREWORD BY THE LATE
ARCHBISHOP LORD LANG OF LAMBETH

PUBLISHED FOR THE

FRIENDS OF CANTERBURY CATHEDRAL

BY LUND HUMPHRIES AND COMPANY LIMITED

LONDON MCMXLIX

BOSTON BOOK AND ART SHOP INC., BOSTON, MASSACHUSETTS

Made and printed in Great Britain by Lund Humphries & Co. Ltd., London and Bradford

TO THE MEMORY OF

WILLIAM RICHARD LETHABY

'It is impossible to explain in words the content of perfect Gothic art. It is frank, clear, gay; it is passionate, mystical and tender; it is energetic, clear, sharp, strong and healthy. It would be a mistake to try to define it in terms of form alone; it embodied a spirit, an aspiration, an age.'

CONTENTS

CONTENTS (*continued*)

ILLUSTRATIONS

FOREWORD

I T is a privilege to be allowed to write a short prefatory note to this book. But it is a privilege of which I am in no way worthy. My only qualification for it is that I have had my 'seat' as Archbishop in two great churches which are singularly rich in ancient stained glass, York Minster and Canterbury Cathedral. Happily in both, thanks to wise foresight and skilful care, this glass has survived the ravages of two wars. At York, a greater quantity of beautiful glass has been preserved; but at Canterbury, in many of the windows, the stained glass dating from the great age of glass painting, the twelfth and thirteenth centuries, there is a richness and beauty of colour unrivalled except perhaps in such great churches as Chartres or Bourges.

There is need of some special and authoritative record, description and interpretation of this incomparable treasure. I know how greatly my own delight in it has been increased by expert guidance. It is hoped that the present volume, for whose publication the Friends of Canterbury Cathedral have made themselves responsible, may supply this need. The text comes from the very special knowledge and judgment and loving enthusiasm of Mr. Bernard Rackham; and the reproductions, both in colour and monochrome, are due to the well-known skill and experience of the publishers, Messrs. Lund Humphries & Co., who have been able to make full use of the latest resources of the art of photography and of colour reproduction. Both they and Mr. Rackham have done their utmost to make the book worthy of its subject.

Doubtless it is primarily those who have some knowledge of ancient stained glass, and of the art which created it, who will specially welcome this volume. But it is the hope of the Friends of Canterbury Cathedral that it may be accessible to all who share their love of that glorious church, and to all who value the treasures handed down to us from the art, the imagination, the reverence of the Middle Ages.

LANG OF LAMBETH
Abp.

November 30, 1945

PREFACE

THE recent war made it necessary to take measures for the protection of the ancient glass of Canterbury Cathedral. Its temporary removal from the windows to a place of safety was a disadvantage not altogether without compensations; for it presented an opportunity, before the glass-paintings were put back into their places, of studying them closely under conditions which are impossible when they are *in situ*. It also provided the occasion for continuing the detailed photographic record which was begun but not completed in 1919, after the earlier great war. In these circumstances it was suggested that a monograph on the subject, with plentiful illustrations, should be produced on a scale such as had never before been attempted. The project was taken up by the Council of the Friends of Canterbury Cathedral, and they honoured me by asking me to write the text of the work now published.

I wish to record my gratitude for help I have received from many quarters in the preparation of the book. In the first place I should like to express my appreciation of the encouragement given at the inception of the work by the late Archbishop Lord Lang of Lambeth, by his gracious consent to contribute a foreword: it is a matter of deep regret that he did not live to see the completion of a project in which he showed so lively an interest. To the Dean and Chapter, and to the whole of the Cathedral staff, I am indebted for granting me needful facilities and ready access to all sources of material contributing to the study of my subject. In particular I must mention Mr. Samuel Caldwell, without whose constant help always given with the utmost willingness in spite of his advanced age, the writing of this book would have been quite impossible; no one living can rival him in his knowledge of the windows, derived from a long life devoted chiefly to their care and maintenance, and many observations in the following pages are due solely to his memory and to powers of observation trained by long and intimate contact with the glass itself. Nor must I pass over the name of his assistant, Mr. George Easton, with whom I spent many pleasant and profitable hours in a close examination of the glass, made possible by the measures taken for its safety during the recent time of trouble. At this point also it is appropriate to speak of the help I have received from the Hon. Steward and Treasurer of the Friends of Canterbury Cathedral—Miss Margaret Babington; I have been obliged to enlist her aid, by letter or by personal importunacy, in dealing with countless small difficulties of a practical kind, and she has always shown the greatest readiness to make light of such additions to a programme of daily work already overcharged.

Preface

Turning to my obligations in the sphere of literature and history, I am glad to acknowledge the generous help given by the late Mr. W. P. Blore, the Chapter Librarian, in placing the resources of the Library at my disposal and in making many valuable suggestions, recorded where appropriate in the text, as to the bearing on my subject of documentary material, much of it unpublished; his Assistant, Mr. William Urry, has also aided me with alacrity in this department of my labours. In this connection also I must not omit my indebtedness to the courtesy of the late Rev. C. Eveleigh Woodruff; Mr. John Harvey has also kindly placed at my disposal relevant observations made in the course of work preliminary to his recent publications.

In matters of heraldry and genealogy I have had the advantage of consulting Commander A. W. B. Messenger, R.N., Mr. H. S. London, Mr. Anthony Wagner, Richmond Herald, and my old friend Mr. A. J. Toppin, York Herald. In connection with the St. Maurice panel in the Royal Window, I have corresponded with the late Professor Hans Lehmann, of Zurich, Professor Jean Helbig, of Brussels, and my former colleague, Mr. A. Van de Put, all of whom were able to give me valuable information for which I owe them thanks. The Rev. Professor Claude Jenkins has, with much appreciated patience, answered lengthy enquiries concerning certain troublesome points of epigraphy and iconography. Among others who have kindly responded to my questions on various matters are Sir Ellis Minns, Mr. John Knowles, of York, Mr. Lewis Edwards and Dr. E. G. Millar, whilst a word of acknowledgment is due in this place to my literary predecessors, the late Dr. A. J. Mason and Canon Crum; their handbooks have a value far greater than might be supposed from the modest scale of their format. Lastly, I am deeply indebted to my wife for her co-operation throughout the long processes of gathering the material on the spot, sometimes under difficult conditions, and of subsequent sorting and preparation for final drafting.

On the technical side of production my thanks are due in the first place to an amateur, Mr. C. E. Sexton, who kindly placed skill, apparatus, and time at my disposal for the taking of photographs used in some of the illustrations; Mr. P. B. Chatwin and Mr. Sydney Pitcher respectively are also to be thanked for two of the photographs reproduced in Plate B, and Mr. C. J. Torr for a film enlarged in Plate 62. Many of the plates are from negatives made officially by the staff of the Victoria and Albert Museum, when the first World War gave an opportunity similar to that which has lately been repeated; it is with the permission of the Director and Secretary that these have been available. Other plates are from photographs by Mr. W. Fisk-Moore, of Canterbury. The photographic work for the colour plates has been in the experienced hands of Thomas Fall Ltd., under the supervision of Mr. E. H. Parker; no small contribution to their excellence was made by their artist, the late Miss Brodrick, whose death shortly after her share in the process had been completed is deplored by all acquainted with her skill in this department of colour reproduction. It may be claimed that the difficult task of rendering on paper the chromatic qualities of stained glass has never been carried through with such fidelity to the effect of the original. Many of the photographs from various sources used for the monochrome plates were also specially adapted for reproduction by Mr. Parker. The diagrams of the windows inserted in the text are from drawings by Mr. Ivo Scarff, of the City of Canterbury College of Art and Crafts, and Mr. Gerald E. Tooke. For the dignified and admirable manner in which the book has been produced my grateful acknowledgments are due to the publishers and printers, Messrs. Lund Humphries & Co. Ltd.; that it has been brought to so high a level of excellence is owing largely to the close personal attention of Mr. Norman Parley, who took the greatest interest in the scheme from the start.

BERNARD RACKHAM

Guildford, 1948

INTRODUCTION

§1 General

IT is reasonable to assume that Canterbury Cathedral, when rebuilt by Lanfranc after the fire of 1067, was intended by its designers, like other major churches of the Middle Ages in western and northern Europe, to be adorned with stained glass. This must however remain a matter of conjecture, since the remnants still existing of Lanfranc's building do not include any vestiges of its windows. Nor have we any indication of the character of the windows in the enlarged and short-lived choir built by Priors Ernulph and Conrad in substitution for that of Lanfranc; we can only surmise what they may have been like from the remnants of Abbot Suger's almost contemporary windows at St. Denis, or from the panels, slightly more recent in date, still to be seen incorporated in the later windows at York Minster.* It is only when we come to portions of the cathedral which were erected after the fire of 1174 by William of Sens and his successor, William the Englishman, under Archbishop Richard, that we have surviving evidence, and evidence in abundance. The glass still remaining from the windows of the reconstructed choir and transepts and from the eastward extension of the church carried out as a sequel to this rebuilding, though a mere fraction of what must once have existed, constitutes the earliest considerable body of stained glass extant in England, and a monument of great importance in the history of medieval European art as a whole.

With the rapid and vast development of the art of glass-painting in the eleventh and twelfth centuries the windows of a large church came to be regarded as an opportunity of presenting, in pictorial form, and in a manner more inescapably conspicuous than could be achieved by the agency of any other craft, the whole

* It is well to point out that the words of the only ancient authority on the subject, William of Malmesbury, in his *Gesta Pontificum* (Rolls Series, London, 1870, p. 138), may imply no more than that the windows were filled with good translucent glass, and do not warrant the assumption that the glass was coloured (*Cantiae dejectam priorem partem ecclesiae, quam Lanfrancus aedificaverit, adeo splendide reerexit, ut nihil tale possit in Anglia videri* in vitrearum fenestrarum luce, *in marmorei pavimenti nitore, in diversicoloribus picturis*).

narrative of Bible history and, by means of allegory, the principles of Christian doctrine. The many windows of a great cathedral like that of Canterbury gave scope for schematic treatment as an orderly concerted whole.

In all discussions of the evolution of stained glass it has to be remembered that far less has been preserved than has been irretrievably lost—arguments based on the body of work still to be seen are apt to be misleading; the early Gothic churches are but few which exhibit connected series of windows so systematically carried through as we find them at Canterbury (allowance being made for the fact that many of the panels in the cathedral have been displaced in the course of the vicissitudes which the windows have undergone, and are now no longer in the positions they are known once to have occupied). Chartres Cathedral enjoys at the present day a primacy in reputation to which on artistic grounds it is fully entitled, although it owes much to the good fortune by which, unlike most other French Cathedrals, it has retained intact all but a very few of its ancient windows; but in the glazing of the church when it was rebuilt in the thirteenth century, after the fire of 1194 which destroyed all but the west end, with its windows, of the earlier Romanesque building, no very systematic sequence was observed. Private individuals and corporations vied with one another as donors of pictorial windows, but these are so far from presenting a logical sequence that, for example, in the seven clerestory windows of the apse, forming the eastward termination of the vista, the subjects of the lateral windows have no express relationship with that of the middle window, which depicts three incidents from the life of the Virgin Mary to whom the Cathedral is dedicated; even in the design of these windows there is no uniformity. For a logical scheme of a didactic nature such as was to be found at Canterbury as rebuilt after the fire of 1174, we may compare later examples such as those of Winchester College Chapel (now surviving *in situ* only in nineteenth-century copies), Great Malvern Priory, Fairford Church and the chapel of King's College, Cambridge; in all these late Gothic buildings the pictorial windows form part of the original architectural conception and were inserted, if not at the outset, at no long interval after the completion of the structure. The Abbey church of Altenberg, near Cologne, offers a rare early Gothic example of non-pictorial glass remaining in its entirety from the inception of the building, dating from about 1300; in accordance with the austere Cistercian rule, its windows, with the exception of that in the west front inserted later, are devoid of pictorial subjects, displaying only a variety of merely decorative patterns.

A worshipper entering the choir of Canterbury would have seen facing him as he raised his eyes towards the clerestory of the apse, behind the High Altar, three windows appropriate to the dedication of the Cathedral Church of Christ; each contained three panels depicting the most important incidents in the Life and Passion of Our Lord, from the Nativity to the Ascension. Flanking these were possibly a pair of windows as now restored by George Austin, the Younger, relating to Moses and John the Baptist as the earliest and latest of the prophets who foretold His coming. These five windows in the apse interrupted a series in the clerestory of the choir, beginning and ending at its western end on the north and south sides respectively. The series displays the lineal descent of Christ from Adam as set forth in the third chapter of St. Luke's gospel (with six figures from the St. Matthew pedigree inserted to give the requisite number). In each window were two figures, one above another. In the upper half of the first window of the series was the subject, now lost, of the Creation of Adam; the lower contained the figure of Adam delving, still existing, but now placed in the West Window of the Nave. The last window of the series, facing the Adam window, was occupied by figures of the Virgin and Christ. For a parallel to this scheme of clerestory windows we may turn to Bourges Cathedral; in the clerestory of its eastern end, slightly later in date than that of Canterbury, we find an easternmost window of two lights filled with figures of St. Stephen as patron of the church and the Virgin and Child, flanked by nineteen figures on each side— on one side, the Prophets together with Moses, David and St. John the Baptist; on the other, the Apostles, the Evangelists and three of the earliest Disciples. A difference from the Canterbury scheme is that at Bourges each light contains a single figure only, standing, whereas at Canterbury there are two figures in each window.

Facing one another at clerestory level in the end walls of the North-East and South-East Transepts were circular windows; the surviving remnants of the northern one show that it was devoted to the illustration of 'the Law and the Prophets', with Moses and the Synagogue in the centre. The corresponding window in the South-East Transept doubtless symbolized the Church and the Gospel as in the modern restoration designed by Austin.

In the aisles of the choir, as we know from an ancient manuscript in the Chapter Library, of which more will be said on a later page, were twelve 'theological' windows illustrating the Gospel narrative and its sequels, together with the subjects from the Old Testament by which these events were held to be foreshadowed. What was here set forth was epitomized in the easternmost window of the Cathedral, the middle window of Becket's Crown, still fortunately remaining for the most part intact. This was doubtless flanked on either side by windows with appropriate subjects; one of these, to be more fully discussed on a later page, contained a 'Tree of Jesse',— the genealogy of Christ concisely represented in symbolical form. The crypt immediately below Becket's Crown served originally as the Lady Chapel; its middle window, as we now know from the remnants of it recently retrieved for the Cathedral, was appropriately devoted to the glorification of the Virgin. The six windows on either side of the Trinity Chapel flanking the spot on which the shrine of Becket stood from the time of the Translation of his body out of its original tomb in the Crypt in 1220 until the shrine was destroyed in 1538, form a sequence of extraordinary interest as being among the few early medieval windows depicting incidents which occurred at no long interval of time before the windows were erected. They are of value as evidence of the costumes, weapons, boats, harness and furnishing, both domestic and ecclesiastical, in use soon after the period of the incidents themselves. For parallels we may turn to the windows with scenes from the life of Becket in the cathedrals of Chartres and Sens; both places had personal connections with the Saint and with Canterbury, the former as the See occupied after his death by his secretary, John of Salisbury, who was present in the Cathedral when he was murdered, the latter as the scene of his exile. Of the twelve Canterbury windows a considerable proportion have been destroyed. Those that remain relate only to miracles reputed to have happened after the death of the Saint, but it may be taken as certain that these were a sequel to others depicting, like those at Chartres and Sens, incidents in his life and martyrdom.

Other portions of the window-scheme in the rebuilding after the fire still remain in medallions from windows relating to two early archbishops, St. Alphege and St. Dunstan, which were doubtless placed originally in the immediate neighbourhood of their altar tombs on the north and south sides of the High Altar. For the original filling of the windows in Lanfranc's Norman Nave, which was remodelled in the fourteenth century after the plans of Henry Yevele,* we have no evidence. The existence of panels with figures of the thirteenth century, now in the Water Tower, which are plausibly conjectured to have been originally in the early Nave windows, seems to suggest that when first built these latter may have been filled, like the Altenberg windows mentioned above, with simple pattern glass for which these remaining figures, doubtless forming parts of a consistent scheme, were substituted at a later stage.

The three great Late Gothic windows at the west end of the Nave and in the two western Transepts have suffered many changes and rearrangements since they were first erected, but of two of them enough remains to show that they also were designed each to form a self-contained series of pictures developing a specific scheme. In both of these, heraldry, entirely absent from the early windows, played a conspicuous part, and in that of the North-West Transept, the 'Royal' window, the donors were not content to be represented by their blazonry alone but were themselves depicted in full-length portraiture. The West Window displayed in the two upper ranges of its main lights figures of the Kings of England; in the small tracery lights above were the Twelve Apostles and the sixteen Prophets, Major and Minor. The Royal Window had a more complex scheme; as will be explained when it is described in detail, its principal theme, as we learn from Richard Culmer whose misdirected zeal was responsible for its mutilation, was the Seven Joys of the Virgin Mary.

---

* See Arthur Oswald, 'Canterbury Cathedral: The Nave and its Designer' (*Burlington Magazine*, Vol. lxxv, 1939, pp. 221–228); also John H. Harvey, *Henry Yevele*, London, 1944.

§2 Development of Stained Glass Technique

FOR readers unfamiliar with the technicalities of stained glass it may be helpful to give a brief account of the development of the art, of which the various stages can be studied in the windows of Canterbury Cathedral. Glass-painting is essentially an art of Western Europe and, in particular, of the Western Church; it was unknown before the Christian era, as indeed was the glazing of windows, which was an outcome of the invention of the blowing-iron, about the time of the foundation of the Roman Empire (small panes of glass seem also to have been made by the Romans by the method of casting in a bed of sand). It was also discovered that by adding metallic oxides to the molten mass of ingredients or 'metal' in the 'pots' in which the materials were fused in the furnace, glass could be dyed or stained to various colours; glass thus stained is known to craftsmen as coloured 'pot-metal', to distinguish it from that which is coloured on the surface only and not throughout its substance. The principal colours thus obtainable are blue from cobalt, green from copper or iron, brown and yellow from iron, deep red or 'ruby' from copper, and mauve from manganese. Already in the early days of the Byzantine Empire it is probable that windows were made in patterns of glass of various colours, held together in a lattice of wood or plaster, as they still are in modern times in the Levant; it was however the invention of flexible 'leads' as a framework for the pieces of glass that made possible the stained-glass window as we know it in the West. Windows could thus be made to display not only regular geometrical patterns but also pictorial compositions in colours.

Exactly when this development came about is unknown; the oldest surviving remnants of stained-glass windows, at Augsburg and Le Mans, dating from the eleventh century or perhaps earlier, are evidence of an art no longer in its infancy. The earliest stained glass in England is somewhat later in date. There are small windows or fragmentary panels at York Minster and elsewhere that are attributed to an earlier period than any at Canterbury; but Canterbury possesses the only considerable quantity of glass in England for which a date before the end of the twelfth century can confidently be claimed.

It is sometimes supposed that enamel painting on stained glass is a relatively late innovation, but this is a misconception. Whilst it is possible to make a patterned or pictorial window entirely of glass and leadwork, without any kind of pigment as an accessory, and such windows have occasionally been produced—rather as a *tour-de-force* by modern artists—this is an exceptional method, of very rare occurrence until the end of the Middle Ages. It is true that in a good stained-glass window the leadwork

5

is always not merely a container for the glass but also an integral part of the design; but the details of a picture, such as the features of a face, folds of drapery, or petals of a rosette, were from the earliest times done by means of painting with a brush in a black enamel pigment derived from iron. In order that this pigment should adhere permanently to the surface of the glass, it is necessary that it should be fixed by fusion, at a relatively low temperature, in a small oven known as a 'muffle'; to protect it from decay due to exposure to the weather the pigment is applied on the inner side of the glass.* Lines thus painted are known by the glazier as 'trace-lines', and the delicate graduation of them with the brush as required, from dense black masses to a tapering fineness which rivals the penwork in the most sensitive of 'Old Master drawings', is eloquent proof of the skill and sure-handedness of the medieval glass-painter. Even in early work we find not only linear brushwork, but also passages of enamel laid as a thin smear where shading is required—sometimes on the reverse or exterior side of the glass, as in a woman's drapery in a medallion of Window XII in the Trinity Chapel (see p. 108)—or to reduce, in places, the vividness of the coloured 'pot-metal', thus throwing up in contrasted brilliancy the unshaded portions. In later medieval glass this method was employed with more calculated refinement and sometimes carried to excess, producing an effect of three-dimensional relief which is hardly compatible with the peculiar properties of the materials; the glazier began to lose sight of the all-important fact that transmitted light is a medium of his craft no less essential than coloured glass, lead, and enamel pigment.

A procedure of which the glass-painter can avail himself with telling effectiveness is that of scratching out a pattern through a coat of black enamel; this was done commonly with the stick of the paintbrush, and where very fine work is needed (more especially in late medieval and Renaissance glass-painting), with a pin or needle point. In the earliest extant stained glass this 'scratching out' technique was used particularly for inscriptions; Canterbury has innumerable examples to show of this method in the inscriptions on the windows of the twelfth and thirteenth centuries, written in superb Lombardic letters, shining through a ground of dense black. In later times the effect was reversed; the ground was left white or coloured, and the inscription, whether in Lombardic characters or—as became customary from about the middle of the fourteenth century—in Gothic 'black letter', was painted in black.

About the end of the thirteenth century a second pigment was added to the glass-painter's apparatus. This was the silver-yellow stain—derived from chloride or sulphide of silver—which, where applied to the surface of glass and fired, imparts to it a golden or brassy yellow hue; in the hands of late medieval and Renaissance glaziers it was developed so as to cover a range from pale primrose yellow to tawny and deep amber tones. M. Jean Lafond, in a recently published paper, has shown

---

* A remarkable and quite exceptional case in which the enamel lines of the drawing are painted of set purpose on *both* sides of a piece of white glass is the subject of comment on p. 64.

that this innovation made its first appearance in France, and about 1310.* This procedure possesses the obvious advantage that whereas, for instance, in depicting a crowned head or a gold-bordered white robe separate pieces of white and yellow glass divided by leads had formerly been necessary, a single piece of white glass could now be employed, coloured where requisite with the silver-yellow stain. The fifteenth-century windows at Canterbury provide ample illustration of this development. By using blue instead of white glass it became possible with the same expedient to render on one piece of glass green trees and a blue sky, and this is a feature frequently to be observed in windows from the last years of the fifteenth century onwards.†

About the end of the Gothic period further additions were made to the glass-painter's palette. First came a red, invented in France and inappropriately known by the name of Jean Cousin, a glass-painter who is wrongly credited with an invention made before his time; this was found especially useful in painting faces, for giving natural hues to lips and complexion, and was also serviceable in heraldry, particularly where a charge in silver or gold on a field of gules or *vice versa* had to be rendered on a small scale in elaborate quarterings. Blue and amethyst-coloured enamels, made by mixing powdered glass of these hues with an oily medium, were the last important innovations of the sixteenth century, much used by Swiss and Dutch artists, as exemplified by two Canterbury heraldic panels of the time of Archbishop Abbot.

Another technicality which needs explanation is that of ruby glass. Unlike other colours, sheets of ruby glass always consist of two layers, a thicker layer of 'white', that is, unstained and approximately colourless glass, and a thin film (known as a 'flash') of ruby, obtained during the process of blowing the glass by dipping a bulb of white 'metal' in a 'pot' of metal stained red with oxide of copper. The copper stain is so potent that a sheet of glass dyed with it throughout its thickness would be so dark as to be almost opaque. This circumstance proved of great value to the glazier when the idea was conceived of removing the ruby film, where required, by grinding on a wheel and thus exposing the underlying white. By this method heraldic charges in argent on a field of gules, or intricate white patterns on a red robe, could be obtained with a single piece of glass, obviating the employment of leads to separate the white from the red. By enlisting the silver-yellow stain already mentioned to give a golden hue to the exposed white portions, a charge of gold on a field of gules could

---

* 'Essai historique sur le Jaune d'Argent' in *Trois Études sur la Technique du Vitrail*, Rouen, 1943 (reprinted from the *Bulletin de la Société d'Émulation*, Rouen, 1943); on pp. 57–65 M. Lafond cites examples from the Cathedral and from St. Ouen, Rouen, dating from the second and third decades of the fourteenth century; he surmises that the evidence of windows in Paris, now no longer in existence, would have shown that the new stain first appeared in that city.

† Though M. Lafond (*op. cit., p. 61*) shows that from its very first introduction yellow stain was used on coloured as well as white glass, its employment as a convenient medium in landscape-painting became general only later.

be similarly rendered, as in the lions of the Royal Arms of England; of this there are many instances in the Canterbury windows, interesting to compare with earlier examples of the same arms where the lions have been laboriously cut out in separate pieces of yellow glass and inserted with surrounding leads in the ruby glass of the field.

In some of the thirteenth-century pictorial panels in the Cathedral great ingenuity has been shown in taking advantage of the ruby 'flash'; thus, in the Passover scene in the East Window of the Corona, there is a touch of ruby on the white glass of the knife in the hands of the sacrificing attendant to represent the stain on its tip from the blood of the victim; for this detail it seems as if part of the sheet of glass had been selected, perhaps near its edge, where the ruby—always liable to be uneven in intensity and 'streaky'—had not 'taken'. Again, in a Miracle scene in Window IV of the Trinity Chapel, the healing blood mingled in the Water of St. Thomas, which is being poured into a bowl, is represented by pinkish glass flashed with ruby.

The method of 'flashing' adopted, for the reason stated above, for ruby glass came to be applied to glass of other colours also, where this was an advantage; thus, in a shield with the Royal Arms in the West window, blue-'flashed' glass has been used for the arms of France Modern in the first and fourth quarters; the three golden lilies have been rendered by grinding away the blue film so as to expose the white, which has then been painted with yellow stain. There are also instances at Canterbury of heraldic charges in which holes have been ground right through a sheet of coloured glass, and charges in glass of another colour inserted in them. A good illustration of this process is afforded by the fifteenth-century shield in the North Transept with the arms of the Salt Fishmongers' Company (see p. 153); here, blue glass has been inserted in holes ground out of the yellow glass in the bows of the keys. A later example is that of the shield with the Tudor Royal Arms given to the Cathedral by Miss Athill (see p. 177); in this case it is the golden lilies of France on a blue field which have been rendered by the process in question.

§3 Development of Window Structure

THE design of a window is affected not only by the methods by which the glass is stained and painted, as described above, but also by the manner in which the coloured glass, when leaded in panels of suitable size, is made fast in the window opening. Lead being a pliable material, it is risky to expose too large a surface of leaded glass to the pressure of the wind without some rigid reinforcement. This is provided by iron rods, cemented into the masonry, to which the panels are attached; the attachment is effected nowadays by copper wires soldered on to the lead borders of the panels, but in the Middle Ages ribbons of lead were used for this purpose. In windows or lights of narrow dimensions a few horizontal rods at intervals are all that is necessary; such rods are known as 'saddle-bars', and in Dutch by the expressive term *windijzers* ('wind-irons'). In larger openings vertical as well as horizontal rods are necessary, and in the great windows of the twelfth and thirteenth centuries before stone mullions were introduced to divide the window into lights, a large framework was employed known by the French name *armature*. The designing of this framework gave the glass-painter great freedom of composition. The wide field at his disposal presented by the window-surface could be broken up in a variety of patterns by planning the framework not only on severely rectilinear lines but also into compartments of other geometrical forms—circular, segmental, quatrefoil, or almond-shaped, combined in endless variety. This development is nowhere better illustrated than in the windows of the eastern part of Canterbury Cathedral. Although in many cases the stained glass with which they were formerly filled has disappeared, the iron *armatures* still remain, differently designed in each case, except for correspondence in some cases in windows occupying the same relative positions on opposite sides of the building; some of them were sadly twisted out of shape through enemy action in the recent war, but have been skilfully repaired in the city by Mr. George Shilling, at the old forge in Best Lane.*

This wonderful diversity introduced by the varied designing of the *armatures* had a relatively short duration, through the twelfth and the earlier part of the thirteenth century, and seems to have been confined to that single artistic province which France and England together at that time formed. We have here an illustration of the mutual interplay of influence of architecture upon glazing and glazing upon architecture. The wide windows of the Romanesque (or 'Norman') and Early Gothic periods were so many arched openings that had to be filled with a medium admitting light and gave the glaziers their wonderful opportunity for varied designing in iron, lead, and coloured glass. As stained glass developed and became an element, ever more impor-tant, in the beautifying of the fabric, the evolution of vaulting, which was at the same time making possible the reduction in mass of the roof-supports, brought about the increasing elimination of the wall-space between the piers; as the windows were enlarged and widened, so it became necessary to subdivide them, and the mullioned window was born, with the result that in the great churches walling gave place to vast screens of glass supported by a network of slender masonry—mullions, transoms, and tracery—filling almost the entire interval between the piers, as we see it pre-eminently in the French cathedrals and in such English buildings as Henry VII's Chapel at Westminster and King's College Chapel, Cambridge. In the nave of

---

* See *F.C.C. Eighteenth Annual Report* (1945), p. 21 and pl. facing p. 25.

Canterbury Cathedral, slightly earlier than these in date, and in the windows of the West end and of the two Western transepts, we find the development has already gone some distance in the direction of these extremes.

We now find, in these later stages, that an evolution begun with a view to yielding greater opportunities to the glazier ended in operating against his freedom of invention in design, as a Dutch writer, Dr. A. van der Boom, has recently pointed out.* The subdivisions between the close-set mullions necessary for supporting the tracery stonework restricted the glass-painter to rectilinear divisions generally narrow in proportion to their height, giving less scope for panels of varied and interesting outline, and for the system of related pictorial compositions of which the early windows of Canterbury, in the Choir Aisles and the Trinity Chapel, give such admirable examples. The way was thus pointed to the standing figure under a canopy as the easiest method of filling the space, perhaps accompanied at its base by a heraldic shield or a small pictorial composition incongruous in scale with the figure. Some very beautiful windows were designed on these lines, particularly where an ever-increasing proportion of shimmering white glass, made all the more brilliant in effect by touches of golden yellow stain, succeeded to the jewelled brightness of colour characteristic of earlier work. Of the intermediate stages in the evolution, as they can be seen at Merton College Chapel, Oxford, and pre-eminently in England at York Minster and in France at St. Ouen, Rouen, Canterbury has almost nothing to show (a small tracery-light remains from a window no longer existing, see p. 115); the 'Decorated' window in St. Anselm's Chapel, now filled with modern glass by Messrs. Clayton and Bell, may well have provided a fine example of this kind. Later stages can be studied in the great windows of the West end and Transepts, in that 'new and national' 'Perpendicular' style, which Mr. John Harvey, developing a suggestion of the late Professor Lethaby, has lately shown to have been the creation of the King's Chief Mason at Westminster Palace, William of Ramsey, appointed in 1336;† of the latest stages of all, when Gothic was giving place to Renaissance, in which under the influence of oil-painting fostered by the diffusion of engravings after the works of its great masters, naturalistic pictorialism became more and more dominant, Canterbury has no examples; the glass-painter, in his ambition to depict a scene with literal accuracy, broke through the restraints imposed by the mullions and, ignoring them, spread his picture right across the lights from side to side of the window. For this stage, in which the French glass-painters showed their skill and ingenuity at Rouen and elsewhere, we must turn in England to King's College Chapel, or the Crucifixion in the East window of St. Margaret's, Westminster.

---

* In his *Ontwikkeling en Karakter der oude monumentale Glasschilderkunst* (Amsterdam, 1943), p. 24; he refers also on this subject to August Schmarsow, *Kompositionsgesetze romanischer Glasgemälde in frühgotischen Kirchenfenstern* (Leipzig, 1916), p. 6.

† *Burlington Magazine*, Vol. LXXXVIII (1946), pp. 192–199; also *Gothic England, A Survey of National Culture* 1300–1500, London, 1947, p. 50.

§4 Authorship and
Production of the Canterbury Windows

THE question of the authorship of medieval church windows has not always been rightly understood. It has been too readily assumed that references to *vitriarius* need necessarily have any relation to coloured glass and glass-paintings. Mr. John A. Knowles, writing of York Minster,* has refuted the idea that the craftsmen who made the stained glass windows were ecclesiastics and 'that the Dean and Chapter had a regular stained glass department in which the windows of the Minster were designed and carried out from first to last'. When payments are recorded to a glazier (*vitriarius*) they are in all probability for plain glazing or repairs. Mr. Urry has found at Canterbury references, in rentals dating from about 1230 and earlier, to *vitriarii* living in the parishes of St. George and St. Alphege. Another *vitriarius*, evidently on the permanent staff of the Priory, received payment for the year 1322 (*pro toto anno*) for himself and his mate (*pro se & garcione suo*); they were employed within the precincts (*infra ambitum ecclesie & curie Cant.*). Again, the late Rev. C. E. Woodruff cites payments made in 1541–2 to a glazier William (Glasyer Willyam *alias* Wm Glasyer *alias* William the Glasier) for various alterations, and 'for new glass for certain wyndowys in the body of the church' and 'in the upper parte of the Church over the north syde'. On the other hand, records† kindly communicated by the late Mr. Blore of payments in 1447–1449 to two London glaziers, Richard Sawyer and John Pyle, may perhaps relate to the stained glass for the Lady Chapel, built shortly before that time, or to the Barnewell window (see p. 153). The original designing of the windows must be considered quite independently of the actual work of painting and glazing. There is much reason for thinking that the monastic scribes who wrote and embellished illuminated manuscripts may also sometimes have provided designs from which cartoons for windows were made, to be used by the craftsmen who actually painted and assembled the stained-glass panels; there is a close similarity in layout between certain pictorial pages of thirteenth-century manuscripts and windows of the 'medallion' type. A roll in the British Museum from Croyland Abbey with a series of circular outline drawings illustrating the life of St. Guthlac is plausibly considered to have been intended to provide designs for such

---

* *Essays in the History of the York School of Glass-painting*, London, 1936, pp. 23–33.
† In a register of various accounts, No. 4.

a window.* The author has already suggested elsewhere† that the monk Eadwine who prefixed such a lifelike self-portrait to his copy of the Utrecht Psalter made about 1150 for the Priory of Christ Church (Plate A), may conceivably have supplied designs for the earliest surviving windows in the Cathedral, those of the eastern Clerestory; to claim that their painting was done by Eadwine's hand would be inconsistent with the obvious difference in handling to be observed between the windows and the portrait, even allowing for a lapse of about a quarter of a century between the two works; though possible, it is not very likely that a miniature-painter would have acquired the peculiar and quite different skill needed for glass-painting—but the 'stringy' treatment of the drapery and the mood, almost grim, in which the figures are conceived—markedly different from the majestic serenity generally observable in Gothic figure-painting after the beginning of the thirteenth century—are characteristics common to the drawing of Eadwine and the tremendous pictures of patriarchs, seeming almost ready to break through the bounds of their enclosing canopies, in the Clerestory windows. In this connection it is interesting to note a case in which influence in the reverse direction can be recognised: in the British Museum is a manuscript written for Robertus de Bello, Abbot of St. Augustine's, Canterbury; an initial letter on one of its pages‡ is filled with a series of tiny pictures among which is one of Adam delving (Plate B(b)); the similarity in pose—in the kilt and the form of the spade—to the Adam of the Clerestory windows is so striking that it is inconceivable that the illuminator was not consciously taking a hint for his composition from this very glass-painting, familiar to him in the church so near to the Abbey for whose head the manuscript was written.

There is good reason for thinking that the 'Royal Window' in the North-West Transept may have been painted—so far as its main lights are concerned—not in Canterbury, but in the workshop of the King's Glazier at Westminster—at that time William Neve§ (this is probably not the case with the tracery lights, which show a marked difference in style from such of the main lights as have survived). The West Window, perhaps a gift from King Richard II, may also with almost equal probability be an earlier example of the art of the same workshop.

The mode of operation in a glass-painting workshop in the Middle Ages—at least in the later centuries—was doubtless much the same as it is to-day. On one small point of procedure Canterbury supplies interesting evidence which seems hitherto to have escaped notice in print. On the glass in the tracery lights of the Royal Window there are glaziers' or painters' marks which may be compared with the masons' marks so frequently met with in medieval buildings. These marks are fully described

---

* See, however, the supplementary note on p. 28 below.

† *Burlington Magazine*, Vol. LII (1928), p. 41.

‡ Reproduced by Dr. E. G. Millar in *English Manuscript Illumination from the Tenth to the Thirteenth Centuries*, Paris, 1926, pl. 76.

§ Information kindly given by Mr. John Harvey.

THE MONK EADWINE, *self-portrait*. Canterbury Psalter. Trinity College, Cambridge. P. 12.

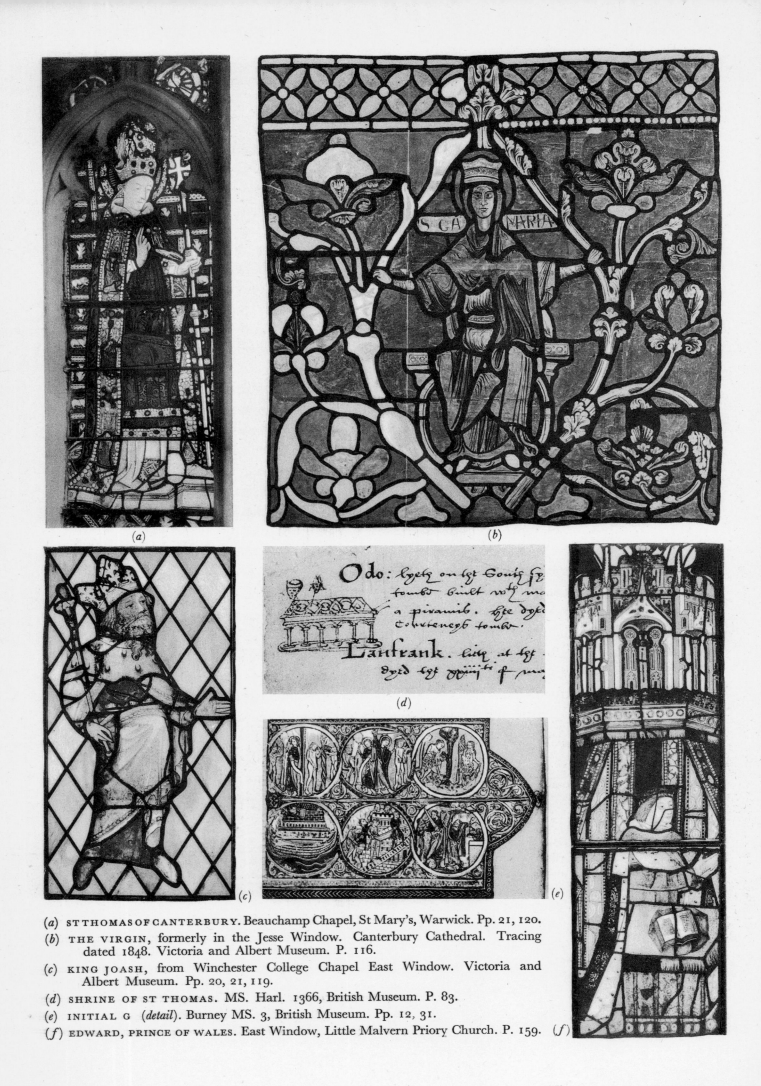

(a) ST THOMAS OF CANTERBURY. Beauchamp Chapel, St Mary's, Warwick. Pp. 21, 120.

(b) THE VIRGIN, formerly in the Jesse Window. Canterbury Cathedral. Tracing dated 1848. Victoria and Albert Museum. P. 116.

(c) KING JOASH, from Winchester College Chapel East Window. Victoria and Albert Museum. Pp. 20, 21, 119.

(d) SHRINE OF ST THOMAS. MS. Harl. 1366, British Museum. P. 83.

(e) INITIAL G (detail). Burney MS. 3, British Museum. Pp. 12, 31.

(f) EDWARD, PRINCE OF WALES. East Window, Little Malvern Priory Church. P. 159.

under the detailed description of the window (pp. 165, 168–9). One of them is done by scratching through a coating of matt grey enamel. In other cases the marks, which show various combinations of short strokes with a small cross, are painted in black; they are to be found on both white and coloured glass, and several times repeated in a single light, differing from light to light. Although an identical mark is to be found on the panes of more than one light, it is likely that the purpose of the marks was to facilitate the arrangement of the panes in assembling and leading them after the firing of the pigment in the muffle kiln; that the marks cannot be personal marks of different painters seems to be the inference from the fact that the same mark is repeated in the panes of lights which differ markedly in manner and in the quality of draughtsmanship shown in their painting. It may be noted here, in passing, that in the early windows no less than the late Gothic windows at Canterbury there is noticeable unevenness in the execution of the designs, suggesting that several hands varying in the degree of their skill were employed in the glass workshop at the same time.

A custom in medieval glass-painting which from a modern standpoint may seem open to criticism is that by which cartoons or portions of them were made to do duty several times over, perhaps with slight variations, and sometimes reversed by merely turning them over. This practice has been fully discussed by Mr. John Knowles.* At Canterbury it is noteworthy that obvious cases of it are not to be found amongst such of the early Clerestory figures as survive; but in the next following phase we may take as examples the figures of St. Thomas and a sleeping man in Panel 3 of Window III in the Trinity Chapel, repeated in the apparition to King Louis VII in Panel 8 of Window IV, and, in the later glass, some of the Kings in the West Window; other instances will be noted in the course of the catalogue descriptions. This labour-saving and therefore cheap expedient of repeating or copying designs may seem surprising to those without a close familiarity with medieval procedure, who are apt to make too high a claim for the dignity of medieval art; but it is an expedient which was not confined to glass-painting and which did not begin or end with the Middle Ages,† nor was it unknown to the great masters. Such plagiarism is to be found, for example, in sculpture; reliefs depicting the story of Achilles on a Roman sarcophagus in the Louvre are repeated with little divergence on another in Rome. In pottery we find, for instance, in Greek vase-painting, stock designs repeated on Attic black-figure vases; in a later age, one of the best of the sixteenth-century maiolica painters of Gubbio did not disdain to paint twice over, slightly altered, a scene of pilgrims at the shrine of St. Ubaldus, the patron saint of his city—an interesting parallel to our Canterbury

---

* J. A. Knowles, 'Medieval Methods of Employing Cartoons for Stained Glass', in *Journal of the British Society of Master Glass Painters*, Vol. I (October 1925), pp. 35–46.

† A modern instance is that of windows with symbolical figures put up as war memorials after the First World War from designs by the late Christopher Whall, which are repeated with slight variations in the parish churches of Ware, Hertfordshire, and Berrow, Somerset, and in the Congregational Church at Purley, Surrey.

glass-paintings. The great masters of painting have not merely repeated motives of their own composition, but have derived ideas from earlier sources and passed them on to their successors; thus Raphael used the figure of St. Peter, in his *Attila* fresco, over again with very little modification for the Almighty separating the Dry Land from the Waters, in one of the ceiling paintings of the Vatican Loggie. He also worked up ideas copied from antique sculptures and early Christian mosaics with which he became acquainted in Rome, and was in turn imitated by Rubens and others, whilst Gaspar Poussin borrowed motives from Titian, giving them a new quality in the environment of his own individual style. In glass-painting, as in these other arts, the manner of rendering is as important as the design of the motive copied or adapted; thus at Canterbury, what were virtually stock motives are transfused, in the hands of a skilful painter, with a spirit and vitality that are lacking in repetitions by less gifted hands.

A word may be said here of the lettering which is so noteworthy an element in the Canterbury windows. In the early windows of the Clerestory, the Corona, and the aisles of the eastern part of the church, there are titles and descriptive legends written in the magnificent Lombardic lettering which was current in Gothic art at the time. As already mentioned, the letters are not painted in black, but left in reserve or scratched out on a ground of dense black pigment, mostly on white glass but occasionally in yellow or other coloured 'pot-metal'. The decorative effect of these inscriptions, especially in the great figure-panels of the Clerestory, is an integral and important element in their general design. There is much variety in the form of letters employed: E's, M's and T's of both angular and rounded form occur alternatively in one and the same inscription. Many abbreviations are used, and ligatures of two letters or even three letters (VAE) combined are of frequent occurrence (it may be mentioned here that the rounded form of T, somewhat like the numeral 5 reversed, was employed also by French glass-painters, as in the Good Samaritan window at Sens (M. Aubert, *Vitraux des Cathédrales de France*, Paris, 1937, pl. 8)). Conformably with early Gothic practice the vowel U has the angular (V) form, except in one surprising instance (see p. 112), where a modern restoration seems to be out of the question. In the 'Theological' windows of the North Choir Aisle and pictorial windows of the 'Miracle' series, most of the inscriptions are in the form of hexameter verse with internal rhyme of the kind known, for reasons which have not been discovered, as Leonine Hexameters.

The names which are found in some of the fifteenth-century windows are in blackletter, and written in black on white glass; the script in these has seldom the high decorative value of the early Lombardic lettering. Here and there among the fragments which have been used to fill out the lights in the South-West Transept Window there are evidences of the existence of inscriptions—notably the Royal motto—in the handsome Roman capitals that became fashionable with the Reformation and the adoption of the Renaissance style under Henry VIII and the later Tudor sovereigns.

§5 Chronological Sequence of the Windows

THERE has been some difference of opinion as to the date of the earliest windows. Sir John Gilbert in his *Fragments towards the History of Stained Glass** suggested that the glass in the North Choir Aisle was already old when the Choir was rebuilt after the fire of 1174, and was of the opinion that it probably came from France; this opinion has not been accepted by any subsequent writer. Winston was content to conjecture the first half of the thirteenth century as the period in which these windows were made. Loftie, writing in 1876, proposed for them a date 'not very much later' than 1185, by which year the building of the aisle was finished; Westlake on the other hand (Vol. I, p. 104) 'cannot agree with him in the early date he would assign to them'. This writer at first regarded the medallion windows of the apse, that is of the Corona and the Trinity Chapel, as likely to have been the first executed—they 'bear the impress of being the earlier'—and dates them as probably not before 1220 (the date of the Translation of the body of Becket from the Crypt to the new shrine in the Trinity Chapel); 'one may therefore', he says, 'fairly reckon the clerestory windows as between this date and 1240'. Westlake seems later to have departed somewhat from this view—a change of opinion to which there will be occasion to refer again elsewhere (p. 18). Mr. L. C. Evetts, writing in *The Burlington Magazine*, Vol. LXXVIII (1941), p. 98, discussed the view sometimes held that the figure of Adam with which the pictorial genealogy in the clerestory begins is later than the remaining figures of the series; he was of opinion that it 'reveals many characteristics typical of work of the early thirteenth century'.

In spite of this diversity of view there can be little doubt that the oldest glass still to be seen in the cathedral comprises the figures now distributed in various parts of the building but formerly set, two in each, in the windows of the clerestory of the Choir. On stylistic grounds these figure panels may be judged to be as early as any other surviving glass of the Cathedral, if not earlier, and it seems likely that the first concern of the builders would be to fill with glass the windows in the highest range— the clerestory—of the new building, and to have them ready for inserting before the removal of the scaffolding erected for the construction of the piers and the high vaulting. What is known of the order followed in the work of re-erection started in 1175, is summarised by Sir Charles Peers in an article on 'William of Sens and his Choir' in the *Seventeenth Annual Report of the Friends of Canterbury Cathedral* (1944, pp. 22, 23). Beginning from the west end of the Choir, the work was complete, including the

---

* For this work and those of other authors cited in this chapter see Bibliography, pp. 185, 186.

East Transepts, as far as the western extremity of the Trinity Chapel by the beginning of September 1178, when an accident to the French master-builder was the cause of its being taken over by his namesake William the Englishman. We may thus assign to the eighth decade of the twelfth century the clerestory windows of the Choir and of the first vaulting-bay of the Trinity Chapel, and with them probably the rose window in the gable of the North-East Transept, which is closely akin to them in draughtsmanship, and its pendant, now for the most part lost, in the South-East Transept. There is a perceptible change of design in the windows of the genealogical series in the continuation of the clerestory in the Trinity Chapel, which was completed by the English William in 1184; this justifies the assumption of an earlier date for the glass of the Choir. The six medallions now in windows of the South Choir Aisle, formerly in the clerestory of the apse, which interrupted these easterly genealogical windows, are undoubtedly of the same date as these latter.

Next in execution probably came the twelve 'Theological' windows of the Choir Aisles, of which the remnants are now gathered in two windows on the north side; for these a date a little before or after 1200 may be conjectured. Possibly, however, the exceptionally heavy payments recorded in the year 1213–14 may be related to the provision of these windows; in that year the Sacrist's expenditure amounted to £120, much higher than in any other year in the thirteenth century—the average for the following ten years being £85.*

Another early window attributable to the last years of the twelfth century is the East Window of the Crypt (the former Lady Chapel, until the building of the present Lady Chapel, also known as the Dean's Chapel), beneath Becket's Crown; this window, of which portions have lately been retrieved for the Cathedral, shows in the wide proportions of its border an earlier type of design than those windows which must be dated to the thirteenth century. The style of foliage recognised as being characteristic of thirteenth-century or 'Early English', as distinct from 'Transitional', glass begins to make its appearance in the ornamental groundwork of the East Window of Becket's Crown, which in view of its primacy of position is likely to have engaged the attention of the glass-painters as soon as this part of the structure was completed; it may be assigned to the beginning of the thirteenth century, and the windows that formerly flanked it—there is evidence of a Jesse window, to be discussed on a later page, on the North—were doubtless approximately coeval with it. Last of the early windows come the series of twelve, six on the north and six on the south, in the aisles of the Trinity Chapel, of which a considerable portion survives; those still extant illustrate the Miracles of St. Thomas, and there are reasons presently to be discussed for the assumption that the series included also scenes from his life, now lost. It seems likely that although these windows may have taken a few years to complete, the work was

---

* Information kindly given by the late Rev. C. Eveleigh Woodruff.

carried through continuously; unlike the windows in Chartres Cathedral, for instance, which were presented by many different persons and corporations and probably at different times, the Becket windows seem to have formed a concerted scheme, perhaps paid for as a single item of expenditure out of the revenues which were coming in steadily out of offerings at the shrine of the saint. For the dating of these windows a definite point is provided by the representation of the shrine in Windows V and XII of the series. Several windows have pictures of his tomb in the crypt, from which no clear inference as to dating can be drawn, but these two windows can certainly have been painted little, if at all, before 1220, the year of the translation of Becket's body from the crypt to the shrine made to receive it in the Trinity Chapel; though the chapel, built specially to house the shrine, was finished in 1184, the coloured windows of its aisles seem not to have been put in hand at once—there may possibly have been an interim period during which the windows were glazed with plain quarry panes. On stylistic grounds the painted windows and remnants that survive can satisfactorily be attributed to the second and third decades of the thirteenth century. Lastly, mention must be made of six thirteenth-century pairs of figures, now in the Water Tower and the East Window of the Crypt; these Mr. Caldwell plausibly conjectures may have belonged to the small Norman windows of Lanfranc's nave, from which they would have been removed when it was rebuilt by Prior Chillenden.

Of the fourteenth century, hardly anything remains earlier than its last decade. To this period belongs such of the glass in the West Window of the Nave as originally formed part of it—some of the tracery lights and, probably, the figures of kings of England in the main lights; the shields of Richard II and his two queens at the top of the window point to a date between his second marriage, to Isabella of France, in 1396 and his deposition in 1399, as almost certainly that of its erection. The tracery lights of the Nave, of which remnants still survive, date also from about this period or a little later.

Two figures recently inserted in the Chapel of Edward the Confessor may be dated about the first quarter of the fifteenth century.* The heraldic glass given by Lady Margaret Holland, Duchess of Clarence, to St. Michael's Chapel is presumed to date from about 1437; nearly contemporary with this glass are the few remnants of the original glazing of the great South Window in the South-West Transept, completed under Archbishop Chichele (p. 140, see A. Oswald, *op. cit.*, p. 222). A little more recent are the windows in the present Lady Chapel, with the Bourchier arms and badges. The great window in the North-West Transept given by King Edward IV in or about 1482 represents the late Gothic style of English glass-painting in its full development; for reasons discussed elsewhere (pp. 157–8) it seems likely that the figures in the tracery lights may be earlier than the main lights of the window. The Tudor arms

* See *C.C.C.*, No. 40, 1944, p. 14.

now occupying a place between the King and Queen in this window, are a fine example of heraldic glass of the end of the Middle Ages. Later developments, when enamel painting was the generally adopted technique and Renaissance had succeeded to Gothic design, are represented by some heraldic panels of the late sixteenth and the beginning of the seventeenth century, the latest glass-paintings in the Cathedral prior to those of the Gothic Revival in the nineteenth century.

§6 The Question of French Influence

THE early glass at Canterbury has been the focus of controversy in the past between the champions of English art and those who are apt to belittle English medieval architecture and ancillary arts as being essentially French in inspiration, if not actually the product of French artists and craftsmen. In the case of glass-painting in particular Westlake, in his great work which no writer on the subject can leave out of reckoning, has been responsible for much misunderstanding, arising out of his inaccuracies of statement. He suggested* that the medallion windows in the aisles of the apse illustrating the miracles of St. Thomas were the first to be executed, and were probably not inserted before 1220; a date between 1220 and 1240 seemed to him 'fair and reasonable' for the genealogical windows of the Clerestory. He drew comparisons between the figures in these latter windows and those of the apse of Chartres, comparing the Isaiah of Chartres with a figure at Canterbury which he named also Isaiah; he misread the name of this figure as ESAIAS instead of RESA, also overlooking the fact that the Prophet Isaiah has no place in the genealogy of Christ. It is true that, in a footnote to the anonymous *Notes* by Miss Emily Williams published in 1897, Westlake is quoted as giving a different opinion; his view was now that the Clerestory windows were the oldest in the Cathedral, and 'may be a little after 1200', adding: 'the style is between those at St. Remi and those at Chartres'. This was a change of opinion in the right direction, for the Clerestory windows in the Church of St. Remi at Rheims are attributable to a date about the end of the twelfth or the beginning of the thirteenth century, whereas the choir of Chartres was not rebuilt, after the fire which destroyed it in 1194, until the second decade of the thirteenth century. Now it has been argued above (p. 16) that the earlier of the Canterbury Clerestory windows can plausibly be given a date not later than 1178; and on stylistic grounds alone they seem earlier than the St. Remi windows. They show a vivaciousness, in some cases almost an agitation, in the pose of the figures, one

* *History of Design,* etc., Vol. I, p. 70.

Plate I

ADAM. This panel, now in the West Window
(L.4), originally formed the lower half of the first
window in the series illustrating the genealogy of
Christ, in the clerestory of the Choir (north side).
About 1178. Pp. 12, 31.

might almost say a picturesque uncouthness, which is in marked contrast with the almost classical restraint—characteristic in general of French Early Gothic art—to be observed in the figures at St. Remi and Chartres.

It has already been suggested (p. 12) that the Canterbury Clerestory figures may owe something of their designing to an English draughtsman, the monk Eadwine of Christ Church, who was the scribe of the Canterbury Psalter, now in the Library of Trinity College, Cambridge. This does not justify a claim that the design of the early Canterbury windows is purely English; for it would be foolish to pretend that in the art of glass-painting of North-Western Europe in the twelfth and thirteenth centuries the lead was not given by France. Glass-painting, though Byzantine in its origin, became pre-eminently a French art. Its earliest supreme achievements were the windows of Abbot Suger at St. Denis, of which only a few remnants now survive unrestored. M. Jean Lafond, who is one of the best living critics of glass-painting, has lately reminded us how unwise it is to argue solely from the monuments still extant.* In particular, it is most important to remember that in Paris before the French Revolution there were to be seen great numbers of stained-glass windows of which not a vestige now remains. From what is recorded of these it is clear, as M. Lafond insists, that in early Gothic times Paris was the great centre of the art, sending forth rays of influence not only throughout France but also across the Channel to England. As is well known, a small panel at York Minster from a twelfth-century 'Jesse' window comes so close to the Jesse of St. Denis as to leave no uncertainty about its paternity; and doubtless if there were still existing in France windows of the twelfth century with large single figures, they would be found to bear such a similarity to the Canterbury figures as to show whence these derived their inspiration. The idiom of Canterbury may be English, but the language is French. The blunder of Westlake was chronological, in arguing that the Canterbury windows were derived from Chartres or St. Remi; he would perhaps have been justified if he had seen in them all derivatives from a single common source and that source in France, probably in Paris.

The recantation of Westlake, taking back the date of the Canterbury Clerestory windows some twenty years, to a little after 1200, was unfortunately published in the small type of a footnote to a little book of limited circulation, difficult to obtain and unlikely to be widely known among French writers. The damage was already done, by his great book, recognised as a standard work on the art. His judgment was accepted without question, and French critics have since been accustomed, until M. Lafond redressed the balance, to decry English glass-painting as an inferior and second-hand art. In this attitude of disparagement the lead was taken by M. Émile Mâle, the distinguished historian of French medieval art. All these writers seem to have forgotten the fact that a French glass-painter, Henri Gérente, writing as long

---

* *Archaeological Journal*, Vol. CIII (1947), 'The Stained Glass Decoration of Lincoln Cathedral in the Thirteenth Century', p. 153.

ago as 1846, took a juster view of the position; of Canterbury he wrote as follows: 'Un peu plus récentes que celles données par Suger à Saint-Denis, plus anciennes que celles des bas côtés et du chœur de la cathédrale de Chartres, les verrières de Cantorbéry égalent les premières et surpassent les secondes. Les bordures encadrant ces fenêtres, les feuillages qui en cernent et réunissent les médaillons, sont du goût le plus noble et de l'exécution la plus parfaite.'* Though these words leave untouched the question of the dependence of the Canterbury glass-painters on French predecessors, they pay just tribute to the high artistic quality of their work as shown particularly in the 'medallion' windows of the Choir, the Trinity Chapel and the Corona. In this connection it is relevant again to refer to the recent paper by M. Lafond on the glass of Lincoln Cathedral.† Included in the thirteenth-century South Rose Window of Lincoln he has discerned fragments of early medallions which he recognises as 'important work of the latter half of the twelfth century'; in these fragments the blue background 'is covered all over with a thin "matt" of paint from which a delicate damask pattern has been scratched out'. He quotes parallels to this decoration at Strasburg about 1200‡ and as 'one of the most remarkable features of Canterbury' (in Window IV of Trinity Chapel); he sees in these Lincoln fragments 'the missing link between Saint-Denis' on the one hand and Canterbury, Sens and Chartres on the other. Such correspondences of technique, no less than the similarities of design which Westlake observed and from which he drew chronologically false deductions, go to emphasise the near relationship of French and English art in the Romanesque and Early Gothic periods. Consistently with the close relations and frequent intercourse between ecclesiastics of both countries and the union of one of them as a single realm with a large portion of the other, Northern and Western France and England at that time formed a single artistic province not, however, devoid of regional variations of idiom.

The later glass of Canterbury belongs to an age in which English Gothic had broken definitely away from French models, and although the glass-painters of both countries were moving along parallel lines and employing in the main the same technical procedure, there was no identity in their manner of treating the content of their designs. The West Window of Canterbury is slightly later in date than the windows of William of Wykeham's two colleges at Oxford and Winchester; in the figures of the Canterbury Clerestory in particular there is some similarity to those of the Jesse window of the Winchester chapel, and amongst the eight figures of Kings of England surviving in the main lights it may be noted that two wear crowns quite different in design from those of their fellows, but not unlike the crowns of the Kings

---

* Quoted by O. Merson, *Les Vitraux*, Paris, 1894, p. 113.

† *Op. cit.*, p. 153.

‡ Compare Fridtjof Zschokke, *Die romanischen Glasgemälde des Strassburger Münsters*, Basle, 1942, figs. 10, 25, 28, 29.

of Judah at Winchester (Plate B(*c*)). The correspondences are not, however, close enough to justify any argument for production in one and the same workshop; indeed, it is generally conceded that the windows of the Wykeham foundations were painted at Oxford—their designer is believed to be Thomas of Oxford, *alias* of Dadyngton—whilst the Canterbury window is likely to have been designed, and perhaps executed, by the King's Glazier at Westminster, Richard Savage, working for the architect, Henry Yevele, who designed the Nave. Correspondences with the later glass, known to be from the Westminster workshop, in the Beauchamp Chapel at Warwick (Plate B(*a*)), will be discussed on a later page. All this work is recognisably English and quite different from anything produced at the same time in France.

The all too scanty remains of the mid-fifteenth-century glass at Canterbury include some work of great beauty and delicacy, such as the delightful figures of St. Catherine and St. Christopher inserted during recent years in windows of St. Edward's Chapel. The great Royal Window of the North-West Transept presents problems, in the disparity of the glass in the tracery lights and the main lights, which will be fully discussed in their turn: the tracery lights seem to be the work of a local designer and painter or painters, and of men not of the first order of competence, whilst the figures and heraldry of the main lights exhibit a much higher degree of skill; they seem to betray a consciousness of the technique of Netherlandish painters in oil and are almost certainly productions of the King's Glazier of a later generation, William Neve. There are a few fine examples of English heraldic design of the Tudor period, notably the magnificent achievement already mentioned in the middle of the Royal Window.

§7 History and Literature of the Windows

THE ancient windows of the Cathedral, although presenting a large aggregate of glass-paintings of several periods, have almost without exception suffered from mutilation, restoration, and transference to and fro from one part of the Cathedral to another. This chequered history can be traced partly from literary records, of which there is no lack. The literature may be said to begin with the famous fourteenth-century MS. in the Chapter Library setting out in detail the subjects of the twelve 'Theological' windows in the Choir Aisles, which was exhaustively discussed in a learned paper by Dr. Montague James;* the MS. will be dealt with further on a later page, in the description of the still existing remnants of these windows (p. 52). Next in order comes another MS., that of R. Scarlet, dated 1599, in

---

* Full details of this and other works here mentioned are given in the Bibliography, pp. 185, 186.

the British Museum (Harl, 1366), consisting in the main of notes, with excellent drawings, of the heraldry in the Cathedral. This MS. deals incidentally with the shields of arms in many of the windows, including some which no longer survive, and so far as it concerns these shields is the basis of the Supplement to the *Heraldic Notices* of Thomas Willement published in 1827. The degree of Scarlet's literacy is shown by the fact that, in giving to Archbishop Whitgift and Dean Nevil the title of Doctor, he spells the word 'dockter'—a spelling which shows incidentally that the abolition of any distinction between the sounds of the vowels in unstressed syllables in common English speech was already beginning in the reign of Elizabeth. There is evidence in this MS. that much heraldic and other glass was then to be seen in the Cathedral buildings which has since disappeared; for instance, 'In the Chapter Howse, nowe used for the preachinge place' there were 'skocheons in glas'. These included some which were still evidently accompanied by figures of the persons by whom the arms were borne; thus there is mention of 'Ricard' Clifford, Episcopus, in glas, standing', and 'Thomas A . . . lett, Archbishop, standing, in glas' (the latter evidently a mis-reading of the name of Archbishop Arundel, the former, Richard Clifford, Bishop of London, 1407–1421). A detail from Scarlet's MS. showing the shrine of St. Thomas is reproduced in Plate B(*d*).

Another document in the British Museum bearing on the Canterbury glass is a manuscript copy made in 1768 by Edward Hasted, the historian of Kent, of much earlier notes relating to churches in Kent (MS.Add. 5479). This book has the title: *Notes taken of Armes, Monuments, etc. in Several Churches in the County of Kent Begun to be taken in the year 1603 to 1624 Communicated to me by Joseph Edmondson Esq* faithfully copied by me Edward Hasted and also a like MSS. of Notes taken of Armes, Monuments, etc. faithfully copied by me from a Curious Book in the possession of the Late John Thorp of Bexley Esq* beginning in this Book at p. 182 Edward Hasted July 1768.* These notes record many shields now lost, as in the 'West window of the S. side of the church', the 'West window in the N. Isle'; several shields now lost are also mentioned in the windows of St. Michael's Chapel ('a Chapel in the Cross Isle on the South Side of the Churche'), and inscriptions relating to the shields in the West window of the North-West Transept, to be described below (p. 152).

The earliest printed allusion to the windows is in the *Antiquities of Canterbury*, dated 1640, by the local antiquarian, William Somner. He briefly refers to the beauty of the glass, 'especially in the Churches upper part', that is, in the Choir and eastwards; he refers to the commendation by William of Malmesbury of the 'glorious choir' of Conrad, adding: 'I thinke his words hold true still'. In an appendix he gives a schedule of the 'verses containing a paralell (*sic*) of the old and new Testament', still to be seen in their entirety in the 'Theological' windows. Within four years of the publication of Somner's work the windows to which he alludes with such tantalising brevity were ravaged and to a large extent destroyed by Puritan fanatics under the

I

Enoch
about 1178
SOUTH-WEST TRANSEPT
p. 32

2

Zorobabel

about 1178

SOUTH-WEST TRANSEPT

p. 42

3

Juda
about 1178
SOUTH-WEST TRANSEPT

p. 43

4

(a)

(b)

(c)

(d)

(a) Ragau
(b) Phalech
(c) Lamech
(d) Mathusala

about 1178
SOUTH-WEST TRANSEPT

pp. 32–34

guidance of Richard Culmer, Rector of Chartham. The account of this onslaught, published as *Cathedrall Newes from Canterbury* in 1644, is our only source of information as to the contents of some of the windows that perished. Thus we read of 'a Cardinalls hat as red as blood, painted in the highest window . . . within Bell-Harry Steeple, over the quire doore, covering the Arch-Bishops Armes'. A picture of 'Austin the Monke, who . . . was the first Arch-Bishop of Canterburie that ever was' is spoken of as being found by the Commissioners in the 'Eastmost window'. This figure of St. Augustine may have been in one of the lateral windows of the Corona: it can hardly have been in the middle window which, there is every reason to think, must have been filled from the outset with the Type and Antitype subjects still to be seen there; these, as illustrations of scriptural events, may have been deliberately spared by the fanatics, apart from those depicting the Crucifixion and the Resurrection, now replaced by modern compositions. There is a detailed description of the North-West Transept Window, to which further reference will be made (p. 153); the description of 'a Minister . . . on the top of the citie ladder, near 60 steps high, with a whole pike in his hand ratling down proud Beckets glassy bones' has been quoted in many later works on the Cathedral. We read also of the defacement of 'many other Images . . . in other windows . . . , severall pictures of God the Father, of crucifixes and men praying to crucifixes, and to the Virgin Marie'; these windows, evidently containing figures of donors at prayer, were probably in the Western Transepts and the aisles of the Nave, where only fragmentary remnants of the old glazing have survived.*

More extensive and reliable information as to the state of the windows is contained in the work of William Gostling, a Minor Canon of the Cathedral, *A Walk in and about the City of Canterbury*, of which the first edition was published in 1774.† This writer tells of the ruinous condition of some of the Becket windows in the Trinity Chapel, especially those on the south side, less protected by buildings than those on the north, 'superstition, the wicked wantonness of unlucky boys, or of bigger and more unpardonable fools, who think there is wit in doing mischief, especially if that mischief is done to show their contempt of what is sacred'. The two windows 'near the door of the organ-loft', in which the 'principal remains' of the twelve Choir Aisle windows had been put together, are described in great detail in the second (1777) and later editions, showing their condition to have been much as it is now. The Genealogical

---

* There is reason to think that Protestants of an earlier age were not guiltless of iconoclasm of this kind; Mr. Urry has found in the *Treasurer's Accounts* for the year ending Michaelmas, 2 Edward VI (1548), a payment of 3s. 4d. '*pro deformacione fenestrarum in communi aula ac extirpand[is] divers[is] histor[iis]*'. The Common Hall or dining hall of the Minor Canons after the Reformation had been the Necessarium of the Priory; the 'fictitious stories' which had to be 'extirpated' from the windows defaced probably, as Mr. Urry suggests, related to Becket or other sainted personages.

† A second edition, supervised by his daughter Hester, with lengthy additions relating particularly to the 'Theological' windows, and several minor corrections, was published in 1777, the year in which Gostling died, aged 81.

windows of the Clerestory are next described, as well as the North-East Transept rose window; a plan with a key showing the positions of the figures then surviving and the titles inscribed on them, has been of value to all subsequent writers in identifying the remnants of this magnificent series of twelfth-century windows. Equally helpful are the lengthy descriptions of the Royal Window in the North-West Transept and of the West Window. There are also brief notices of the windows in 'the beautiful chapel of the Virgin Mary, now called the Dean's Chapel', and in St. Michael's Chapel.

Shortly before Gostling's book, in 1772, there was printed an account of the Cathedral by J. Burnby,* a Cambridge solicitor, of which a second edition came out anonymously in 1783. This adds little to earlier descriptions of the windows, but tells us that 'the name of Chillenden was formerly at the bottom of the west window, over the door', of the Chapter House; the account continues: 'And in one of the south windows are the arms of Arundel. In all the windows, which are nearly in the same taste as those in the body of the church, are some remains of coloured glass, and in the upper lights of the west one are several handsome emblematical figures with the nimbus or circle about the heads representing the orders of the hierarchy with the titles underneath.' Nothing now remains of these figures, evidently of the Orders of Angels, which occupied the tracery of the west window in the Chapter House, but this account lends plausibility to the conjecture that this building was the source of supply for much of the glass used at the end of the eighteenth century in the rearrangement of the West Window of the Nave.

The great window of the South-West Transept, which was 'falling into decay', was rebuilt about the end of the eighteenth century, under Dean Powys. Hasted, in Vol. IV of his *History of Kent*, published in 1799 (p. 521, footnote), records this as a recent occurrence, and states that the glass for it, 'taken from different parts of this church and the neighbourhood of it . . . was selected and arranged with much care and industry by Mr. John Simmonds, one of the vesturers of the church, to whom the arrangement of it was committed by the dean and chapter'.† It was apparently during this reconstruction that figures to fill the three ranges of main lights in the window were brought from the clerestory of the Choir and Trinity Chapel; traces of this operation are to be seen in the names of William Burgess and Thomas Pottinger as repairers of the window in 1792 scratched with a diamond on one of the tracery lights.

This reconstruction of the great South Window seems to have been preceded by a similar rearrangement of the glass in the West Window. Mr. Woodruff drew attention to a resolution of the Chapter recorded in the Dean's Book in 1787 (Midsummer

---

* Not *Barnby*, as given by Miss Williams in her *Notes on the Painted Glass*.

† Miss Williams in her *Notes* (p. 44) quotes these statements with several inaccuracies; she inserts 'in 1799' before the words 'was selected and arranged'. Mr. Urry has found record of payment for this work in the Treasurer's Book under the date 26th June, 1792.

Chapter) which gave authority for the transference of glass to this window from the Chapter House: 'That the painted glass in the Sermon House (*i.e.*, the Chapter House) be removed to the West Window in the Church and replaced by the plain glass from thence and that in future the Consistory Court be holden in the Sermon House'. Speaking of the West Window, Hasted (*op. cit.*, p. 529) states that 'there are very little remains' of the names in black-letter under the Kings of England; of the aisle windows of the Nave he writes: 'the compartments of the windows . . . have each a slender border, of no meaning and as little beauty; in the midst of each throughout the whole, is a shield of arms'. He is the first writer to mention (p. 375) the figure of St. Martin 'on horseback, cutting off part of his cloak to cover a naked beggar', still remaining in the window of St. Martin's Chapel in the North-East Transept (see p. 111 below).

The architect and glass-painter Thomas Willement gives lengthy references to the shields in various windows in his work, already mentioned, on the heraldry of the Cathedral, published in 1827. He prints as an appendix to this work the MS. notes dated 1599 of R. Scarlet (cited above) so far as they relate to heraldry. The earliest published reproductions of any of the windows in their entirety are those in crude chromolithography by Sir John Gilbert in a folio published in 1842, which was intended to be the first instalment of a work, never continued, on the history of stained glass.*

A year earlier, in 1841, J. G. Joyce made for Willement coloured drawings of many details of the windows gathered into an album with the title *Specimens of the Ancient Stained Glass in Canterbury Cathedral*, which is now in the Victoria and Albert Museum. These drawings show that much of the glass at that time was in a very defective and disordered state, but their value as documents is impaired by the fact that they are in many particulars palpably inaccurate. They comprise eleven panels from the North Choir Aisle windows, seven from 'Miracle' windows in the Trinity Chapel, of which the true import was so little understood that the title 'Martyrdom of St. Stephen' was written on the copy of the frog-stoning scene in the story of Robert of Rochester (see p. 98), five from the East Window of the Corona (including the Virgin from a 'Jesse' which then occupied the place of the Crucifixion—see p. 74), and three which were at that time in windows of the North Choir Triforium—namely, two scenes from the story of St. Alphege still in that position, and what is curiously described as 'the Death of Rufus', actually the shooting of Adam the Forester, now in Window VII of the Trinity Chapel.

The middle of the nineteenth century was the period in which the most serious efforts were made to restore the windows from the state of disarray into which they had fallen through the neglect, indifference and ignorance of earlier generations. Nothing seems to have been done in the way of restoring the windows until after 1840; the

---

* See p. 54 below.

Dean's Books from 1792 to that year have no mention of glass, nor is anything said of purchases of *stained* or *coloured* glass in the Treasurer's Accounts from 1798 to 1832.* Such glass as was obtained seems to have been plain glass for filling the openings in Henry of Eastry's choir-screen after the removal of the wainscotting about 1825, and in the screen erected by the elder George Austin, Surveyor to the Cathedral, behind the High Altar in 1826. It is true that at a much earlier date, in 1677, we learn from a fragmentary document of that year of 'glassing about Christchurch', and of payments 'for 9 foot of painted glasse repaired and leaded', and 'for 2 foot of painted glasse repaired besid the oardit-house' (the Audit Room, no longer existing, adjacent to St. Andrew's Chapel), 'at 9d. the foot'; and in June 1678 there is record of more 'painted glasse' as well as 'new glasse' paid for at the same rate per foot 'in the vpper north joyle' [aisle] and 'in the window beside the oargen', presumably the first window in the North Choir Aisle.† There are also indications that old glass, presumably displaced by Culmer's iconoclasts, was to be found loose on the Cathedral premises; an inventory of 1689 includes under the heading 'Glaziery' 'some old painted glass' as well as 'stock of plain glasse upon seaven shelves', and at later dates (1745, 1752, 1761) we find recurring the entry 'a quantity of small pieces of glass' in what is presumably the same place, described as 'the Glazing Room'.‡

An obituary notice§ of Austin, who died in 1848, tells us that the stained glass was much in need of repair, and that Austin 'undertook himself to restore the worst lights, and the vacancies of one or two other lights of figures he filled with new glass—though without the slightest previous knowledge of the art'. The work of restoration was carried on by his son, George, elder brother of his successor as Surveyor of the Cathedral, Harry Austin.

Mr. Blore drew the Author's attention to receipts for payments to the younger George Austin in respect of window repairs and restoration during the years 1853–1855. In 1853 the upper half of the 'East Window—Trinity Chapel', presumably the middle window of the clerestory in the apse, was re-leaded and repaired and 'figures and portions of subjects' were restored; another item in the same account relates to the South Window: 'Re-leading repairing and restoring portion of this window containing fourteen feet at 7/6'. In 1854 the 'East Window in Beckett's (*sic*) Crown' was taken in hand. The lower portion was re-leaded and repaired and 'missing figures' were 'restored and replaced'; 'fifteen new medallions of Figure subjects Scrolling and Borders' were made 'containing together thirty nine and a half feet at One pound ten shillings per foot'. The West Window was also dealt with in

---

* Information kindly given by the late Mr. W. P. Blore.

† These are more items of information which the Author owes to the kindness of Mr. Urry.

‡ See Legg and Hope, *Inventories of Christ Church*, 1294–1780, pp. 304, 309, 312 (communicated by Mr. Blore).

§ Quoted from *The Builder* in *The Gentleman's Magazine*, N.S., Vol. XXXI (1849), p. 660.

this year; 're-leading and restoring the Portion of this window containing "Adam" and the parts below 6 ft. 8 in. by 2 ft. 7½ in.,' that is, the middle light in the lowest range, cost £6 0s. 0d. In 1855 another part of the West Window was re-leaded and restored, 'consisting of the figure "Seth" and shields etc. below it—The Head feet and many parts missing restored with new glass' (this is the figure of Semei, with the name incorrectly restored as SETH). Payment was also made in 1855 for the 'restoration of the Easternmost Window in the North Aisle illustrating the miracles supposed to have been performed by, and at the shrine of, St. Thomas à Becket'; in this bill there are two items—'re-leading and restoring the missing portions of the medallions etc. of the upper part of the window consisting of the old glass', and 'nine medallions of new glass to complete the old subjects—six lights of ground work new and six lengths of border and two corner lights also new glass at 30/- per foot.'

A paper on the early glass by W. J. Loftie published in the *Archaeological Journal* in 1876 gives the earliest printed examination of the window from the point of view of art criticism and history; for the first time an attempt was made to explain the subjects in the aisle windows of the Trinity Chapel by reference to the accounts of the miracles of St. Thomas by his contemporaries Benedict of Peterborough and William of Canterbury, then newly published in the Rolls Series. Loftie makes some useful comparisons with early illuminated MSS., although he dates the windows too early. The next important study of the windows was in the first and third volumes of N. H. J. Westlake's monumental work on painted glass, published respectively in 1879 and 1886. Westlake showed the fine appreciation of an artist for the æsthetic qualities of the glass and did great service to students in the way of stylistic comparison between the various national schools; but his survey of the remains at Canterbury is marred by the prejudices and inaccuracies, affecting not only his text but also his otherwise admirable drawings, which so greatly impair the usefulness of his book.

The earliest monograph on the Canterbury windows is the *Notes on the Painted Glass in Canterbury Cathedral*, by Emily Williams, published anonymously with a preface by Dean Farrar; this, though not free from inaccuracies of transcription, is invaluable as an account of the distribution of the glass at the time of its publication (1897), and contains excellent illustrations in outline of many of the earlier panes based on tracings made by the younger Austin. The description of the windows given in Chapter IX ('County Lists of Ancient Glass') of Dr. Philip Nelson's work on English stained glass, published in 1913, in the series entitled 'The Antiquary's Books', is in the main a repetition of Miss Williams's schedule, and includes on a reduced scale some of her illustrations. This was preceded in 1911 by a paper in *Archæologia Cantiana*, by the late John Le Couteur, discussing the 'Royal Window' of the North-West Transept. There are short chapters on the windows in S. A. Warner's *Canterbury Cathedral* (1923), in the *Memorials* (1912) of Woodruff and Danks, and in Miss Babington's *Canterbury Cathedral* (1933). Valuable critical references to the glass will be found, together with coloured illustrations, in the work on English and French stained glass by Saint and Arnold (1913), and in Dr. Herbert Read's *English Stained Glass* (1926). By far the most authoritative work on the ancient windows as a whole is the modest little *Guide* published by the late Dr. A. J. Mason (1925), in which the identification of the Miracle subjects in the Trinity Chapel is carried further than by any previous writer. Similar information in a more condensed form is given in the *Notes on the Old Glass* by Canon Crum, first printed in 1930, in which visitors to the Cathedral will find an admirable and clearly arranged first introduction to the windows. Articles on the earliest glass at Canterbury have been published in the *Burlington Magazine* by the Author and Mr. L. C. Evetts. The information contained in various articles by the Author which have appeared in the *Canterbury Chronicle* and in the *Annual Reports* of the Friends of Canterbury Cathedral is recapitulated and revised in the present work.

SUPPLEMENTARY NOTES

In a book (*Vitraux des Églises de France*, Paris, 1947, p. 6) which came to the notice of the Author only when the present work was already in the Press, M. Louis Grodecki accepts arguments for a relationship contrary to that suggested on p. 11; according to these the earlier illuminated MSS. derive their scheme of designs from stained-glass windows. M. Grodecki concedes independence of design to miniatures from the second half of the thirteenth century onwards, but gives reasons for refuting the theory of J. L. Fischer (*Handbuch der Glasmalerei*, Leipzig, 1914, p. 76) that the reversal of influence dates from the production of the Psalter of St. Louis in 1260. The case of the Adam in the Bible of Robertus de Bello, cited on p. 31 below, is also relevant in this connection.

* * * *

A few words may be added here in explanation of a feature of decoration which occurs in several of the thirteenth-century windows of the Trinity Chapel and Corona (pp. 75, 84, 88, 104, 106) and, in its most beautiful form, in those of the North Choir Aisle (pp. 55–64). This is a repeating motive found especially in the borders of medallions which sometimes has the appearance of, and has been mistaken for, a series of crowns but is actually derived ultimately from an Arabic word *alafia* (meaning 'blessing') written in the stylized script known as Cufic, from the name of the town of Cufa, in Irak, a seat of Mohammedan learning. The word was frequently employed as a decorative formula in Islamic applied art, notably in the silk fabrics which were largely imported from the Levant and used in the make-up of liturgical vestments and church furnishings; from these it was adopted in glass-painting and other forms of the early Gothic art of the West, often as 'mock Arabic' which has become illegible.

CHAPTER I

THE EARLY GLASS

§1 The Genealogical Windows (Clerestory of the Choir, Eastern Transepts and Trinity Chapel)

IT is now generally agreed that the earliest surviving windows of the Cathedral are those of the clerestory in the Choir and Eastern Transepts and the first vaulting-bay of the Trinity Chapel. As already stated (p. 15) they may probably be dated about 1178 or a little before, and the rose windows which interrupt the series in the north and south walls of these Transepts were probably carried out about the same time. The windows continuing the clerestory series in the Trinity Chapel, some of which show a perceptible difference in style and design, come later and may be assigned to the last years of the twelfth or the beginning of the thirteenth century. These latter windows, however, must have been part of the intended scheme from the first, for the sequence of subjects is continuous, beginning at the western end of the north side of the Choir and including the side windows of the Trinity Chapel before coming to an end in the windows of the south side of the choir, facing where it began; the difference is one of treatment, not of subject. The theme of the series has already been explained (p. 3), the genealogy of Christ from Adam, with a break, in the apse, to admit the most important incidents from His Life and Passion.

From a plan with descriptive list given by Gostling in his *Walk* (first edition, 1774, pp. 215–218)* we have valuable evidence as to the figures and subjects originally occupying the windows; he quotes the names which then still remained, entire or in a fragmentary state, in the several windows. A comparison of these names with the sequence in the Biblical text shows that already in Gostling's time there had been a certain amount of disturbance and rearrangement in the order of the figures. In each window of the genealogical series were two figures, one above another, shown—with the exception of Adam—seated on a throne or a high-backed chair. The figures at the beginning and end of the series—those in the windows of the Choir and eastern

---

* Considerably amplified and corrected in the second (1777) edition.

Transepts—are set under shrine-like canopies, with the exception of those in the first six windows, where the evidence of the surviving panels indicates that the canopy was absent, the lower of the two figures occupying a rectangular panel, the upper panel having a plain lancet top. The shrine-motive here so well exemplified has recently been traced back, by Mr. John Summerson,* through Carolingian miniatures and Byzantine mosaics to the *aediculae* or shrines for the statues of the deities in Roman temples, adopted as a purely ornamental feature of the design in the wall-paintings of Pompeii; he cites as an early example in glass-painting the canopy enclosing the Virgin and Child in the 'Belle Verrière' at Chartres dating from about 1250.

The canopy system is kept up in the first two windows on the North side of the Trinity Chapel (of the original panels belonging to the opposite windows on the South side only incomplete remnants of one survive); in the windows eastward from this point, where the building narrows and the bays become smaller, a change of design and treatment appears, suggesting that a different artist provided the cartoons; the figures are now set in compartments of vesica-shaped, quatrefoil and other outline with foliage or diaper, of a kind consonant with a date early in the thirteenth century, to fill up the spandrels or other remaining areas. All the windows had originally a wide ornamental border varying in design from window to window. Only nine of the original figures now remain in these clerestory windows, and of these only two (Nos. 23 and 61) are in their original places, the others having been transferred from one window to another. The remaining figures that survive are now distributed in the West Window of the Nave, the South Window of the South-West Transept, and a window of the North-East Transept, see pp. 132, 142, 41.

All the windows of the clerestory retain their original iron frameworks (armatures). The first fifteen on the north side and the last fifteen on the south (not including the rose windows on both sides) are simply divided by three horizontal saddle-bars into four panels, two for the upper and two for the lower figure in each window. The remainder are divided into compartments of various shapes, not always corresponding on opposite sides of the church, as severally described below.

Most of the clerestory panels now in other parts of the building were drastically reduced and altered to adapt them to their present positions; in some of the figures the hands or feet have been truncated in this process. The compartments enclosing those of the figures which came from the Trinity Chapel are not all of their original form, nor can the patterned groundwork by which they are surrounded or separated be accepted in most instances as that which belonged to them; this being so, it is difficult or impossible in the case of the eight panels lettered A to H in the subjoined description to say from which window in the clerestory they came.

---

* In 'Heavenly Mansions: an Interpretation of Gothic'. *Journal of the Royal Institute of British Architects*, 3rd Series, Vol. 54 (1947), pp. 159–167.

5

(a) Joanna
    about 1178
    SOUTH-WEST TRANSEPT

(b) Joseph
    about 1178
    WEST WINDOW

(c) Noe
    about 1178
    SOUTH-WEST TRANSEPT

(d) Esrom
    about 1190–1200
    WEST WINDOW

    pp. 33–43

6

(a)

(b)

(a) Semei
   about 1178
   WEST WINDOW

(b) Abraham
   about 1178
   SOUTH-WEST
   TRANSEPT

(c) Abia
   about 1190–1200
   WEST WINDOW

(d) Jeconias(?)
   about 1190–1200
   WEST WINDOW

   pp. 35–45

(c)

(d)

(a)

(b)

(c)

(d)

7

(a) Sem
NORTH-EAST TRANSEPT
east side, *Window IV*

(b) Isaac
NORTH-EAST TRANSEPT
east side, *Window IV*

(c) Aram
WEST WINDOW

(d) Rhesa
SOUTH-EAST TRANSEPT
east side, *Window II*
about 1178

pp. 33–42

8

(a) David
(b) Nathan
(c) Ezekias
(d) Ozias

about 1190–1200

SOUTH-WEST TRANSEPT

pp. 37–39

(a)

(b)

(c)

(d)

In the descriptions given below the numbers in brackets appended to each figure indicate the Biblical sequence, which is doubtless that of the original arrangement of the panels in the series; in each window the upper figure is given first. The numbers preceded by 'G' are those given by Gostling to the entire series of clerestory windows in the Choir, Eastern Transepts and Trinity Chapel, thus including the rose windows of the Transepts and the apse windows as well as those of the genealogical series.*

CHOIR, NORTH SIDE
WINDOW I (G1)

The original border remains (branching leaves interlaced with leaves paired to form lyre-like motives).

1 (1). THE ALMIGHTY, missing; 'quite defaced and probably so for having been a design to represent the Almighty' (Gostling).

2 (2). ADAM (the figure panel now in the West Window, L4, p. 134). He is delving with a mattock beside a tree, with a band of cloud above, naked except for a fleece round his loins. His name: ADAM inscribed above his head. Blue background.

See Mason, p. 10. Reproductions: Read, pl. 6; *Burlington Magazine*, Vol. LII (1928), p. 41.

The figure may be compared with that, slightly later in date, in the rose window of the North Transept of Lincoln Cathedral (in which Adam is accompanied by Eve spinning). Another example is in a late fourteenth-century window in Halam Church, Nottinghamshire.† In all these the spade or mattock is of the form still commonly used on the Continent with blade shaped as on playing cards; the handle at Lincoln and Halam is T-shaped.

It is important to compare the figure also with that at the beginning of *Genesis* in the Bible of Robertus de Bello, Abbot of St. Augustine's, Canterbury (1224–1253), now in the British Museum (Burney MS. 3, f. 5v°);‡ the resemblance is so close as to leave no doubt that the illuminator was consciously copying the window or else some earlier design from which both the window and the Bible illustration were derived. It may be remarked that in later designs such as those in the Chester Beatty Psalter by W. de Brailes and the Bible of William of Devon (British Museum Royal MS.1DI, f.5) Adam is shown wearing a loose shirt, not a fleece.   Colour Plate I.

WINDOW II (G2)

Described by Gostling as 'all plain'.

---

* The numbering is as in Gostling's second edition; in the first it is faulty, owing to a miscalculation of the number of windows in the eastern limb, and the transcription of the names varies in several cases from that of the second and later editions.

† Reproduced in *The Journal of the British Society of Master Glass-Painters*, Vol. IX (1946), pl. facing p. 132.

‡ Plate B (e). Reproduced also by E. G. Millar, *English Illuminated Manuscripts from the Xth to the XIIIth Century*, Paris, 1926, pl. 76.

1 (3). SETH, missing (the figure now bearing the name SETH is probably that of Semei, No. 68 in the series, *q.v.*, p. 43).

2 (4). ENOS, missing.

WINDOW III (G3)

'All plain' (Gostling). The original border remains (clusters of trefoils enclosed between continuous stems which open out to form ogee loops and meet again in a rosette).

1 (5). CAINAN, missing.

2 (6). MALELEEL (Mahalaleel),* missing.

WINDOW IV (G4)

1 (7). JARED (the figure now in the South-West Transept Window, Q4, p. 150). Robe green with gold borders of trellis-pattern at the neck, scale-pattern at the wrists; white mantle with a similar scale-pattern border in mauve at the bottom; shoes dark blue-grey. Seat gold, footstool ruby and green. Inscribed: IARETH (the first letter partly replaced with an L from elsewhere; in Gostling's first edition the name is printed as IARE). The spandrels above the pointed top in the present location of the panel have been filled with coloured leafy scrollwork on a ruby ground brought from a window, probably in the Trinity Chapel, later in date (early thirteenth century) than the panel.

See Mason, p. 13. Reproduction: Read, frontispiece (in colours).

2 (8). ENOCH (the figure now in the South-West Transept Window, Q8, p. 150). The patriarch turns vigorously on his seat, with left hand raised, looking over his shoulder towards the hand of God which emerges from a cloud above, seizing his right wrist for his 'translation' to Heaven. His robe is white, with pale yellow girdle, over an undergarment with green sleeves and pale yellow scale-patterned wrist-bands, his mantle pale murrey, his shoes white; the sleeve of the divine arm is also pale murrey. The seat pale yellow, with green lozenge-diapered cushion; background blue. His name: ENOCH inscribed behind his head (so given in Gostling's second edition though printed as ENO in the first). The Translation of Enoch is repeated in the East Window of the Corona (see p. 78). Plate 1

WINDOW V (G5)

The original border remains (a repeating tier of frond-like leaf-buds in pairs on either side of a middle trefoil).

1 (9). MATHUSALA (Methuselah) (the figure now in the South-West Transept Window, Q5, p. 150). Seated with right knee raised to prop his right arm whilst he strokes his beard, his left hand resting on his left knee. Robe green with murrey borders patterned with quatrefoils across the shoulders, lozenges and ovals down the front; a yellow-sleeved undergarment with green scale-pattern at the wrist seen on his left arm; white mantle, pale grey shoes, gold throne with green lozenge-diapered

---

* The names in each case are given in the New Testament form, followed by that of the Old Testament (*Genesis, Numbers, I Chronicles,* and *Ruth*), in cases where it differs, in brackets. The Latin names inscribed on most of the panels correspond in most instances with those in the Vulgate.

cushion. His name: MATVSALE behind his head. The spandrels above the pointed top filled to fit the present location of the panel in the same manner as in No. 7 above.

Reproductions: Saint and Arnold, pl. 3 (in colours); Le Couteur, fig. 14; Sanders, fig. 37; *C.C.C.*, No. 33 (July, 1939), p. 34. Plate 4d

2 (10). LAMECH (the figure now in the South-West Transept Window, Q1, p. 150). He sits looking to the right, his knees turned towards the left. He has a murrey hat with point on the top, green robe with murrey lozenge-diapered band at the top and scale-patterned cuffs, white girdle, yellow mantle with pale blue patterned border at the bottom, and murrey shoes. His name: LAM*E*CH* behind his head (the E appears to have been missing when Gostling wrote, being enclosed in brackets in the second edition, although the name is printed as LAMACH in the first edition). The white throne has a high back with rows of arcading and a pale blue cushion; green footstool.

Reproduction: *Burlington Magazine*, Vol. LII (1928), p. 41. Plate 4c

NORTH-EAST TRANSEPT, WEST SIDE
WINDOW I (G6)

The original border remains (quatrefoils connected by two stems which open out in loops to enclose symmetrical leaf-buds springing from the quatrefoils).

1 (11). NOE (Noah) (the figure panel now in the South-West Transept Window, Q2, p. 150). He sits with left knee drawn up, right hand on hip, left hand raised and open with a rhetorical gesture. White robe with gold borders, green tippet or scapular, girdle and sleeves (gold-cuffed, of undergarment); murrey cloak, pale blue shoes; green throne with gold arch, ruby footstool. The trefoil-arched canopy has roofing and turrets in fragmentary condition in the spandrels, and ruby supporting columns with gold and pale blue foliated capitals.

Reproduction: *Burlington Magazine*, Vol. LII (1928), p. 37. Plate 5c

2 (12). SEM (Shem) (the figure panel now in the North-East Transept, East Side, Window IV, p. 35). He sits with right hand extended and left hand supporting a scroll on his knee. His hair murrey-coloured. Murrey robe with green lozenge-diapered band across the chest, white cloak, pale blue shoes, gold throne. Canopy with semi-hexagonal top, with turret above, resting on ruby shafts with gold capitals. His name: SEM on a white band with ruby edges behind his head. Plate 7a

WINDOW II (G7)

The original border, now missing, remained when Gostling wrote, as also in Window III.

1 (13). ARPHAXAD, missing.

2 (14). CAINAN, missing.

WINDOW III (G8)

Border recorded by Gostling, now missing (see on Window II above).

---

* Here and throughout the book in quoting inscriptions italic capitals are used for modern restorations or irrelevant insertions; lower case italics within square brackets indicate letters now entirely missing.

33

1(15). HEBER (Eber). The upper half of the panel only survives and has at present no location in the Cathedral. His hair pale blue, face and beard pink. He wears a pink robe with green ornamental band across the chest, white cloak. Low-arched canopy with a turret and roofing above and white and mauve foliated capitals on golden-yellow shafts. The name: .BER in white on a ruby-bordered panel behind the head (the initial E and final R defective).

In Gostling's list this figure is named as being, above Sala (see below), in Window II (G11) on the east side of this transept.

2(16). SALA (Salah), now missing; the name SALA* is given in Gostling's list as in Window II of the east side of the Transept (G11).

NORTH-EAST TRANSEPT, EAST SIDE
WINDOW I (G10)

Described by Gostling as 'plain', the figures being given by him as in Window III below. Both figures are under canopies with a trefoil arch ornamented with spots at intervals and remains of turrets above; of the lateral columns only fragments of the capitals remain.

1 (17). PHALEC (Peleg) (the figure-panel now in South-West Transept Window, Q6, p 150.). He sits with his right hand raised and forefinger extended, in his left hand a scroll supported on his knee. Robe green with a gold disc-patterned band across the shoulders, white sleeved undergarment, murrey cloak with pale blue band near the bottom, fastened with a bright blue morse at the neck, green shoes; throne white, green and ruby, background blue. His name: PHALECH behind his head.

Plate 4b

2 (18). RAGAU (Reu) (the figure-panel now in South-West Transept Window, Q7, p. 150). Seated with his right hand pointing with forefinger extended towards the spectator's right, his left clasping a scroll on his knee. His hair murrey. Robe green with gold tippet, belt and borders, white undergarment, pale murrey cloak with white and blue bands, yellow shoes; from his right shoulder depends what is apparently a border of his cloak, pale grey-blue, with a geometrical pattern. Throne white, gold and green; footstool ruby. His name: RAGAV inscribed behind his head.   Plate 4a

WINDOW II (G11)

In Gostling's list EBER and SALA (see above, Nos. 15, 16) are given as in this window.

1 (19). SARUCH (Serug), missing.

2 (20). NACHOR (Nahor), missing.

WINDOW III (G12)

The original border remains, consisting of two wavy interlaced white stems enclosing symmetrical clusters of foliage; the ground blue in the middle, ruby on either side.

---

* Thus in the second edition; in the first it is printed SARAES.

Plate III

COSAM. The figure and the quatrefoil enclosing it belonged originally to the series illustrating the genealogy of Christ, and occupied the lower half of Window VIII in the clerestory of the Trinity Chapel (south side); they have been enclosed within ornamental borders contemporaneous with them in order to fit them for their present position, in a window of the lowest range in the North-East Transept (west side). About 1190–1200. P. 41.

The places of the original figures are now occupied by two unidentified figures (see G, H, p. 46). The original figures, described below, are both under canopies with segmental notched arch supporting roofing and battlements; the leafy capitals and supporting shafts differ in colouring. In Gostling's list these figures are given as being in Window IV (see below); in his first edition no name is inserted for the lower half.

1 (21). THARA (Terah) (the figure now in the South-West Transept Window, Q3, p. 150). He sits with right hand extended from a fold of his cloak, a green scroll supported on his knee in his left hand. He wears a ruby hat, with a spike, pale blue robe with green border at the top, patterned with discs, gold cloak and green shoes; throne pale green, footstool ruby. His name: THARE inscribed in two lines behind his head. Capital pale murrey and white, shafts ruby.

Reproduction: *Burlington Magazine*, Vol. LIII (1928), p. 37.   Colour Plate II.

2 (22). ABRAHAM (the figure panel now in the South-West Transept Window, M1, p. 148). He sits with left hand raised, fingers spread, his right hand not seen. Hair pale purple, robe white, green cloak, yellow stockings diapered with trellis-pattern, pale grey shoes. His name: ABRAM inscribed behind his head (the form of the M, resembling H and O conjoined, is to be observed, and may have caused Gostling to transcribe the name in the fuller form). Murrey throne, ruby footstool. Green and gold leafy capitals, gold shafts.   Plate 6b

WINDOW IV (G13)

The original border remains—two white bands parting to form a series of vesica-shaped compartments enclosing clusters of foliage, ground colours as in Window III. In Gostling's list THARE* and ABRAHAM (see above) are given as in this window. The places have now been filled with figures of Isaac (reinstated) and Sem (from G 6).

1 (23). ISAAC. He sits with right hand resting on a lozenge-patterned scroll and left hand raised. His hair is deep murrey. Robe white with green band across the chest and pale blue undergarment showing below its hem, murrey mantle, stockings ruby, shoes white. Throne white, green and ruby, patterned in the middle to imitate porphyry. Low arch with two turrets and battlements above, ruby shafts with green and gold foliated capitals. Name: I.....C (mutilated) behind his head.   Plate 7b

2 (24). JACOB, missing. This position is now occupied by Sem (No. 12, see. p. 33).

TRINITY CHAPEL, NORTH SIDE
WINDOW I (G14)

The original border remains (pairs of opening fronds with a pointed leaf between, springing from butterfly-like foliations and enclosed between two looped continuous bands).

1 (25). JUDA (Judah) (the figure now in Window II of the South-East Transept, East side (G38) see p. 42). He has his right hand raised and holds a pale pink

---

* In the first edition HARE.

scroll in his left hand. Pink robe with green patterned border at the neck, white mantle, seat green and gold with lozenge-diapered pale blue cushion. Canopy with half-hexagonal top bordered with acanthus cresting, with turrets above; ruby columns with amber-coloured foliated capitals. Name: IVDA behind his head on a white band edged above and below with ruby.

2 (26). PHARES (Pharez) (the figure now in the same window as No. 25, see p. 42). He sits with left hand raised in a gesture of exposition and right hand swathed in his mantle, supporting on his knee a murrey scroll. He wears a deep green robe with light blue wristband and hem, white mantle with pattern of foliations along the folded edge, and white shoes. Seat gold; trefoil arch with battlements and roofing above, ruby columns with white capitals. Name: PHARES on a deep amber band behind his head.

WINDOW II (G15)

The figures are both under canopies with notched trefoil arch and foliated capitals of which the supporting columns are missing.

1 (27). ESROM (Hezron) (the figure now in the West Window, L1, p. 134). He sits holding a yellow scroll on his right knee with his right hand, his raised left hand and bare arm protruded from his mantle. His hair is deep murrey, his robe of the same colour, over an undergarment of grey-blue, his mantle and shoes white; his throne has a dark green seat, ruby high back decorated with arcading, and high golden feet. His name: ESROM (partly mutilated) behind his head. The panel has been filled out at the sides with fragments of fifteenth-century pinnacles.   Plate 5d

2 (28). ARAM (Ram) (the figure panel now in the West Window, L7, p. 134). He wears a brown wide-brimmed hat, a white robe, murrey cloak and green shoes; in his right hand he holds a pale blue extended scroll, his left hand raised in gesticulation. Throne green and gold, with foliage at the corners, ruby footstool. Behind his head the name: ARAN. Only one capital (murrey and white) remains. The sides of the panel are filled out with fifteenth-century fragments with pinnacles, rosettes, part of a quarry with oakleaves and acorn, and the letters OI (probably from the Royal motto *Honi soit*...).   Plate 7c

WINDOW III (G16)

The armature gives a field lancet-headed and bulging outward in three equidistant pairs of lobes, the whole subdivided horizontally by three bars. Both figures are under a low arch now without lateral shafts.

1 (29). AMINADAB (Amminadab) (the figure now in the West Window, L6, p. 134). In his left hand he holds a scroll of the same colour as his flesh. His hair is deep murrey; robe white with amber belt and band below the knee and olive-green wristband, mantle murrey, stockings ruby, shoes blue. Throne ruby, with green between the legs; footstool murrey. The blue background studded with ruby spots. Of his name only fragments remain (...H(?)A..AD..). Among the fifteenth-century architectural fragments with which the panel is filled out at the sides are two with inscriptions in open-outline black-letter (*Ec,A*).

2 (30). NAASSON (Nahshon) (the figure now in the West Window, L2, p. 134). Olive-green hair, green robe with gold borders figured with circles, white sleeves and

hem showing of undergarment, murrey mantle and shoes. Throne white and ruby, footstool white. Background as in No. 29 above. Name: NAASON behind his head on a white band with ruby edges.

WINDOW IV (G17)

Divided by the armature into two large circles with a smaller between and small semicircles above and below, connected with one another and with the sides of the window by vertical and horizontal bars. The original border and ground remain (pairs of leaves flanking a white bud and springing from a yellow leaf, pointing inwards and outwards on alternate sides of a continuous wavy band and coloured alternately green on a ruby ground and murrey on blue; the intervals between the large circles which contained the figures are filled with coiled foliated stems springing from the outer border of the circles).

1 (31). SALMON.

2 (32). BOOZ (Boaz).

These figures are cited by their names SALMON and BOOZ by Gostling. These names no longer survive, but Dr. Mason conjectures that the two 'unidentified' figures in the South-West Transept Window (described as A and B on p. 44 below) 'may from their shape and size be said with some assurance to be Salmon and Boaz, though the scrolls on which their names were carried have been cut away' (M., p. 13)

WINDOW V (G18)

Divided by the armature into two quatrefoils with a lozenge between them, connected with one another and with the sides of the window by vertical and horizontal bars.

1 (33). OBED (the figure now in the West Window, I2, see p. 132). He sits with a scroll in his left hand, wearing a grey cap, white robe with gold band below the knee, murrey mantle, ruby stockings and gold shoes. His chair green and gold, footstool green and murrey. His name: OBETH inscribed behind his head.

2 (34). JESSE (the figure now in the West Window, 16, p. 132). Sitting with scroll in his left hand. Hair olive-green, robe white with gold bands across the chest and below the knees, gold belt, mantle with olive-green scarf hanging loose, stockings ruby, shoes gold. Footstool white. His name: IESSE inscribed behind his head.

WINDOW VI (G19)

Divided by the armature into two large lozenges truncated at their points by a small circle between them (connected by horizontals with the sides) and half-circles above and below. Both figures are enclosed in hexagonal panels (to fit the truncated lozenges) with a green border of acanthus-leaves on a cross-hatched ground (now largely missing in No. 36 and replaced with various fragments from elsewhere) and blue background studded with white stars. At the extremities of the panels are half-medallions with foliage and in the spandrels ruby discs on a blue ground.

1 (35). DAVID (the figure now in the South-West Transept Window, H4, p. 146). He sits on a gold bowed seat with a fold of his cloak in his right hand, his left turned up

as if to support the pale blue scroll on which his name is written: DAVID; he wears a gold crown, a green robe with narrow gold patterned bands below the knee, murrey mantle with white bands, and white shoes.

Gostling unaccountably gives the name as DAVID REX; the panel has no appearance of having been cut down sufficiently to have admitted the Royal title.

Plate 8a

2 (36). NATHAN (the figure now in the South-West Transept Window, H5, p. 146). He sits holding in his left hand a sceptre topped with a dove to which he points with his right forefinger. He wears a pale blue pointed cap or mitre, a green robe with gold patterned belt and wristbands and blue border over a white undergarment, murrey cloak with white stripes fastened with a brooch, and yellow shoes; the throne green and gold. Name: NATHAN above his shoulders.

Plate 8b

WINDOW VII (G20)

Divided by the armature into two large vesicas connected by vertical bars traversed between them by a horizontal. The figures are both enclosed in vesica-shaped panels with a ruby inner border, enclosed in their present position by an outer border of later fragments. The original border remains (leaf-buds springing inwards in pairs from half-rosettes and enclosed within semicircular bands).

1 (37). ROBOAM (Rehoboam) (figure now in the West Window, I3, p. 132). He sits with a scroll in his right hand, his left hand raised. His hair is dark brown, his robe white with gold disc-patterned belt, wristbands and band below the knee, murrey cloak and green shoes; throne green and gold. His name: ROBOAS behind his head. The outer border of the vesica is composed of fragments of white fifteenth-century glass painted with canopy work; the spandrels are filled with thirteenth-century glass including portions of figures of soldiers in chain mail. The panel is filled out laterally with fifteenth-century fragments among which can be recognised foliage, pinnacles, crowns and parts of black-letter inscriptions (*Pi*, probably for *Prior*, ..*num,osi*(?) on a scroll; also ..*num* in the same open-outline script as the fragments under No. 29 above.

This figure and Nos. 38–42 are interpolations in the Luke genealogy from *Matthew* I 7–12. Gostling gives the name as ROBOAN*, although the present title is clearly as transcribed above and original.

2 (38). ABIA (Abijah) (the figure panel now in the West Window, I5, p. 132). He sits on a brownish arc-shaped seat, with right hand raised palm outwards and a scroll in his left hand. He wears a green skull-cap, murrey robe with olive-green patterned band across the shoulders and gold rosettes on the thighs, white mantle and green shoes. His name: ABIAS† behind his head. As in No. 37, the outer border of the vesica consists of fifteenth-century fragments, here showing canopy work and the word *Sit;* thirteenth-century fragments in the spandrels, including part of a chain-mailed figure.

Plate 6c

WINDOW VIII (G21)

Divided by the armature into two quatrefoils with a small circle between them, all connected by vertical and horizontal bars with the margins.

---

* In the second edition; in the first it is given as ROS CAS.
† Given as ARI AS in Gostling's first edition.

9

Moses and the Synagogue
about 1178
NORTH ROSE WINDOW
p. 48

10

(a) Prudence
(b) Temperance
about 1178
NORTH ROSE WINDOW
pp. 48, 49

(a)   (b)

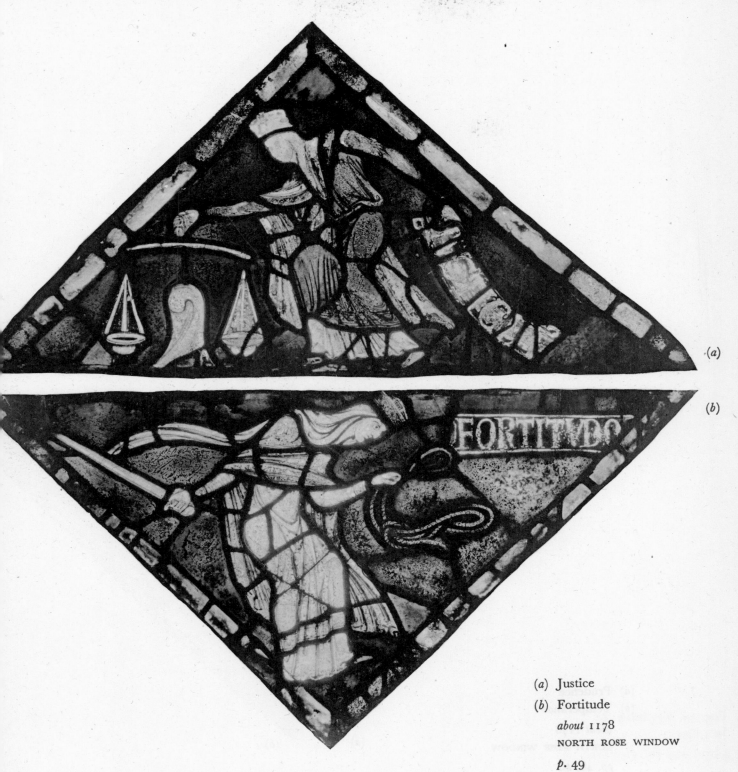

(a) Justice
(b) Fortitude
about 1178
NORTH ROSE WINDOW

p. 49

12

(a)

(a) Pharaoh dismissing the
    Israelites
(b) Christ and the Heathen
    about 1200
    NORTH CHOIR AISLE
    Window II
    pp. 55, 56

(b)

1 (39). EZEKIAS (Hezekiah) (the figure panel now in the South-West Transept Window, M3, p. 148). He sits with legs crossed, holding in his right hand the Dial of Ahaz, his left resting on a knob of his throne. He has a gold crown, a white robe with disc-patterned border in the form of an archiepiscopal pallium, green-lined murrey mantle, ruby stockings and green shoes. The dial gold. The throne ruby and gold, the footstool murrey. Behind his head his name: EZECHIAS*. The allusion is to the shadow turning backwards on the Sundial (II *Kings* XX 8–11).

 Reproduction: *Burlington Magazine*, Vol. LII (1928), p. 37.   Plate 8c

2 (40). OZIAS (Josiah) (figure panel now in the South-West Transept Window, M6, p. 148). He sits holding in front of him at arm's length the Book of the Law (in the form of a long scroll unrolled, inscribed in mock Hebrew characters). A gold crown is on his head; he wears a murrey robe with disc-pattern at the neck, a gold-lined green mantle and gold shoes; his seat is gold and white. Behind his head his name: IOSIAS. The allusion is to the re-discovery of the Book of the Law (II *Kings* XXII 8–XXIII 2).

 Reproduction: Nelson, pl. II.   Plate 8d

WINDOW IX (G22)

Divided by the armature into two large vesicas with a small rectangle between them, all connected by vertical and horizontal bars with the margins.

1 (41). JECONIAS (Jeconiah). This figure is identified by Dr. Mason as the figure now at I1 in the West Window (described as C on p. 45 below); it was at one time at I4 in the same window. Gostling in his second edition gives in the upper panel of the window IE; it is difficult to account for the legend TEA ABPE given in this position in his first edition.

2 (42). SALATHIEL. Identified by Dr. Mason as the figure now at I7 in the West Window (described as D on p. 45 below). Gostling gives this panel as 'broken'.

TRINITY CHAPEL, SOUTH SIDE

Gostling gives Windows I–IV (G28–32) as 'plain glass'.

WINDOW I (G28)

Divided by the armature in the same manner as G22.

1 (43). MATTATHA, missing.

2 (44). MENAN, missing.

WINDOW II (G29)

Divided by the armature in the same manner as G21.

1 (45). MELEA, missing.

2 (46). ELIAKIM, missing.

---

* Given as EZECHIEL in Gostling's first edition, but corrected in the second.

WINDOW III (G30)

Divided by the armature into two large vesicas connected by a small circle between them and joined by vertical bars with the apex and base of the window.

1 (47). JONAN. See note on No. 48.

2 (48). JOSEPH. It is possible that this and its companion No. 47 may be the figures (described as E, F on p. 45 below) now at H3 and H6 in the South-West Transept Window (see p. 146). The question is discussed on p. 46.

WINDOW IV (G31)

Divided by the armature in the same manner as G19.

1 (49). JUDA, missing.

At this point Austin's diagram (reproduced by Miss Williams, p. 2) unaccountably gives the name 'Jude', 'Juda' being given at G39. The panel inscribed IVDE belongs rightly in G39, together with Joanna; when Gostling wrote they were in the adjoining window G38 (see below, p. 43), G31 being described by him as of 'plain glass'. It should be pointed out that there is no authority in the Vulgate for the form 'Jude'; the name, which in all three verses of the Authorised Version (*Luke* IV, 26, 30, 33) appears as 'Juda', is given in the Vulgate in this form in vv. 30, 33 only: in v. 26 it appears as *Judae*, genitive of *Judas*.

2 (50). SIMEON, missing.

WINDOW V (G32)

Divided by the armature into two large quatrefoils nearly in contact with one another and breaking into the border.

1 (51). LEVI, missing.

2 (52). MATTHAT. This figure may possibly be the one with undecipherable name now in G12 (G on p. 46 below, but compare also No. 70).

WINDOW VI (G33)

The armature similar to that of G19. The original border remains (a white band based on the inner edge of the border, rising at regular intervals to form alternately a small trefoil and an arch which is intersected by sprays of foliage springing symmetrically from a half-rosette at the centre of the arch).

Gostling gives SUS and SHER (Nos. 55, 56) as being here—in the second and subsequent editions; in the first the window is described as 'mixed'.

1 (53). JORIM, missing.

2 (54). ELIEZER, missing.

WINDOW VII (G34)

The armature similar to that of G32 except that the quatrefoils are separated by a small circle. The original border remains (a row of half-rosettes along the inner edge from which spring alternately buds in pairs on curved stems and, intersecting these, a continuous zigzag band). Both figures are now in panels lancet-pointed at the top and bottom and bordered with 'crown' ornament, the spaces above and below being filled with leafy scrollwork on a ruby ground, probably not their original setting. Gostling describes this window as 'plain', and gives SUS and SHER as in Window VI.

1 (55). JOSE (the figure now in the South-West Transept Window, H7). He sits with right arm akimbo, legs drawn vigorously apart, and a scroll in his outstretched left hand. His hair is murrey; white robe confined by an amber belt twisted into a knot and having a broad green neck-band patterned with quatrefoils in squares, murrey mantle, ruby stockings, brown shoes; the throne green with white cushion. Name (mutilated): *LESV* behind his head; the L is an error or a later insertion for the I of the Vulgate *Jesu*.

2 (56). ER (figure now in South-West Transept Window, H2, p. 146). He sits with arms extended, the hands being partly concealed behind the borders. His hair is blue, his robe green with diapered gold band across the shoulders, his mantle murrey, stockings ruby and shoes yellow. Seat white, with gold trellis-patterned cushion. His name: HER (preceded by a leafy scroll which was misinterpreted by Gostling and Dr. Mason as an initial S) behind his head.

WINDOW VIII (G35)

From this point onwards the windows are merely divided by three horizontals, as in the corresponding windows on the opposite side of the church.

Described by Gostling as 'plain'.

1 (57). ELMODAM, missing.

2 (58). COSAM (the figure now included in a restored window of the lowest range on the west side of the North-East Transept). He points with his right hand towards the scroll which his left hand supports on a corner of the bench on which he sits. He is beardless, with yellow hair. He wears a pale blue robe over a green undergarment with gold wristbands, a murrey cloak and yellow shoes. The bench is white, with ruby supports. His name (now partly obliterated, CO...?) is written behind his head. The quatrefoil with ruby, white and green border in which the figure is enclosed probably does not represent the original setting.

Reproduction in (colours): *Burlington Magazine*, Vol. LII (1928), p. 35.

Colour Plate III

WINDOW IX (G36)

The original border remains (paired tufts of leaves springing from a quatrefoil and enclosed between two looped bands).

Gostling gives NERI (No. 61) and NI as being in this window.

1 (59). ADDI, missing.

2 (60). MELCHI, missing.

SOUTH-EAST TRANSEPT, EAST SIDE

WINDOW I (G37)

The original border remains—a trellis of white bands with gold rosettes in a cluster of green foliage at the intersections, forming lozenge-shaped compartments in which are triple sprays of leaves in white and murrey; blue ground, with ruby lateral bands. Gostling gives IOROBABEL (No. 63) and RESA (No. 64) as in this window.

1 (61). NERI. He sits with left arm akimbo and right forefinger raised. His hair light blue. He wears a ruby spiked, broad-brimmed hat (the 'flash' of which has almost disappeared), white robe with green wristbands, murrey cloak lined with green, pink stockings and blue shoes; seat gold. Trefoil arch supported on ruby columns with gold foliated capitals. Name: NERI behind his head.

2 (62). SALATHIEL, missing. Part of the name of this figure may be that given by Gostling as NI in his 36th window.

WINDOW II (G38)

The original border remains—leaves with alternate changes of colour springing in threefold clusters from a continuous lateral stem in white. This window is now occupied by Juda and Phares (Nos. 25, 26, from Window G14, p. 33).

1 (63). ZOROBABEL (the figure now in the South-West Transept Window, M8, p. 148). His hair is blue, his robe white with a green trellis-pattern band across the chest, mantle murrey, shoes yellow; the throne pale green. His name ZOROBABEL in a semicircle above his head. Round-arched canopy with golden columns having white and murrey foliated capitals. Gostling, who reads the name IOROBABEL, gives this figure as in the preceding window.   Plate 2

2 (64). RHESA (the figure now in Window I, adjacent). His left hand is on his knee; in his right, which is swathed in his mantle, he holds a scroll; his hair murrey. Ruby hat similar to that of Neri (No. 61), murrey robe with transverse white stripes, ruby sleeve and grey cuff of undergarment showing on left arm, green mantle, ruby stockings, grey shoes. Throne white and gold. Round-arched canopy with two turrets above; white shafts with gold foliated capitals. Name: RESA behind his head. Given by Gostling as in the preceding window.

Reproduction: Westlake, Vol. I, pl XXXIX*a*, where the figure is wrongly identified as the Prophet *Esaias* and false deductions are drawn from certain resemblances to the figure of *Isaias* at Chartres (particularly the shape of the hat 'although in these hats there is the only exact identity, both in form and colour').   Plate 7d

WINDOW III (G39)

1 (65). JOANNA (the figure now in the South-West Transept Window, H1, p. 146). He sits with his right hand clasping his left forearm and a murrey scroll in his left hand, which is wrapped in a fold of his mantle. His hair is pale mauve, his robe green, with a golden disc-patterned band at the neck and a pale blue border at the

bottom, his mantle and shoes white. His name: JOHANNA in a semicircle above his head under the round arch of the canopy, which has white and murrey foliated capitals and golden shafts; ruby footstool.

Reproduction: *Burlington Magazine*, Vol. LII (1928), p. 40.   Plate 5a

2 (66). JUDA (the figure now in the South-West Transept Window, H8, p. 146). He sits supporting a pinkish scroll with his right hand on his left knee, his left hand raised as in exposition. His hair blue, robe green, murrey sleeve of an undergarment showing on his right arm, white mantle, pale blue shoes. Throne murrey. His name: IVDE in a semicircle above his head under the round arch of the turreted canopy, which has gold shafts with green and blue leafy capitals.

Although in Austin's diagram 'Jude' is given in G31, the similarity of the setting to that of Joanna (No. 65) shows that this figure belonged to this window, not to G31, where the armature would have required a setting similar in form to that of David and Nathan (Nos. 35, 36), on the opposite side of the Choir (see also note on No. 49 above).   Plate 3

WINDOW IV (G40)

1 (67). JOSEPH (the figure now in the West Window, L5, p. 134). He sits sideways, with his right hand raised, his left resting on his left knee. His hair is light blue, his robe green, mantle white and shoes light blue; the throne murrey, light blue and gold. Of his name: *IOSEPH*, behind his head, on a golden instead of the customary white band, the first four letters are a modern restoration. The canopy has pale murrey and green foliated capitals and white shafts. The panel has been filled out on each side with fragments of fifteenth-century glass (two crowns from borders and pinnacles and foliage from canopies).   Plate 5b

2 (68). SEMEI (the figure now in the West Window, L3, p. 134). His beardless face is shown in striking profile to right, his right hand rests on his left thigh, his left on the top of a pale blue book or scroll. Green robe with pale murrey borders, a white under-garment showing below it at the skirt, yellow mantle and shoes; green and white throne with murrey band on the pedestal. Only one capital (to the left, murrey and green) of the trefoil-arched canopy remains. Of his name: *SETH* the last two letters are a modern restoration, wrongly identifying him as the second genealogical figure in the series, which was missing when Gostling wrote.

Reproduction: Westlake, Vol. I, pl. XL (as *Seth*).   Plate 6a

SOUTH-EAST TRANSEPT, WEST SIDE
WINDOW I (G42)

1 (69). MATTATHIAS, missing.

2 (70). MAATH, missing unless this figure is to be identified as one now in Window G12 (see note on No. 52 above).

WINDOW II (G43)

1 (71). NAGGE, missing.

2 (72). ESLI, missing.

WINDOW III (G44)

1 (73). NAUM, missing.

2 (74). AMOS, missing.

CHOIR, SOUTH SIDE

WINDOW I (G45)

1 (75). MATTATHIAS, missing. See note on No. 76.

2 (76). JOSEPH, missing. This figure is identified by Dr. Mason (p.12) with that now in the South-West Transept Window at H3, described as F on p. 45 below, where reasons are discussed against this identification, and that of No. 75 as its companion, E (H6).

WINDOW II (G46).

1 (77). JANNA, missing.

2 (78). MELCHI, missing.

WINDOW III (G47).

1 (79). LEVI, missing.

2 (80). MATTHAT, missing.

WINDOW IV (G48).

1 (81). HELI, missing.

2 (82). JOSEPH, missing.

WINDOW V (G49).

1 (83). THE VIRGIN MARY, missing.

2 (84). CHRIST, missing.

UNIDENTIFIED PANELS AND FRAGMENTS

Eight figure-panels survive of which the names have either been lost or are so far effaced or mutilated that they cannot be read with certainty.

A. Unidentified figure, perhaps SALMON (No. 31), now in the South-West Transept Window (M2, see p. 148). In a vesica-shaped panel with blue background studded with ruby discs and border with leaf-and-dot pattern on a gold band, the spaces above and below being filled with scroll foliage on a ruby ground. He sits in a high-backed chair with both hands raised in a gesture of argument. His hair blue, robe white with gold belt patterned with circles, neck and wrist-bands, mantle green, shoes yellow; the chair murrey.

For a discussion of the identity of this and the following figure see under Nos. 31, 32, p. 37 above.

B. Unidentified figure, perhaps BOOZ (No. 32), now in the South-West Transept Window (M7, see p. 148). The panel and setting as in A above except for the border, which is patterned with cross-hatched circles in squares. He sits with right hand raised (partly cut off by the border) and left forefinger extended. The head a modern restoration. Green robe with broad band across the shoulders and wristbands, all gold with a pattern of circles, white mantle, shoes pale grey-blue, stockings ruby; chair as in A, but with details in ruby, blue, green and murrey.

See note on A above.

C. Unidentified figure, perhaps JECONIAS (No. 41), now in the West Window (I1, p. 132). He sits with both arms raised, in his left hand a book, in his right a white bowl full of silver coins. His hair pale buff, robe murrey, mantle green with white lining, stockings ruby, shoes gold; the throne blue and gold. The name on a yellow band with ruby line below, behind his head, has perished beyond legibility, but it may perhaps be read as PHO..A..., which does not, however, tally with any otherwise unidentified name in the genealogy. When Miss Williams wrote, the figure was in the middle of the row, where the eighth King of England now is (I4); it was identified by her, without reason given, as Jeconias. It may be admitted that the vesica form of the panel containing the figure is in conformity with the position originally occupied by Jeconias in the Trinity Chapel Clerestory (G22). The symbolism of the bowl of coins remains unexplained. The vesica has a border of fifteenth- and sixteenth-century fragments which include, besides architectural fragments and decorative crowns (from borders), a hand holding the hilt of a sword hung from a belt and a fragment of plate armour with chain mail beneath (probably both parts of a single figure), also illegible black-letter inscription and GHU in Roman capitals.   Plate 6d

D. Unidentified figure, perhaps SALATHIEL (No. 42), now in the West Window (I7, p. 132). He sits with right hand on his thigh, his left raised as in exposition. Hair dark greyish, robe white with amber-coloured band across the chest and green wristbands, ruby belt, mantle murrey, shoes yellow, throne green, white and ruby. The name, behind his head, is almost obliterated but SI....C can perhaps be made out. The figure is in a vesica-shaped panel with white border.

The figure was pieced together by Mr. Caldwell and put where it now is when Phares was removed to the South-East Transept (Window G38); it is identified by Dr. Mason as 'probably Salathiel', doubtless because its setting shows it to be a suitable companion with C (above) which, if accepted as Jeconias, would have been originally in the same window (G22) of the Trinity Chapel Clerestory; the second Salathiel (in Window G37 of the South-East Transept Clerestory) would almost certainly have been in a panel of a different form (similar to that of Neri in the same window).

E. Unidentified figure, now in the South-West Transept Window, H6 (p. 146), possibly JONAN (No. 47). He sits pointing upwards with his left forefinger, his right hand being lost. He wears a greenish 'Phrygian' cap, green robe with white disc-patterned band at the top and belt, murrey mantle and shoes. The seat is white and amber. Part of an inscription (ACLC?) remains on the left. See note on F below.

F. Unidentified figure, now in the South-West Transept Window, H3 (p. 146), possibly JOSEPH (No. 48). He sits with a leaf-topped white sceptre in his left hand, his right hand extended, back downwards. His hair is white. He has a round murrey cap and a robe of the same colour with disc-patterned white border at the top, green mantle, and gold shoes. The name: IOSEP is placed in disordered arrangement to the left.

The identification of this figure and of E above is uncertain. Gostling (second edition) gives IOSEPH and MA (*sic*) respectively as the lower and upper figures in the first window of the apse (G23), where they were almost certainly out of place. The position of the titles in both panels makes it uncertain whether they actually belong to the figures, or may have been inserted arbitrarily when the panels were adapted for their present locations (in almost all other surviving cases the names are placed either behind the shoulders of the figure or arched over the head). If the name IOSEP can be accepted as belonging to the figure it accompanies, this figure must almost certainly be No. 48 in the series (Window G30) and its companion No. 47, Jonan, in spite of the fact that the broken lettering has no connection with this name (it cannot indeed be identified with any other name in the genealogy). Dr. Mason has suggested that the Joseph is No. 76 in the series, and the companion consequently Mattathias (No. 75); but it seems probable that these figures, like all those surviving from the Choir and Transepts, would have been enclosed under an arched canopy, not in a shaped medallion like those of the more easterly windows. The same is likely to have been the case with Joseph, husband of the Virgin, and his companion Heli (Nos. 82, 81). From these considerations it seems almost certain that these two figures, whoever they may be, belonged in any case originally to one of the now untenanted windows on the south side of the Trinity Chapel. The fact that the quatrefoil shape of the panels now containing the figures does not concord with the vesicas of the armature of Window G30 is not an insuperable difficulty, since the present form of the panels of A, B above indicates that in many cases the shape of the panels was extensively altered when they were transferred from their original places to their present positions in the West and South-West Transept Windows. The green border of opening fronds on a cross-hatched ground which is common to the panels containing E and F is doubtless original, and shows signs of having been adjusted to a shape for which it was not originally designed; the same may be said of the leafy scrollwork, growing out of a continuous stem closely adhering to the border, which fills the spaces above and below the panels.

G. Unidentified figure now in Window III (G12), in place of No. 21. He sits with left arm akimbo and right hand raised as in exposition. His hair is murrey, his robe white with gold border on the arms, below which the sleeves of a murrey undergarment with blue cuffs protrude, his mantle green and shoes pale blue. The throne gold. The canopy has a low trefoil arch with a turret above and ruby shafts with gold foliated capitals. The name, on a white ruby-edged band behind his head, seems to read: M....AT. The figure may perhaps be identified as either Matthat or Maath (Nos. 52, 70 in the series).

H. Unidentified figure now in Window III (G12), in place of No. 22. Sitting with right hand on thigh and left raised with forefinger extended. His hair murrey. Robe white with gold trellis-diapered band at the chest and wristbands of the same colour, green-lined murrey mantle, ruby belt, dark green shoes, gold throne. Canopy with trefoil arch and shafts as in G above. White ruby-edged name-band (illegible) behind the head.

I. Bearded head of an unidentified figure, twelfth century, from the Clerestory series. This and J (below) have been brought to light recently by Mr. Caldwell. It is impossible to say to what figures they belonged, but from its style it seems likely that I was in the Choir or Transepts.
Plate 50a

J. Bearded face, twelfth century, perhaps from the Clerestory series. See note on I above.
Plate 64a

13

(a) Solomon and the Queen of Sheba

(b) Joseph and his Brethren

about 1200

NORTH CHOIR AISLE

Window II

p. 56

14

(a)

(a) Eli receiving Samuel

(b) The Presentation in the
  Temple

about 1200

NORTH CHOIR AISLE

Window II

pp. 57, 58

(b)

(a)

(b)

(a) The Church with the Sons of Noah

(b) Virginity, Continence, and Marriage

about 1200

NORTH CHOIR AISLE

Window II

p. 60

16

(a)

(c)

(a) Balaam

(b) Isaiah

(c) The Magi
   and the Star

(d) The Magi
   and Herod

(e) The Adoration

(f) The Dream
   of the Magi

about 1200

NORTH CHOIR
AISLE

Window II

pp. 55–57

(e)

§2 Rose Windows of the North- and South-East Transepts

FACING one another at the clerestory level in the end walls of the East Transepts are two circular rose windows of which only that in the north wall still retains any of its original pictorial glass. The subject is the Old Dispensation, 'the Law and the Prophets', represented by Moses and the Synagogue in a square panel in the middle surrounded by four triangular panels forming a second square set diagonally about the inner square and containing figures of the Cardinal Virtues; these again are surrounded by four semicircular compartments with figures of the Major Prophets, the whole being inscribed within a circle and the interspaces between the semicircles filled with symmetrical foliated ornament on a blue ground. The outer part of the window is now filled with plain white glass but retains its original armature; this forms four main segmental divisions, each bisected radially and separated by trilobed panels so as to provide twelve compartments which, as Dr. Mason has very plausibly suggested, may have contained figures of the Minor Prophets, now lost. The date of the north rose is about 1178 (see p. 16).

The facing window in the south wall retains a considerable proportion of the original foliage work in the intervals of the figure-subjects but none of the latter. New figures were supplied by Austin in 1850, doubtless correctly, to illustrate the New Dispensation; Christ and the Church in the centre are surrounded by the symbols of the Four Evangelists, the Christian Virtues, Faith, Hope, Charity and Humility, and eight of the Apostles.

Reproductions: (North Rose) Westlake, pl. XXXIX*b* (the armature, pl. XL*a*); (South Rose) *C.C.C.*, No. 1 (October 1928), pl. facing p. 12.

NORTH ROSE WINDOW

1, 2. MOSES AND THE SYNAGOGUE. Standing figures, each on a greensward under a round arch springing from foliated capitals with battlemented turrets above them: Moses holding the tables of stone delivered on Sinai (in the form of a jewelled and clasped book), and the Synagogue, a woman with the Tables of the Law in her hands. The heads of both figures are restorations by Austin. Moses is without the horns on his forehead, which are his usual but not invariable attribute in medieval art; the same is the case in the only other representation of him at Canterbury—in the 'Burning Bush'

47

panel of the East Window of the Corona (see p. 77), but there the omission is in accordance with the sequence of his life's narrative.* The woman symbolising the Synagogue is veiled. It is possible that the original head would have shown her blindfolded also (as Austin's new face does not); this is usual in at least a large number of early medieval representations, as for instance a miniature of a German manuscript Book of the Gospels of about 1200 in the Cathedral Treasury at Treves† (where she stands with a banner on a broken staff as a pendant to the crowned figure of the Church, at the foot of the cross, in a Crucifixion group), in a similar scene on a thirteenth-century Limoges enamelled reliquary in the treasury of Chartres Cathedral,‡ in the abovementioned window at Bourges, in a twelfth-century glass panel from Châlons-sur-Marne now in the Musée de Sculpture Comparée, Paris, and in the almost identical design on the enamelled portable altar at Stavelot, Belgium;§ The famous statue of the south door of Strasburg Cathedral, and another in the south front of the transept of Rheims Cathedral show similar treatment. The symbolism of the veil is carried further in a window formerly in St. Denis Cathedral, in which Christ is shown standing between Ecclesia and Sinagoga and placing a crown on the head of the former whilst he tears the veil from the latter. ‖ On the other hand, the figure of the Synagogue is *unveiled* in a miniature of the Psalter of Robert de Lineseye, Abbot of Peterborough, dating from before 1222, belonging to the Society of Antiquaries.¶ Of the names inscribed behind the shoulders of the two figures, MOYSES and SINAGOG, the last three letters of the former and the first four of the latter are restorations by Austin, as is shown by Gostling's account of the window.

Reproduction: *F.C.C. Fifteenth Annual Report*, 1942, pl. facing p. 32.   Plate 9

3–6. THE CARDINAL VIRTUES. All four are crowned and have their names appended on a label.

Prudence (PRVDEN). She stands on a green mound with a dragon-like winged serpent in her right hand and two doves in her left. Dr. Mason gives the reference *Matth*. X, 16, but speaks of 'a dove' where actually two birds are to be seen, as does also Canon Crum.

Reproduction: Read, pl. IV.   Plate 10a

---

* Moses is also hornless in the statue, slightly later in date than this window, of the North Porch of Chartres Cathedral, although he is holding the Tables. He has horns in the nearly contemporary 'New Alliance' window at Bourges Cathedral (E. Mâle, *L'Art Religieux du XIIIe Siècle en France*, Paris, 1919, fig. 78), in a window of the Sainte Chapelle, Paris (J. D. Spencer, *Les Vitraux de la Sainte Chapelle de Paris*, Paris, 1932, pl. facing p. 24), and in a fragmentary French Jesse window of the same period at the Victoria and Albert Museum (see B. Rackham, *Guide to the Collections of Stained Glass*, 1936, p. 32). Mrs. Spencer (*loc. cit.*) notes that the horns are also absent, correctly, in a medallion of the same window of the Sainte Chapelle in which the scene of the Burning Bush is depicted; but in later Gothic Art the horns are sometimes shown, anachronistically, even in this subject, as in a sixteenth-century stained glass panel from Mariawald, near Treves, now in the Victoria and Albert Museum (reproduced in the *Burlington Magazine*, Vol. LXXXV, 1944, pl. 268).

† Reproduced by H. Swarzenski, *Vorgotische Miniaturen*, Königstein im Taunus, 1927, pl. 73.

‡ E. Houvet, *Monographie de la Cathédrale de Chartres*, Chartres, n.d., pl. 66, 67.

§ Reproduced respectively by G. Heinersdorff, *Die Glasmalerei*, Berlin, 1914, pl. I, and E. Mâle, *L'Art Religieux du XIIe Siècle en France*, Paris, 1922, fig. 127.

‖ Reproduced by Mâle, *op. cit.*, fig. 130.

¶ Reproduced by E. G. Millar, *English Illuminated Manuscripts from the Xth to the XIIIth Century*, Paris, 1926, pl. 69a.

Justice, stooping forward with a pair of scales in her right hand and her left upholding her name-scroll: IVSTICIA. Beneath the scales is what Gostling and subsequent writers have described as 'a golden bag', the relevance of which is not obvious.

Reproduction: *F.C.C. Fifteenth Annual Report*, 1942, pl. facing p. 32.   Plate 11a

Temperance walking on a greensward with a flaming torch in her right hand and, in her left hand, a bowl full of water; her name TEMPANTIA is on a scroll thrown over her left wrist.

Reproduction: Read, pl. 4.   Plate 10b

Fortitude, leaning forward, holds in her left hand a sword, in her right hand what Dr. Mason, who presumably never saw the figure at close quarters, wrongly describes as a green dragon but what is in reality a twisted cord (Westlake also describes the figure erroneously as 'Fortitude slaying a serpent'). Inscribed: FORTITVDO.

Reproduction: *F.C.C. Fifteenth Annual Report*, 1942, pl. facing p. 32.   Plate 11b

What follows is quoted from the author's note on the window in *F.C.C. Report*, XV, 1942, pp. 30, 31: 'The Virtues are masterpieces of adaptation to their very exacting compartments. Their representation here is noteworthy, because the numerous French series of Virtues cited in his monumental works by M. Émile Mâle, though including many of the virtues described by Ruskin as "only north-north-west", not cardinal,* apparently omit altogether Justice, for whose representation in glass-painting we consequently seek in vain for a parallel . . . [the twisted cord] may be taken to refer to the binding power of Force, the Virtue of police as well as soldiery, unless indeed there may be here some allusion to Gordian Knots to be cut by prowess of arms. No such attribute is carried by Fortitude as depicted elsewhere, by Giotto for instance, who shows her in the Arena Chapel at Padua as a warrior with lion-skin hood and arrow-pierced shield, or in the reliefs of the French cathedral doorways cited by Monsieur Mâle. This Canterbury window has, therefore, an importance for Christian iconography quite apart from its value as a work of art'. It will be noticed that Moses and the four Prophets have haloes.

7. ISAIAH. Leaning forward, with left knee raised, on a bench decorated with circles; in his left hand a scroll with his name: YSAIAS.   Colour Plate IVa

8. JEREMIAH. His pose is similar to that of Isaiah. Scroll inscribed: IEREMIA P (*Propheta*).

Reproduction: *F.C.C. Fourteenth Annual Report*, 1941, pl. facing p. 18. Colour Plate IVb

9. EZEKIEL. He sits upright on his bench, with right leg extended, right hand raised, and his name-scroll (EZECHIEL) in his left hand.

Reproduction: *F.C.C. Fourteenth Annual Report*, 1941, pl. facing p. 18. Colour Plate IVc

10. DANIEL. He holds his name-scroll (DANIEL) with both hands; his right leg outstretched. His throne has a leafy finial.   Colour Plate IVd

---

* *The Stones of Venice*, II, viii, 46.

§3 Apse Clerestory

THE five windows of the apse which interrupt the genealogical series were filled by Austin in 1861–2 with new designs as follows:—*

(1) Giving the Law, Moses striking the Rock; (2) The Magi, The Agony, The Transfiguration; (3) The Nativity, The Crucifixion, The Ascension; (4) Flight into Egypt, Flagellation, The Resurrection; (5) Beheading S. John Baptist, Baptism. These appear to have no relation to the original contents of the windows. Of these the panel depicting the Crucifixion, from the middle window (No. III), has been restored, partly with old glass, by Mr. Samuel Caldwell, Junior.† The medallions described below, originally set one above another vertically in Nos. II and IV, the windows immediately north and south of the middle, were reconstituted by Mr. Caldwell and placed by him where they are now, in Windows III and I of the South Choir Aisle Triforium (see pp. 72, 73); they may be assigned to the same period as the later windows of the genealogical series (see p. 29), the end of the twelfth century.

WINDOW II

This window illustrated the Infancy of Christ.

1. THE NATIVITY (now in Window III, 1, of the South Choir Aisle Triforium, p. 73). The Infant Christ lies, half draped, on straw laid over a low trestle bed. The Virgin kneels in adoration on the right; behind her stands a young shepherd leading a lamb by a halter. St. Joseph stands on the left, his left hand resting on a staff. In the background are an ass and an ox, with palings behind them. A lamp hangs above. The figure of the Child is a modern restoration. Plate 22a

2. THE ADORATION OF THE MAGI (now in Window III, 2, of the South Choir Aisle Triforium, p. 73). The Virgin sits on the right, the Child with right hand raised in benediction on her knee; before them are the three Kings, crowned, one kneeling, the others standing; two of them hold offerings in globular boxes, the third points at the Star of Bethlehem above them. Plate 22b

3. THE PRESENTATION IN THE TEMPLE (now in Window III, 3, of the South Choir Aisle Triforium, p. 73). The Virgin holds out the Infant above an altar into the arms of Simeon, who stands with Anna on the right; two candles (in reference to Candlemas) are burning on the altar, the end of which is diapered. On the left stands St. Joseph, holding a basket with a pair of turtledoves in it. Dr. Mason seems to have been mistaken in seeing a book lying on the altar. Plate 23a

---

* The titles are cited *verbatim* from the diagram on p. 2 of Miss Williams's *Notes on the Painted Glass.*
† Reproduced in *F.C.C. Twenty-first Annual Report*, 1948, facing p. 31.

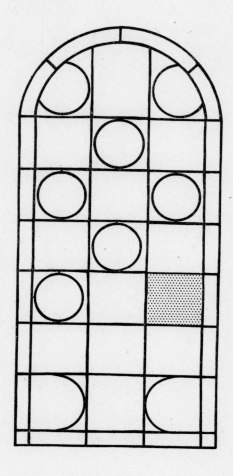

17′ 6″ × 6′ 6″

Plate V

THE PARABLE OF THE SOWER: the
seed falling by the wayside and upon stony places.
Panel from the 'Theological Windows' of the
North Choir Aisle, originally in Window VI, now
Window II, 15. About 1200. P. 58.

1. THE DORMITION OF THE VIRGIN (now Window I, 1, of the South Choir Aisle Triforium, p. 72). The Virgin lies with eyes closed and hands clasped in prayer on a bed with five of the Apostles gathered round it, one kneeling in front, the others in the background. This may be compared with a medallion showing the same subject in the contemporary Shoemakers' Window of the nave of Chartres Cathedral* in which all twelve Apostles are grouped round the dying Virgin. Plate 26a

2. THE ASSUMPTION (now in Window I, 2, of the South Choir Aisle Triforium, p. 72). The Virgin, barefooted, rises through two banks of clouds with the Dove hovering above her; 'as in the vision of the Apocalypse, she carries her Child, on the left arm' (M). She is surrounded by eight angels in particoloured robes in postures of adoration, two above and two below on either side. Plate 26b

3. THE CORONATION OF THE VIRGIN (now in Window I, 3, of the South Choir Aisle Triforium, p. 72). She sits with a palm-branch in her right hand on a stone bench decorated with quatrefoils facing Our Lord, who is placing a crown on her head. Among clouds on either side of them are angels swinging censers. Plate 27a

§4 Windows of the North and South Choir Aisles

THESE windows are the subject of an exhaustive examination by the late Dr. Montague James in a publication of the Cambridge Antiquarian Society (see Bibliography, p. 185), and all that here follows is based mainly on his work. There were formerly in the aisles of the Choir and in the two Eastern Transepts a series of twelve windows with medallions varying in number in the different windows, illustrating 'antitypes' and 'types', that is, New Testament subjects with the incidents in the Old Testament by which they are foreshadowed. The antitypes occupied panels set one above another in the middle of each window and were flanked by two panels with related types. These windows are sometimes known as the 'Theological Windows', a term derived ultimately, as Dr. James states, from the monograph by Cahier and Martin on the windows of Bourges Cathedral. They formed 'one of the most exhaustive and complete sets of types and antitypes which were to be found in any English church; and . . . England was the country in which this special product of medievalism found its most copious expression in artistic monuments'. 'The series finds its counterpart in many well-known instances' but differs 'in the full treatment accorded to the Parables of our Lord'. Early in

---

* Reproduced by Claudel and Aubert, *Vitraux des Cathédrales de France, XII*e *et XIII*e *Siècles*, Paris, 1937, pl. IX.

the thirteenth century this scheme of Old and New Testament subjects was codified in the 'Poor Man's Bible' (*Biblia Pauperum*)* and later in the 'Mirror of Human Salvation' (*Speculum Humanæ Salvationis*), both of which when made widely accessible in the fifteenth century by printing, supplied designs which were frequently copied or adapted in late Gothic stained glass.

In the Chapter Library there is a manuscript (C. 246) on three parchments joined with pins to form a continuous roll, written, according to Dr. James, early in the fourteenth century and giving a list in Latin of the subjects depicted in these twelve windows and copies of the inscriptions on them. Dr. James considered that the writer may very well have been the same who made the Inventory of Prior Henry of Eastry (British Museum, Cotton MS. Galba, E. IV). A copy of the Canterbury MS. is in the Library of Corpus Christi College, Oxford,† written by William Glastynbury, a monk of Christ Church, Canterbury, who died in 1478; this copy is comprised in a book (MS. C.256), with other miscellaneous records relating to the Cathedral and Priory, blank pages in which were subsequently filled with antiquarian notes by John Twyne, a Canterbury schoolmaster of the sixteenth century.‡ This copy bears the heading, now lacking in the original roll: *Fenestræ in superiori parte ecclesiæ Christi Cant. incipientes a parte septentrionali;* Dr. James conjectures from this that the roll was probably intended to be hung up near the windows as a guide to them, where visitors could see it.

From this roll it is clear that the small remnants of glass now surviving from these windows are not for the most part in their original positions. Dr. James discusses the location of the twelve windows described in the roll and concludes that the first six were the three windows in the North Choir Aisle and the windows in the lower range on the west and north walls of the North-East Transept; the placing of the remaining six is uncertain, but the last two in the series were probably the two more easterly windows of the South Choir Aisle; a thirteenth window necessary to complete the series of types and antitypes according to the normal scheme, which would have occupied the westernmost opening in this aisle, is conjectured never to have been completed, since there is no record of it in the roll. Turning to the windows as they are now, we find that the first in the North Choir Aisle was blocked up to make room for the staircase by the organ-loft which was once above the stalls on the north side of the Choir. Nothing is now left of the glass from this window. The second window still contains its original glazing as regards the four uppermost ranges of

---

* See H. Cornell, *Biblia Pauperum*, Stockholm, 1925.

† Not Corpus Christi, Cambridge, as stated by Westlake, p. 104.

‡ The book was afterwards in the possession of Twyne's grandson, Bryan Twyne, which circumstance gave rise to the misconception that the copy contained in it of the roll describing the windows was written in the seventeenth century; see C. Eveleigh Woodruff, 'The Chronicle of William Glastynbury, Monk of the Priory of Christ Church, Canterbury, 1419–1448' in *Archæologia Cantiana*, Vol. XXXVII (1925).

panels, twelve in all, and two (Nos. 13 and 14 in the diagram) of the next range below; the remaining subjects (Nos. 15-21) all belonged originally to Window VI (as also perhaps a fragment of lettering mentioned on p. 101). Window III is still filled with ancient glass, but only the subjects numbered 1–4 are now in their original positions; of the remaining eight, six were originally in Window IV and two came from Window VI. The former location of these eight panels within their windows will be indicated in the detailed descriptions of them given below. Of Windows V and VII–XII there is now nothing left.

The date of these windows is about the beginning of the thirteenth century, probably slightly before that of the 'Miracle' windows in the Trinity Chapel;* the date suggested by Loftie,† about 1174, on the evidence of similarity to an illuminated psalter written for a nun of Shaftesbury Abbey, now in the British Museum, is inadmissible on stylistic grounds.

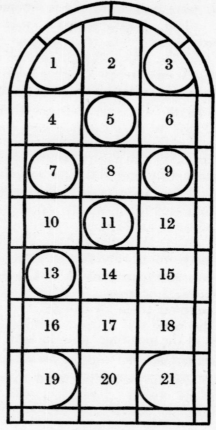

17′ 6″ × 8′ 6″

NORTH CHOIR AISLE
WINDOW II

The original scheme of this window, now only partially surviving, consisted of a middle column of seven panels with New Testament antitypes, without explanatory legends, flanked by others in pairs with Old Testament types, each with an inscription; the whole was surrounded by the surviving outer border of foliage springing from interlaced stems. The ground of the medallions is blue throughout; the border has a blue ground outside the loops of the stems and a ruby ground within them.

In the successive alternate ranges, a rectangular middle panel with an ornamental border was flanked by a circular medallion inscribed within a square, with a palmette filling each of the four spandrels; the intervening ranges show the reverse of this arrangement, the circle occupying the middle position and the squares the outer ones. In the two uppermost ranges the outer divisions are reduced where they come into contact with the arching of the border, following the shape of the window, so that what would otherwise be circular medallions on the flanks of the first range are somewhat less than half a circle in form. In the three lowest ranges the scheme

---

* Winston, p. 40; Westlake, p. 104; James, *loc. cit.*, p. 38.
† *Archaeological Journal*, XXXIII (1876), p. 12.

is now broken by the insertion of panels from another window (VI) of the series.

The window is reproduced in its entirety by Dr. Nelson (*Ancient Painted Glass*, etc., pl. IV). Its three upper ranges are reproduced in colours, very inaccurately, with the title, 'Upper half of the large North Transept (*sic*) window Canterbury Cathedral' on pl. I of Sir John Gilbert's *Fragments towards the History of Stained Glass* (see Bibliography, p. 185), on p. 19 of which it is described in laudatory terms as follows: 'The artist has spared neither time nor labour in endeavouring to do justice to this magnificent window, and the most ancient, perhaps, that remains to enrich and enliven the cathedral of Canterbury. The drawing of the horses of the three kings, in the upper centre square, is graceful and spirited, considering the remote period at which it was executed. The glass is of unusual thickness and strength, and has happily struggled through and escaped the destruction that continually menaced it. The two sides contain the history of the Israelites, the three centre pictures are from the life of Christ. . . .

'This superb window, which for brilliancy of drawing and execution surpasses every effort of which we have any knowledge either in this country or in any other, was in all probability old, when it was called to enrich the cathedral of Canterbury. The power of Henry II and the untiring zeal and refined taste of Becket, enabled them to command works of the most exalted genius. They had likewise the means of possessing themselves of whatever of excellence the Christian world had to offer. Its age, and the country that produced it, must therefore be a matter of conjecture, though in all probability it came from France. Of this, however, we are certain, that its rank as a masterpiece of genius must at all times have been of an exalted character, and indeed may be regarded, like *The Last Judgment* of Michael Angelo, far beyond the power of any other mortal hand.

'We shall gratify many of our subscribers by presenting a likeness of the head of this superb animal, taken from the group of the three kings in the upper centre of the window. The classic beauty and fiery expression given to the animal by the artist in the original, is wonderful; and it is fair to presume that he took his model from some exquisitely executed Grecian Sculpture that adorned the palaces or the temples of that era.

'The words of the artist who has so successfully copied this beautiful portrait, however modestly expressed, will perhaps be the best guide to its merits. "With regard to the head of the war-horse, I send you a drawing with as much of the spirit it contains as I could convey. The trappings are copied exactly from those of the glass. The more I have examined this head, the more am I astonished at its Grecian beauty and strength, and even now, my drawing, although I have spared no pains with it, does not appear to me to be nearly equal to the original."'

In the catalogue which follows the panels are numbered to correspond with their present arrangement in the window, but they are described in the sequence which they originally occupied, either (as explained above) in the window itself or in other windows of the series from which they were brought, antitypes being taken in order before their related types. The descriptive Latin titles are those given to them in the fourteenth-century parchment roll in the Chapter Library.

Reproduction: See above.

2. *Tres reges equitantes* (uninscribed). The Magi riding, point upwards to the Star among the clouds above them; the leader is already entering the Gate of Jerusalem. Gostling comments: 'They seem to be in doubt of the way'. It will be

(a)

17

(b)

(c)

(d)

(e)

(f)

(a) Lot

(b) Jeroboam's
      Sacrifice

(c) Christ and
      the Pharisees

(d) The Sower

(e) Julian and
      Maurice

(f) The Three
      Righteous Men

about 1200

NORTH CHOIR AISLE

Window II

pp 57–59

The Miraculous Draught
of Fishes
about 1200
NORTH CHOIR AISLE
Window III
p. 64

TEC DVODENNIS IN MEDIO DOCTO RVM

(a)

(b)

(c)

(d)

(e)

(f)

(a) Christ among the Doctors
(b) Moses and Jethro
(c) Daniel and the Elders
(d) The Miracle of Cana
(e) The Six Ages of the World
(f) The Six Ages of Man

about 1200

NORTH CHOIR AISLE

Window III

pp. 62–64

20

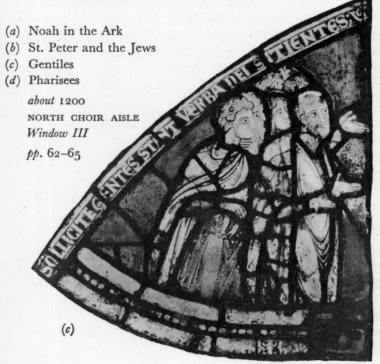

(a)

(b)

(c)

(d)

(a) Noah in the Ark
(b) St. Peter and the Jews
(c) Gentiles
(d) Pharisees

about 1200
NORTH CHOIR AISLE
Window III

pp. 62–65

noted that they wear the loose trousers familiar as the dress of Orientals from the figures of Persians in Ancient Greek art as, for instance, in the battle-scenes on the so-called Sarcophagus of Alexander at Constantinople. At the same time it must be stated that Sir John Gilbert's curious conjecture quoted above, as to the source from which the artist may have drawn inspiration direct for the rendering of the horses, will not find acceptance with modern art-historians.   Plate 16c

1. *Balaam.* The prophet is seen 'on his ass riding eagerly forwards with his cloak floating behind him, and stretching both hands towards the same Star [*i.e.*, in the middle panel]' (M). Inscribed: BALAAM and, on the border: ORIETVR STELLA EX IACOB ET CONSVRGET VIRGA DE ISRAEL ('There shall come a Star out of Jacob, and a Sceptre shall rise out of Israel'). The parchment roll in the Chapter Library (C. 246, see p. 52) gives *exurget homo* for *consurget virga*. Miss Williams, following Gostling, reads *consurget virgo*, which, as Dr. Mason points out, would suggest that the original word was *homo* as given in the roll; but in spite of the decayed condition of the glass the reading given above can be distinctly made out.   Plate 16a

3. *Ysaias et ierusalem* (Glastynbury reads: *Ysagas & civitas ierusalem*). 'Isaiah, standing at the gate (presumably) of Jerusalem, and pointing like Balaam to the star [in the middle panel]' (M). Inscribed (beside the prophet's head) : YSA and : AMBVLABVNT GENTES IN LVMINE TVO ET REGES IN SPLENDORE ORT' *BENIAMˢ* ('The Gentiles shall come to thy light, and kings to the brightness of thy rising'). Only the first five words are quoted in the roll. The end of the original inscription had already, when Gostling transcribed it, been lost and replaced by BENIAMˢ, doubtless from the circle originally occupying the left-hand space at the foot of the window, with the slaughter of the tribe of Benjamin (*Judges* XX), as shown by Glastynbury's transcription.   Plate 16b

5. *Herodes et Magi* (Glastynbury: *Tres reges cum pharone* [*sic*, for *herode*]). 'Herodes sitting in a pensive attitude', stroking his beard, 'receives the account of the three wise men who are standing before him; over their heads is the Star, and under them TRES MAGI . . .; behind his chair stands a person with his right hand expanded, as if in astonishment' (Gostling), 'doubtless a priest or scribe telling where the Christ should be born' (M). Below Herod (not above, as Gostling, followed by Miss Williams and Dr. Mason), his name: HERODES; equally inaccurate is the introduction of the inscription TRES MAGI to occupy the full length of the band below the subject as shown in Gilbert's chromolithograph, copied in the woodcut in *Archaeological Journal*, Vol. XXXIII, p. 9.   Plate 16d

4. *Pharao et moyses cum populo exiens ab egypto.* Pharaoh with crown and lily-headed sceptre sits in the door of his house, with an attendant, dismissing Moses from his land; the architrave above him is inscribed: PHARAO REX EGIPTI (not EGYPTI, as Gostling). To the left, Moses, his rod in his left hand, pointing with his right hand towards the waters of the sea which 'stand in a heap' (M) in the left lower corner of the panel, and leading 'a group of Israelitish men, women and children' (G); above is the pillar of fire as a flaming column, with the legend: ISRL SEQVENS COLVMPNAM ('Israel following the pillar'). Above and below the panel the inscriptions: EXIT AB ERVMP*N*A *POP*LVS. DVCENTE CO*LV*MPNA and STELLA MAGOS DVXIT: LVX XPC VTRI*SQ* RELVXIT ('The people go out of the wilderness led by the pillar. The star led the Magi; to both Christ shone as a light'). Mock Arabic lettering at the sides of the panel.   Plate 12a

6. *Christus et gentes.* 'The conversion of the heathens' (G) from idolatry to the faith. 'On the right is a pale blue idol on a pedestal in a temple, with a heathen altar at the foot. The idol is horned and holds a staff. Our Lord carries a scroll, representing the Gospel, and leads the people up steps into a church, in which is an altar with a cross upon it, and by the steps is a baptismal font. In the air above the people a winged devil attempts to persuade them not to abandon the false god' (M). The inscriptions which, as Dr. Mason points out, express the relation of the picture to the central scene (in No. 5) read: (above) STELLA MAGOS DVXIT: ET EOS AB HERODE REDVXIT; (below) SIC SATHANAM GENTES FVGIVNT: TE XPE SEQVENTES. ('A star led the Wise Men and led them back from Herod; thus the Gentiles flee from Satan, following Thee, O Christ'). Mock Arabic lettering at the sides (compare p. 28, note).

It will be noticed that the idol is represented as an Antique nude statue, horned like a satyr (a similar naked but hornless idol is depicted in the nearly contemporary window at Chartres Cathedral with the story of St. Eustace). The inscription formerly on the scroll held by Christ has entirely disappeared.

Reproductions: Williams, pl. 1; Nelson, fig. 26; J. D. Le Couteur, *English Mediæval Painted Glass*, fig. 13. Plate 12b

8. *Maria cum puero. Magi et pastores.* The Adoration of the Magi (to the left) and the Shepherds (to the right). The Virgin sits with the Child on her knee on a high-backed throne, with her feet on a footstool, beneath a canopy of which the pillars are painted to imitate veined marble; she looks straight in front of her, as in the famous window at Chartres known as the *Belle Verrière;* the Child holds up his hand in blessing and looks towards the Magi, of whom two bring caskets and the third (kneeling) a handful of coins.

It will be noted that the coins, being painted on the same piece of glass as the hands, are white; at a later period, by the use of yellow stain, they could have been more realistically shown as gold. The star is seen above them in the left corner of the panel, which has a border of rosettes and no inscription. The three shepherds, barefoot and trousered, carry staves. Plate 16e

7. *Rex salomon et regina Saba.* Solomon to the left, sceptre in hand, on a throne with arcaded arms, receives the Queen of Sheba, who enters a doorway with double door and is followed by two 'members of the king's household' (M) turning to receive gifts from two attendants, one of whom has negroid features and curly hair, seen to the right mounted on camels (with the head of a third camel). A large saddlebag is shown on the nearest camel. Below are the names: REX SALOM, (not SALLOM as transcribed by Gostling), REGINA SABA. Inscribed round the edge: HIS DONAT DONIS REGINA DOMVM SALOMONIS. SIC REGES DOMINO DANT M[un]ERA TRES TRIA TRINO ('The Queen bestows these gifts on the house of Solomon. Thus the kings give three gifts to the threefold Lord'). Miss Williams wrongly reads the first word as HIC. Plate 13a

9. *Joseph et fratres sui cum egyptiis.* Joseph, with his name IOSEPH above him, sits in the middle on a throne with steps in front between groups of his brethren on one side and Egyptians on the other, some of whom carry bowls filled with coins. Below, the legend: FRS IOSEPH + EGIPTII. Inscribed round the edge: AD TE LONGINQVOS IOSEPH ATTRAHIS ATQ' PROPINQVOS: SIC DE*VCI* [for *deus*] IN CVNIS IVDEOS GENTIBVS VNIS ('Thou, Joseph,

drawest to thyself men from far and near; thus, O God, thou dost unite Jews and Gentiles at the cradle [of Christ]').

'The head (of Joseph) is not the original head, but belongs to the same period, and was well chosen by those who repaired the window (presumably) in the eighteenth century' (M).

Plate 13b

11. *Admoniti sunt magi ne herodem adheant* (sic). The Wise Men warned in a dream not to return to Herod. The Three Kings lie asleep, crowned, in a single bed with a high arcaded tester over which a curtain is thrown; on the right an angel flies down towards them with a scroll inscribed: NE RDEATIS AD HERODEM (the original wording has been replaced since the publication of Miss Williams's book, which records it as HERODE preceded by SECU inserted from elsewhere.) The panel may be compared, as Miss Williams points out, with a panel dating probably from about 1100 at Le Mans Cathedral, reproduced by Westlake, Vol. I, p. 11, in which, however, one of the kings is awake, looking towards the angel; the same is the case in a picture of this subject in the illuminated MS. in the British Museum mentioned above (p. 53), reproduced by Loftie (*op. cit.*, p. 13), where the angel is standing, not flying, and the crowns of the kings are ranged symbolically in a group together, in the top left corner.

Reproduction: Westlake, Vol. I, pl. LIX*d*.

Plate 16f

10. *Subuersio sodome et loth fugiens*. The destruction of Sodom and the escape of Lot. Two angels are leading Lot and his two daughters away, up a hill on the right, with a tall tree in the background; in the middle is his wife, looking back over her shoulder at the burning and collapsing ruins of Sodom, and already turned into a pillar of salt, as shown by the white glass used for her entire figure instead of the pinkish glass which would otherwise have been employed for her face. Inscribed: (above) VT LOTH SAL[*v*]ETVR NE RESPICIAT PROHIBETVR; (below) SIC VITANT REVEHI PER HERODIS REGNA SABEI ('Lot is forbidden to look back so that he may be saved; so the Sabeans avoid riding back through the realms of Herod'). Mock Arabic lettering at the sides.

Reproduction: Read, pl. 7.

Plate 17a

12. *Jeroboam immolans*. Jeroboam's sacrifice and the warning to the man of God (I *Kings*, XIII, 9). The prophet, indicated by the title PPH'A, a halo, and the scroll in his left hand, is on the left with a flock of sheep behind him, approaching with right hand raised in admonition King Jeroboam, who is in the act of slaughtering with a small knife a lamb laid on a square blood-red altar; the name REX IEROBOAM is written on a band above, in line with a scroll inscribed with the warning words: NE REDEAS VIA QA VENISTI ('Return not by the way by which thou camest') held by a hand from Heaven (indicated by a line of clouds). Behind the altar stand four attendants; in front of it is 'a large vessel, either to catch the blood, or to hold libations of wine' (M). Inscribed: (above) VT VIA MVTETVR REDEVNDO: PPH'A MONETVR; (below) SIC TRES EGERVNT: QVI XPO DONA TVLERVNT ('The prophet is warned that his road should be changed as he returns; thus did the three act who brought gifts to Christ'.) Mock Arabic lettering at the sides.

Plate 17b

14. *Oblatio pueri in templo et symeon*. The Presentation in the Temple (Candlemas). The Virgin holds out the infant Christ above the altar towards the outstretched hands of Simeon, behind whom stands an attendant carrying a long white candle

topped with a flame in ruby glass; behind the Virgin stands Joseph, holding also a candle as well as a basket containing a pair of turtle doves. The altar, on which are laid a book and drapery, is covered with a richly diapered cloth fringed at the bottom; behind is an arcade draped with a curtain. Border of quatrefoils reserved on a cross-hatched ground. No inscription. 'Mr. Caldwell has substituted a new head, on old glass, for the head of the Mother now restored to its proper place above. This is the only new work in the whole window. . . . Originally this scene was flanked on the right by Melchisedech "offering bread and wine for Abraham". This is unfortunately lost; but on the left is the corresponding scene—the presentation of Samuel' (M).

Plate 14b

13. *Oblatio samuelis*. 'Eli in the Temple receives Samuel from Hannah. Over his head HELI SACERDOS' (G). Elkanah stands beside her, and on the right is a woman attendant carrying an amphora of wine. In the foreground are other offerings, three young bullocks and 'three baskets of cakes or corn. Upon the altar lies the ark, half open, identified by its contents—Aaron's budded rod, the two tables of the Law, and the golden pot of manna' (M). The contents of the baskets are probably intended for grains of corn, the 'flour' of the A.V., and may be compared for their exaggerated size with the seeds scattered by the Sower in panel 15. Inscribed: SIGNIFICAT DOMINVM SAMVEL PVER. AMPHORA. VINVM. . . *A . . RE*: . . RA. GEMINVM. TRIPLEX OBLATIO. TRINVM. ('The child Samuel signifies the Lord, the amphora the wine; the threefold offering the triune form of that which is by nature twofold'.) The MS. roll shows that the defective word was *natura;* that the lettering employed for filling the blank was originally in another panel of this series of windows seems to be indicated by the form of the ornament (derived from mock Arabic lettering) following the letters RE, which occurs again at the end of the inscription of panel No. 19 below. Plate 14a

The following seven panels were originally in Window VI of the series and will be described in the sequence in which they were there placed, the antitypes in each case being taken before the corresponding types (where the latter exist).

15. (from Window VI, 5) *Seminator et uolucres*. The Parable of the Sower, first scene. The sower, holding the seed in the fold of a cloth thrown like a cloak over his shoulders, is scattering it broadcast with his right hand; some of it falls on a road which curves upwards on the right, where it is being devoured by six birds of various colours (three others fly towards a tree in the background); some is lying on 'stony places' represented by coloured rocks on the left and long curving strips of yellow soil. No inscription; border of beads within mock Arabic lettering; small rosettes in the four spandrels.

Reproductions: O. Elfrida Saunders, *A History of English Art in the Middle Ages*, Oxford, 1932, fig. 38; *C.C.C.*, No. 35 (May 17, 1940), p. 12.

Colour Plate V

17. (from Window VI, 6). *Pharisei recedentes a ihesu*. A group of Pharisees shod in buskins, on the left, are walking away from Christ, who stands barefooted on the right holding a scroll inscribed: NISI MANDVCAVERITIS CARNEM F *HEBES.NHVIVS* (St. John, VI, 53: 'Except ye eat the flesh of the Son of Man'; the italicised portion is an insertion from elsewhere and difficult to decipher). Dr. Mason comments: 'This seems to fix the scene as that of *St. John*, VI, 66. The number of hearers departing is indicated by the tops of heads which have no feet or other parts belonging to them.' Miss Williams wrongly transcribes: NISI

17′ 6″ × 6′ 6″

(*a*)

Plate VI

(*a*) THE CALLING OF NATHANAEL:
two scenes are included—Christ approaching
Nathanael beneath the fig-tree, and 'Whence
knowest Thou me?'. Medallion from the
'Theological Windows' of the North Choir
Aisle, originally in Window IV, now Window
III, 10. About 1200. P. 63.

(*b*) WILLIAM OF KELLETT: the accident
at the carpenter's bench. Medallion (9) in
Window VII of the series illustrating the
miracles of St. Thomas of Canterbury, in the
aisles of the Trinity Chapel. About 1220. P. 101.

(MANDUCA) CAVERITIS. Inscribed above and below the panel: SEMEN RORE CARENS EXPERS RADICIS ET ARENS HI SVNT QVI CREDVNT. TENTANTVR SICQ; RECEDVNT. ('Seed lacking dew, having no root and parched, these are they who believe, are tempted and thus fall back.') Miss Williams, following Gostling, wrongly reads RATIONIS for RADICIS. Border of bead ornament within quatrefoils. This panel was originally on the right of No. 15; on the left was 'The Pharisees tempting Jesus', now lost. Plate 17c

20 (from Window VI, 8). *Semen cecidit inter spinas—semen cecidit in terram bonam.* The Parable of the Sower, second scene. The sower, this time carrying his supply of seed in a two-handled basket, walks to the left. In the foreground are thorn-bushes with a garment, probably the sower's cloak, lying amongst them; the bare soil behind is the good ground. In the background are trees on hillocks, with clouds above. To the left of the sower's head part of an inscription: ' . . . IDIATOR'; has been inserted. This has been read by authors hitherto, wrongly, as '[SEM]-INATOR'. That the band bearing the inscription is an insertion from elsewhere is proved by the fact that it is of golden-yellow glass and, if complete, would come in contact with the yellow glass used for the tree on the left (from which it is now separated by a piece of blue glass filling the defect in the inscribed piece); this would be in violation of the practice of mediæval glass painters who, like the heraldic designers of the period, avoid the contact of two passages of the same colour except where it represents part of the same element in the picture, such as sky, a robe or building. At each side, a bead border within a band of quatrefoils. This panel was originally flanked, as now, by Nos. 19 and 21. Plate 17d

Reproduction (in colours): Read, pl. 1.

19 (from Window VI, 7). *Diuites huius mundi cum pecunia.* 'The rich men of this world, in whom the life of the seed is choked. Their names are *Iulianus* and *Mauritius* [sic]. The names are unexplained: but probably they represent two emperors, Julian (the famous Apostate) and Maurice (the opponent of St. Gregory), whom the saint denounces in vehement language. They wear crowns, and have a heap of gold coins at their feet, and servants to wait on them. . . . The circle in which they sit was too large for its present position, and has been cut down to suit the space' (M). The crowned figures sit on benches with footstools and between them are a bowl full of coins, other pieces of plate and rolls of cloth; beside each is his name: IVLIANVS, MAVRICIVS. Two attendants stand behind under a double arcade, with rich fur-lined cloaks (not curtains, as suggested by Dr. Mason) thrown over a rod. Inscribed on enclosing band: DELICIOSI NIL FRVCTVS REFERVNT QVONLNƎ TERRESTRIA QVERVNT . . . NOSI. ('These thorny ones are the rich and luxurious; they bear nought of fruit since they seek earthly things'—the inverted letters have been substituted for the original IAM of *quoniam*.) Branching palmettes in the spandrels to the right.

The MS. roll shows that the inscription originally began: *Isti spinosi locupletes deliciosi* —of which the termination of *spinosi* has now been inserted at the end of the band. Plate 17e

21 (from Window VI, 9). *Job. Daniel. Noe ce. i t.bo.* (for *ceciderunt* [or *cemen* for *semen*] *in terram bonam*). The three righteous men of *Ezekiel* XIV, Daniel, Job, and Noah, representing the seed sown in good ground. They sit on a single bench, holding each a scroll bearing his name: DANIEL, IOB, NOE. On the head of each a square crown is being placed by three angels descending from a cloud above.

Beneath the right foot of Noah is a rainbow. The panel has been cut down on the right, so that only part of the original inscription remains, and in a disordered state: VERBA PATRIS SEVIT DEV . . . ONA CTVS SIBI CREVIT: IN TELLVRE BON SVA (*Verba patris sevit deus hijs fructus sibi crevit. In tellure bona triplex sua cuique corona*—'God sowed the words of the Father; to these fruit was brought forth. In the good ground to each was given a triple crown.') Miss Williams wrongly reads SERVIT for SEVIT. In place of the portion cut away, there has been inserted part of the inscribed border belonging to another medallion in the same window, with the subject of the good and bad fish from the Parable of the Draw-net cast into the Sea (*St. Matthew*, XIII, 47): REPROBANTVR: PARS EST A DO (*Hij qui iactantur in leuam qui reprobantur. Pars est a domino maledicta cremanda camino*— 'These who are cast to the left are they that are rejected This part, cursed by the Lord, is destined to be burnt in the furnace.') In the spandrels are portions of branching acanthus foliage.   Plate 17f

The panels 16 and 18 originally flanked, as antitype in the middle, the subject of the Parable of the Leaven or Three Measures of Meal.

16 (from Window VI, 10). *Tres filii noe cum ecclesia.* The Church with the three sons of Noah, who were symbolical of it. The Church, represented as a woman holding a long scroll with a mock inscription, stands to the left with the title: *ECCLESIA* (partly restored) above her. The names: SEM, CH*EV*, IAPHET are written above figures of Shem, Ham and Japhet, who stand holding the round world (lettered MVNDVS) between them and pointing each to his own portion, distinctively coloured green, gold and pink. The map of the world is encircled by a band inscribed: PARTE NOE NATI MICHI QVISQ; SVA DOMINATI ('Noah's sons ruling for me, each in his own part'). Above the panel is the legend: VNA FIDES NATIS EX HIS TRIBVS. ET DEITATIS ('From these three sons one faith in the Godhead'); the penultimate word is written in error, for EST, which is read, but wrongly, by Miss Williams. Below is a mutilated inscription made up of fragments from elsewhere: VERIT SVM P RO S EO DE ABEL DE SH BORAT. Dr. Mason conjectured that the final fragment might be from Window IX (*coram Pharaone laborat*) or Window V (*dum mundi cura laborat*) and identified ABEL DE as belonging to the original panel 18 in this window (Window II), with the subject of Elijah fleeing from Jezebel and Ahab as type of the Flight into Egypt; his first conjecture gives the clue both to BORAT and to VERIT, which belong to the inscription accompanying panel 4 in Window V, Peter fishing and John reading, type of Martha and Mary at Bethany (*Equoris unda ferit hunc. ille silencia querit. Sic requies orat dum mondi cura laborat*—'The one is smitten by the wave of the sea, the other seeks out silence. Thus quietness prays whilst the care of the world labours'). Equally certainly SEOD, and SH and RO belong to the same couplet as ABEL DE (*Ut trucis insidias jezabel declinat helyas. Sic deus herodem terrore remotus eodem*— 'As Elijah shuns the plots of the butcher Jezebel, so God shuns Herod and is removed from the same terror'). The remaining fragment (SVM) eludes identification.

Reproductions: Williams, pl. 2; Nelson, fig. 27.   Plate 15a

18 (from Window VI, 12). *Virgines. Continentes. Coniugati.* The three blameless states of life, Virginity, Continence and Marriage, represented by three figures under a triple arcade. The scrolls held by them with the titles: VIRGO, CON-TINENS and CONIVGATVS are filled out with mock inscriptions which seem

to be based respectively on Hebrew, Arabic and Latin. Above the arcade is the inscription: ATA TRIA TRES FRVCTVS OPERATA; this inscription was originally: *Fermentata sata tria tres fructus operata.* The whole has been shifted to the left and mock Arabic lettering inserted to fill the gap on the right. At the foot, completing the couplet but (as observed by Mr. Woodruff in *Archæologia Cantiana*, Vol. XXXVII, p. 144) not recorded in the MS. roll, are the words: SVNT VXORATIS ET VIRGINIBVS VIDVATIS ('Three seeds when leavened produce three fruits, for the espoused, the virgin and the widowed'); mock Arabic ornament fills up the band. A border of quatrefoils above and below.

Reproduction: Read, pl. 5. Plate 15b

WINDOW III

This window comprised originally four medallions, one above another, displaying New Testament anti-types, flanked by half-medallions and quarter-medallions with corresponding types set at a level half-way between the main medallions. Of these only one medallion (No. 1) and three half-medallions (Nos. 2, 3, and 8) remain; the places of the rest have been given to medallions and half-medallions (Nos. 4, 7, 10, 5, 6, and 9 respectively) from Window IV and two quadrants (Nos. 11 and 12, at the bottom corners of the window) from Window VI. In the subjoined catalogue, as in that of Window II, the divisions are numbered to correspond with their present arrangement, but they are described in their original sequence, whether in the window itself or in those from which they were removed to take their places here, antitypes coming before their related types; as before, the Latin titles given are taken from the fourteenth-century roll. The arrangement of the medallions has been altered since the publication of Miss Williams's *Notes on the Painted Glass, etc.,* and of Dr. Nelson's *Ancient Painted Glass in England* (1913); medallions 4 and 8 were then in the places now occupied by 5 and 7 and *vice versa.* The three interpolated middle medallions (4, 7, 10) are smaller in diameter than No. 1, the difference being made good by the addition of outer 'crown' borders. The ground of the window is filled up with sprays and tufts of foliage springing from coiled stems which are interlaced with one another and encircle the large pictorial medallions; the stems form also smaller medallions set in the intervals of the larger and filled with quadripartite symmetrical groups of acanthus-leaves and sprays. The ground of both larger and smaller

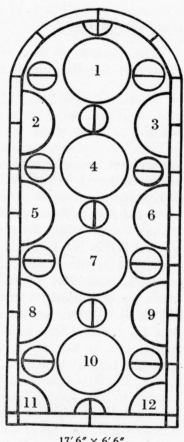

17′ 6″ × 6′ 6″

medallions is blue, that of the interspaces ruby; the medallions have an inner border consisting of trelliswork seen in perspective, a typical Late Romanesque pattern. The border of the window is filled with bunches of grapes—gold, blue, and green—and white leaves on vine-stems twined about a gold rod which divides the particoloured background, ruby on the inner side of the border and blue on the outer.

Reproductions: Nelson, *Ancient Painted Glass*, pl. V (where the window is shown as before subsequent rearrangement); (in colours) Saint and Arnold, pl. 4.

1. *Ihesus sedet in medio doctorum*. The boy Christ sits with a scroll in his left hand in the midst of two groups of bearded doctors, four on either side, who emphasise their arguments with animated gestures of the hands; one of them holds an open book with mock lettering. At the back, an arcade of round-headed arches on two planes, the supporting columns set alternately; below, the inscription: IHC DVODENNIS IN MEDIO DOCTORVM ('The twelve-year-old Jesus in the midst of the doctors').

Miss Williams transcribes in error *doctrum*. In the omission from the scene of the figures of Mary and Joseph this medallion differs from many versions of the subject, as in the 'Canterbury Gospels' (6th or 7th century) at Corpus Christi College, Cambridge, and from later works such as those in Giotto's fresco in the Arena Chapel at Padua and the window in the Transept of Great Malvern Priory Church (see Rushforth, *Medieval Christian Imagery*, pp. 382, 3). Plate 19a

2. *Moyses et Jetro cum populo*. Moses receiving advice from the Gentile Jethro (*Exodus*, XVIII, 13–26), as a type of the humility of Christ. Jethro stands with gestures of warning to the right of the high-backed seat of Moses, at whose feet a crowd of Israelites sit on the ground, looking up towards him. Their names: MOYSES and IETHRO are appended beside them. Inscribed: HIC HOMINES AVDIT ÐS (for *Deus*). HINC VIR SANCTVS OBAVDIT GENTILIS VERBIS. HVMILES SVNT FORMA SVPERBIS ('Here God listens to men. Hence the holy man pays heed to the words of the Gentile. The humble are a pattern for the proud'). Miss Williams and Dr. Nelson give erroneous readings (*sic, hinc* for *hic, i sic* for *ds*). The subject is repeated in the Corona window (p. 79, No. 24). Plate 19b

3. *Daniel in medio Seniorum*. Daniel among the Elders. 'The . . . roundel illustrates the wisdom of the holy Child. A type is found in the sagacity of the youthful Daniel, as told in the story of Susanna. Susanna does not appear in the picture, but the wicked Elders stand in the foreground on trial. Daniel, with admiring Elders, sits on a bench above them' (M). The name: DANIEL inscribed above; the onlooking Elders—three are visible—raise their hands in gestures of astonishment. Inscribed round the border: MIRANTVR PVERI SENIORES VOCE DOCERI SIC RESPONSA [*Dei sen*] SVMQVE STVPENT PHARISEI ('The Elders marvel at being taught by the utterances of a boy; thus the Pharisees are amazed at the answers of God').
Plate 19c

8. *Noe in Archa*. 'Noah, at the open window of the ark, receives the return of the dove with the olive-leaf; in the foreground a rock rises above the waters of the flood, and on it is a raven' (M). The ark is in two storeys, having pilasters crowned with foliated capitals attached to the walls; the window out of which Noah is leaning opens in the roof with a shutter provided with ornamental iron hinges. At the foot, the words: NOE IN ARCHA. Round the border the inscription: FLVXV CVNCTA VAGO SVBMERGENS PRIMA VORAGO OMNIA PVRGAVIT BAPTISMAQVE

Plate VII

THE VIRGIN AND CHILD ENTHRONED.
Crypt, East Window (upper part). About 1190–
1200. Pp. 65–67.

SIGNIFICAVIT ('The first devouring flood, submerging everything with its pervading flow, purified all things and signified baptism').

This panel, which originally occupied the position of No. 5 in the window, is one of the two types of the Baptism of Christ (the original No 4, now lost); the subject is repeated in the Corona window (p. 77, No. 12). Dr Nelson wrongly reads *fluxa*.

Reproduction (in colours): Saint and Arnold, pl. 4.   Plate 20a

10. *Vocatio natanael iacentis sub ficu*. The Calling of Nathanael. The medallion combines two scenes. 'On the right is Nathanael under the fig-tree, which is conspicuously marked as FICVS. His head rests upon his left hand in an attitude of meditation. His name [NATHANAEL] is in the background. Philip [named PHILIPP'], with his right hand upraised, is pointing to where Jesus stands. In the middle of the picture Nathanael is seen a second time, with his name over him. He bears a scroll, with the words: VNDE ME NOSTI ("Whence knowest thou me?"). Our Lord meets him with a similar scroll, nearly obliterated CVM ĒĒS S [*ub ficu*] VIDI [*te*] [("When thou wast beneath the fig-tree I saw thee")]. Two disciples stand behind whose names are given above, PETRVS and ANDREAS' (M). Below, a yellow band with zigzag ribbon ornament. Foliated 'crown' border (see p. 28, note).

This medallion was originally No. 1 in Window IV.

Reproduction: Williams, pl. 4.   Colour Plate VIa

4. *Christus mutauit aquam in uinum et sex ydrie*. The Miracle of Cana. 'Our Lord is seated at the right-hand end of the table, with his Mother next to Him. Next to her is one of the disciples—perhaps the Evangelist—as denoted by the nimbus. Next are the bride and bridegroom, and at the left end the governor of the feast [wearing a mitre]. One of the servants is bearing to him a bowl of the miraculous wine; the other is still filling the waterpots ["*hydriae*"] with water, and looking up at the Lord for direction. The six waterpots are prominently displayed in front. Three of them have side handles, three have not—perhaps with reference to the difference of their capacity, but this is not insisted on in the interpretation' (M). On the table are dishes of viands (that in front of Christ contains symbolically a fish) and round loaves; at the back, a curtain thrown over a doorway. The diaper pattern of the table-cloth is painted on the outside of the glass and seen through its folds, 'thus tempering its whiteness' (M). No inscription, the significance of the subject being explained in the legend to the type (No. 5) of which this is the antitype. Foliated 'crown' border.

Originally No. 4 in Window IV. Reproduction: Williams, pl. 3.   Plate 19d

5. *Sex etates mundi*. The Six Ages of the World, referring to the mystical meaning of the six water-pots of No. 4. The explanation SEX ETATES SVNT MVNDI is written above. The names of the representatives of these ages, ADAM, NOE, ABRAH, DAVID, IECHONIAS, are given over the heads of the seated figures (except in the case of Christ, who is distinguished by a crossed nimbus). 'Adam is depicted as fully clothed with a hoe in his hand; Noe with the Ark; Abraham with the fire [in a bowl] and knife [or sword]; David with crown and harp; Jechonias with crown and sceptre; and last Our Saviour with the open book of the Gospels' (M). Round the border, the verses: YDRIA METRETAS CAPIENS EST QVELIBET ETAS. LIMPHA DAT HISTORIAM Vᵒ' [*vinum*] NOTAT ALLEGORIAM ('Any one of the ages is a waterpot containing firkins. The water gives the story, the wine signifies the allegory'.) Miss Williams erroneously transcribes: *lympha*.

Originally No. 5 in Window IV.   Plate 19e

6. *Sex etates hominis*. The Six Ages of Man, continuing the interpretation of No. 4. In the field above is the title: SEX ETATES HOMINIS. The ages are represented by standing figures—each with his name attached on a label—respectively of a babe (INFANTIA), a boy carrying 'a ball with a hole in it and a curved stick, like a hockey stick' (M) (PVERITIA, 'boyhood'), a youth 'bearing a sort of sceptre, perhaps as an academic distinction' (M) (ADOLESCENTIA), a bearded young man with a sword which, *pace* Dr. Mason, he holds in his right hand only, not in both hands (IVVENTVS, 'young manhood'), a man, also bearded, of middle age, with 'perhaps a wallet and loaf' (C) (VIRILITAS, 'manhood'), and an old man, bald and bearded, with a crutch (SENECTVS, 'old age'). Dr. Mason describes the last-named as holding in his right hand a scroll, 'perhaps containing his life's history', but this appears rather to be the turn-over of the dependent label bearing his title. Round the border the inscription (in part nearly obliterated): PRIMVM SIGNORVM DEVS FACI-ENDO SVORVM IN VINVM MORVM CONVERTIT AQVAM VITIORVM ('By working the first of his signs God converted the water of vices into the wine of good morals'). Miss Williams gives the words of the title inscription in the wrong order, the word *etates* having been replaced since she wrote; in the last inscription Dr. Mason mistakenly reads *prodendo* for *faciendo*.

The medallion was originally No. 6 in Window IV. To make it fit the border surrounding the original medallion which it replaces, it has been filled out with parts of other inscribed borders reading: ATVR IN PACIO D MARIS RBRIS. These fragments embody part of the legend, in a disordered state, belonging to the original No. 6 of Window III, the Passage of the Red Sea, as the second type of the Baptism— *Unda maris rubri spacio divisa salubri Quae mentem mundam facit a vitio notat undam;* they comprise also perhaps part of a descriptive title: *[Baptiz]* ATVR D *[ominus]*, which may have belonged to the Baptism itself (No. 4). They appear in part to have been inserted since Dr. Nelson wrote his book and in substitution for the fragments there quoted; he omits the legend appropriate to No. 6 (originally Window IV, 4) itself and gives: IN VINVM from the lost legend of No. 4, and SVB *[mersio]* FARAON from the title of the drowning of Pharaoh's host in the Red Sea (Window III, 6).

Plate 19f

7. *Piscatores* (sic) *apostolorum*. The Miraculous Draught of Fishes. Our Lord sits with right hand raised and a scroll in his left hand, in the stern of a boat on the left in which are also St. Peter and St. Andrew; St. James and St. John (beardless) are in a second boat on the right. All four Apostles are drawing up the same net full of fishes, of which some are escaping through the broken meshes; the sails of both boats are furled. Below is the inscription: PISCATIO APL'ORVM VBI RETE RVPITVR ('The fishing of the Apostles, when the net breaks'). 'Crown' border.

Originally No. 7 in Window IV. A technical feature of great interest is the fact that the escaping fishes are painted half on the inner surface of the white glass and half on the outer, so as to be seen realistically in part through the meshes of the net. Miss Williams and Dr. Nelson omit *ubi* in their transcription. It is interesting to compare this rendering of the subject with Raphael's in the Vatican tapestry cartoon (now in the Victoria and Albert Museum), in which Christ is shown in a similar attitude.

Plate 18

9. *Sanctus petrus cum ecclesia de iudeis*. This medallion 'depicts St. Peter with the church from among the Jews; S PETRVS above, and ECCL'IA DE IVDEIS below, tell their story. On the right of the picture two PHARISEI walk out of the church; "the

net brake" ' (M). The church has a low dome and an arcade; below the platform on which St. Peter sits, with a crutch in his left hand and his right hand raised, is a crowd of men and women converts. Inscribed on the border: VERBVM RETE RATIS PETRI DOMVS HEC PIETATIS: PISCES IVDEI QVI RETE FORANT PHARISEI ('The word is the net; the boat of Peter is this house of piety; the Jewish fishes who make holes in the net are the Pharisees').

Originally No. 9 in Window IV; the companion type on the left (No. 7) was St. Paul with the Church of the Gentiles. It is open to question whether Dr. Nelson is right in making the title *eccl'ia de iudeis* apply only to the woman sitting with her chin on her hand in the front of the congregation. Both Miss Williams and Dr. Nelson regardless of the sense read *ferant* for *forant*.   Plate 20b

11. *Gentes audiunt.* A group of Gentiles, seen three-quarter length, standing with gestures of attention and approbation; a young man on the left seems hesitant, hand to chin. The border inscribed: SOLLICITE GENTES STANT VERBA DEI SITIENTES ('The Gentiles stand anxiously thirsting for the words of God').

Originally No. 2 in Window VI, as type of Jesus speaking in parables. Miss Williams erroneously reads *solicite*, and *sunt* for *stant*, Dr. Nelson also *solicite*. Plate 20c

12. *Pharisei contempnunt.* A group of Pharisees, also seen three-quarter length, with looks of incredulity. The border inscribed: HI SVNT VERBA DEI QVI CON-TEMPNVNT PHARISEI ('These are the Pharisees who despise the words of God').

Originally No. 3 in Window VI, as companion type to No. 11 above. Miss Williams and Dr. Nelson omit *p* in *contempnunt;* the latter gives *que* for *qui*. Plate 20d.

§5 East Window of Crypt

IN 1938 Mr. Caldwell acquired for the Cathedral at a sale at St. Alban's Court, Nonington, a panel from a lancet window with the Virgin and Child enthroned which on stylistic grounds he recognised as being part of the early glazing of the Cathedral. A note in the *Seventeenth Annual Report* of the Friends (1944, p. 15) in which the author described the panel and discussed its original position may be quoted here: 'The Virgin is shown seated on an altar-like throne, crowned, with the Holy Child on her knee. His right hand is raised in the gesture of Benediction; in his left he holds the book of the Gospel. The angels kneel on one knee, swinging censers of globular shape. Above the Virgin's head the dove of the Holy Ghost is seen descending in a wreath of clouds. That we have here the upper part of a window in honour of Our Lady is obvious. The situation of this window in the Cathedral is not known; it has been suggested that it was in one of the Choir Transepts; but it may perhaps be argued with greater plausibility that the subject indicates the place of honour in the original Lady Chapel, that is to say, the eastern-most chapel of the crypt, immediately below Becket's Crown, and in this connection attention may again be drawn to the width of the border, greater than that of the surviving windows of the upper parts of the church.

'When the composition is examined in detail, certain characteristics will be noticed. The treatment of the subject is in general that of the famous *Belle Verrière* of Chartres, where the crowned Virgin is similarly seated on a throne of masonry with the Dove descending towards her and the hands of the Child are similarly employed; at Chartres also there are flanking angels, but the proportions of the dominant figure to the size of the window have made possible the introduction of three pairs instead of a single pair of angels, and of these, four hold censers whilst the remaining two are supporting candlesticks. The conception of sovereign majesty, coming from Byzantium, related originally to Our Lord, and thus continues, for instance, in the uppermost medallion of the Becket's Crown window, where Christ is enthroned between angels kneeling, not with censers but with their hands joined in adoration. This subject of Christ throned in majesty is found in tympanum sculptures of the splendid twelfth-century doorways of the great French churches and is not unknown in England, as for instance somewhat rudely carved in the humble Gloucestershire church of Little Barrington.* Its transference to the Virgin was a feature of the cult which developed in the twelfth century; in the following century this cult underwent a modification resulting in the concentration of thought less on the royal majesty than on the womanly motherhood of Our Lady, and a subtle trace of this change of sentiment may perhaps be recognised in our glass-painting. In many representations the Virgin is not merely crowned but holds in her right hand a lily sceptre; we see this in the fragment of an early window at Compton, near Guildford, and, nearer Canterbury, in a medallion at Upper Hardres, and in the thirteenth-century seals of Merton and other abbeys. In a window at Laon Cathedral the sceptre gives place to a rose. In French glass brought from Touraine now at Rivenhall, Essex, the descending Dove is there, as in the early symbolism, but flies down, not ceremonially from above, but in more naturalistic manner from one side, breathing a message as it were in the Virgin's ear; the Holy Mother herself, as she bares her breast, rests her cheek lovingly on that of her child. The same nursing mother is presented in a second window at Chartres where, though censing angels are still in attendance, she is no longer enthroned but stands. A harbinger of this growing sentimentalism of the thirteenth century, to which the preaching of St. Francis was to give a powerful stimulus, may perhaps be detected in the gesture by which, in our newly acquired panel, Mary supports with her own right hand the infant weakness of the little hand raised in the act of blessing. It is in such slight details as this that the individual designer could contribute out of his own imagination to the code at first so rigidly imposed and handed down by ecclesiastical tradition; and thus sentiment taking symbolism in hand

---

* Compare p. 80 below.

(a)

(b)

(c)

(a) SS. James the Greater and
Matthias

(b) SS. John the Evangelist
and James the Less(?)

(c) Isaiah, Jeremiah, Jacob
and Isaac

Early 13th CENTURY
WATER TOWER
Windows III, V
CRYPT
East Window

pp. 113, 114

22

(a)

(a) The Nativity

(b) The Adoration of the Magi

about 1200
SOUTH CHOIR AISLE
TRIFORIUM
Window III
p. 50

(b)

(a)

(a) The Presentation in the
Temple

(b) The Crucifixion

about 1200–1220
SOUTH CHOIR AISLE
TRIFORIUM
Windows III, II

pp. 50, 72

(b)

24

(a)

(a) The Resurrection

(b) The Ascension
about 1220
SOUTH CHOIR AISLE
TRIFORIUM,
Window II
p. 72

(b)

brought into being the immense diversity so noticeable when later Christian art is compared, for instance, with the less variable formulas of the religions of the East.'

The panel has been found to fit exactly in the head of the East Window of the Crypt within the magnificent wide border of the window, consisting of rosettes alternating with palmettes, which has been preserved. The date and style of the panel and border are discussed in the note, already quoted above, as follows: 'Those familiar with the development of window design will immediately be struck by the generous proportions as well as the magnificent pattern-organisation of the border. In the earliest Gothic windows it is observable that there is a progressive diminution in the width of the border, with an accompanying decline in its decorative vitality. In the work before us we see a border of remarkable width, composed of rosettes in circles separated by motives derived from the classical palmette; the kinship with the acanthus of the individual leaves in these motives differentiates them at once from the coiled bud, as of opening fronds of bracken, so characteristic of thirteenth-century design in painting as well as sculpture, seen for example in the border of the East Window of Becket's Crown (see p. 73). The border, in fact, comes near in spirit and character to that in Abbot Suger's Jesse window at St. Denis, dating from about 1150, of which a single unit may be seen in the Victoria and Albert Museum; it is concordant also with the "Canterbury capitals", with their Corinthian-looking acanthus sculpture, of the choir of William of Sens, and of such imitative work as the nave arcade of Reigate Parish Church. The inference from these observations is that the glass comes from a window of relatively early date, perhaps before rather than after 1200.' It may further be remarked that there is every reason to suppose that this window, on account both of its accessibility and of the importance of its situation as the eastern termination of the Lady Chapel, would be among the earliest to be taken in hand when the Cathedral was extended after the fire of 1174.

To fill out as far as possible the remainder of the window, in the absence of its original glazing, with glass not incongruous or widely separated from the original in date Mr. Caldwell has inserted glass formerly in other parts of the Cathedral. Below the Virgin and Child are two panels with figures of Apostles and others from the same series as the four now in windows of the Water Tower (see p. 137); these Mr. Caldwell plausibly conjectures to have been made originally to fill the windows of the Norman nave which was pulled down in the fifteenth century to make way for Prior Chillenden's still existing nave. They are described on p. 114 below. To separate these figures from the panel above with the Virgin and Child, a strip of foliage has been introduced which probably belonged originally to the Jesse Window (see p. 115); below them is a panel of uncertain significance which may have come from one of the vacant 'Miracle' Windows in the Trinity Chapel and is described in full on p. 112.

Colour Plate VII

§6 South Window of South-West Transept

WHEN this window was rebuilt (see p. 140), the deficiencies in its original glazing were made good, partly by inserting thirteenth-century ornamental glass belonging originally to the clerestory windows of the Eastern Transepts;* the portions of the window so filled are named in the detailed description of it (pp. 142–144). They comprise the majority of the small tracery lights, each containing a length of early border, as well as the row of seven square panels at the foot of the lowest range of main lights. These latter are almost uniform; they are described by Dr. Mason as 'squares containing green rosettes in quatrefoils. The corners of the squares are filled with demi-semi-circles. These demi-semi-circles came from one of the windows of the North-East Transept where they formed eight complete circles. The rosettes in quatrefoils come from the South side of St. Thomas' Chapel' (the Trinity Chapel). In 1920 the two six-sided figure-panels described below, of glass dating from about 1200, were reconstructed by Mr. Samuel Caldwell, Junior, and inserted in the middle of the mid-most range of main lights, in place of two panels which were put back where they rightly belonged in Window III of the Trinity Chapel (see p. 85).

1. DAVID. He sits crowned, in white and pale green robes, on a murrey throne, playing a harp. The background is made up of a white trellis, with ruby discs at the intersections against a blue field. The panel has a deep green border. Colour Plate XIII

2. UNIDENTIFIED FIGURE, bare-headed, in pale brownish-murrey and white robes and amber-yellow shoes, seated on a green throne, holding a pale green scroll with reticulated pattern. Background and border as in No. 1, above.

§7 North Choir Aisle Triforium

THE three windows of the North Choir Aisle Triforium are triple-lobed at the top and are filled each with three pictorial medallions set among scrollwork within a border of foliage. The armatures and, in the main, the ground patterns and border are original and may be dated about 1200. The medallions, though of approximately the same date, were not originally in these positions but, as

---

* John Brent, *Canterbury in the Olden Times, from the Municipal Archives and other Sources,* Canterbury, 1860, p. 108.

Mr. Caldwell has convincingly suggested, must have belonged to the windows of the Choir Aisles immediately east of the eastern Transepts, north and south of the High Altar, in the immediate neighbourhood of the shrines and altars respectively, of St. Dunstan and St. Alphege (or Alphage), who occupied the archiepiscopal throne in 960–988 and 1005–1013 and whose lives the pictures commemorate. The reassembling of the medallions in their present positions is the work of Mr. Caldwell. All three windows have borders of foliage in mauve, yellow, green, and white on a blue ground, similar in style but in each window of a different design; the scrollwork filling the intervals between the medallions is on a ruby ground in all three. The medallions in the first two windows relate to the story of St. Dunstan, those in the third to St. Alphege.

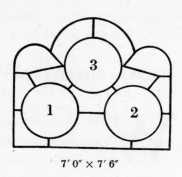

7′ 0″ × 7′ 6″

WINDOW I. ST. DUNSTAN

1. KING EDWY'S RELEASE FROM HELL. St. Dunstan in mitre and vestments stands in front of a pillared building on the left beckoning towards the King who is seen crowned, among three other figures in torment amid flames, half emerging from Hell (represented as a monster with gaping jaws within an embattled vesica-shaped enclosure). Two other victims are being dragged down by two demons from clouds above towards the open mouth. Dr. Mason comments: 'The interpretation of the topmost roundel cannot be doubted. Osbert says that while St. Dunstan was engaged in prayer, the soul of Edwy was shown him by certain beings resembling wicked men, or blackamoors. St. Dunstan burst into a flood of tears, which continued until he recognised that his prayer was heard, and saw the angry blackamoors return empty-handed.'

Plate 27b

2. AN ORDINATION SCENE (perhaps Archbishop Odo ordaining St. Dunstan). The archbishop stands in mitre, pallium and chasuble, before an altar draped with a cloth diapered with a chequer pattern of quatrefoils and cross hatching; on the altar are a chalice and a book, above it hangs a lamp. The archbishop holds his cross in his right hand and extends his left hand towards a chalice held by a kneeling priest behind whom, on the right, stand two others, one of them holding a book. Dr. Mason writes: 'The "Ordination of St. Dunstan" (October 21) was kept as a festival, with its eve, in the calendar of the Cathedral—as was the case also with that of St. Alphege (November 16). But here comes a difficulty. Does "ordination" mean what it means in modern usage—ordination to the priesthood, or, as was frequently the case in older times, "consecration" to the episcopate? Dunstan was ordained priest by Alphege, called "the Bald", of Winchester; but the ordaining prelate here wears the pall (the cross in his hand had lost its top, but the pall shows that it must have been a cross, not a pastoral staff). Again, the chalice and vestments which are being delivered from off the altar to the newly-ordained—apparently two—would suit an ordination to the priesthood, and not a consecration to the episcopate. But why, in that case, the vestment and chalice? Why more than one? Why does the Archbishop—doubtless

69

Odo—stand alone, without assistant consecrators? Perhaps these questions of interpretation can never be settled.'

3. 'DUNSTAN DIVIDING THE STRICTER MONKS FROM THE SECULAR "CLERKS". His were days of a revival in monasticism' (C). The archbishop stands fully vested, cross in hand, in the middle of a columned building, his arms outstretched towards two groups of men who turn outwards to left and right respectively. 'No one vivid scene of that nature is mentioned in Osbert's life of St. Dunstan as taking place by action of the saint himself; but the procedure of Oswald at Worcester and of Ethelwold at Winchester had his warm approval, and may well have supplied the glass-painter with a model' (M). Dr. Mason's further comment ('the group on the Archbishop's right hand appear to be going upstairs—perhaps to take possession of the dorter') seems to involve a stretch of imagination.

WINDOW II. ST. DUNSTAN

1. ST. DUNSTAN'S VISION. Quatrefoil-shaped. The saint lies asleep, mitred and vested and clasping his archiepiscopal cross, on a bed in a building with two gables and columns in the background. Our Lord appears above in an inverted arc of clouds, His right hand raised in blessing and a book in His left hand, between two angels who hold each one end of a scroll with an inscription of which only a few letters are legible (DI' . . . P . . T . . . A . . . A . . PEŁ). Dr. Mason explains the scene as follows: 'It is difficult to say which of St. Dunstan's visions is intended. If the words on the scroll held by the angels were still legible, the question might be settled; but they are gone. The most probable interpretation is that the picture represents a vision which he received one Ascension Day, or its eve, at Canterbury. The night office was finished, and St. Dunstan was left alone in St. Saviour's, when a multitude of blessed spirits burst into the church, and brought him an invitation from our Lord to spend the day with them in heaven. He asked some of them who they were; they answered, "We are Cherubin and Seraphin". But Dunstan replied that it was his duty to give the people their communion, and to preach to them that day, and so declined the offer.'

2. DUNSTAN AND THE DEVIL AT GLASTONBURY. Quatrefoil-shaped. The saint kneels before an altar with a lamp hanging above it in a church outside which, to the left, a winged devil with tail ending in a serpent's head flees before an angel who flies down from above. 'An incident in the early life of Dunstan as a monk at Glastonbury. Dunstan came to the church to give thanks after a great illness, in spite of the intimidation of the devil; and, finding the door fastened, climbed up a ladder to the roof, and got in without knowing how. An angel set him before the altar, where he was found in the morning' (M).

Plate 32a

3. THE MIRACLE OF CALNE (the subject was thus identified by Dr. Mason). The saint, mitred and vested, seated on a raised platform to the left, stoops to lay his hands on the face of a young man who steps up with hands joined, whilst another with hands in a similar gesture falls backward behind him. Behind, a group of men rush forward, in chain mail and helmets, one of them carrying a large heater-shaped shield. Behind the saint a monk stands with cowl thrown back and hand under chin apprehensively watching the warriors. 'The adversaries of the saint—chiefly sons of married clergymen—"armed" with the advocacy of a skilled speaker, met him in an upper chamber. He had scarcely made his reply, when the floor gave way under them, and they fell to the ground. Dunstan and his company sat unharmed' (M).

Plate VIII

(a) THE SIEGE OF CANTERBURY BY
THE DANES.

(b) THE MASSACRE OF THE MONKS
BY THE DANES; St. Alphege blesses the
dying. Two medallions originally in a window
adjacent to the Altar of St. Alphege, now in
Window III (1, 2) of the North Choir Aisle
Triforium. About 1200. P. 71.

WINDOW III. ST. ALPHEGE

1. THE SIEGE OF CANTERBURY BY THE DANES. The city is represented as a battlemented fortress with an inner tower and a gate between columns; the gate has a double door with scrolled hinges. Of the four defenders two hurl stones at the enemy from the inner tower, the other two are thrusting their long lances through the bodies of two opponents; two more Danes in the foreground attack the defenders with a sword and a lance. Danes and Saxons alike wear chain armour and conical helmets with nose-pieces similar to those depicted in the Bayeux Tapestry. Their shields are almond-shaped, with a border of scallops inside and outside. The chain mail is rendered by rows of short curved strokes as in illuminated MSS. of the period and, in stained glass, in early fourteenth-century fragments in the Lady Chapel at Wells Cathedral,* and in the window of the South Transept of Chartres Cathedral depicting St. Denis giving the Oriflamme to Henry Clement, Marshal of Metz† (to name only two examples at random).

Reproductions: Williams, pl. 6; Nelson, fig. 28; *C.C.C.*, No. 22 (October 1935), pl. facing p. 1; also (two of the figures) in a woodcut in *Archæological Journal*, Vol. XXXIII (1876), facing p. 11. Colour Plate VIIIa

2. 'ST. ALPHEGE, DURING THE MASSACRE OF THE MONKS, BLESSES THE DYING' (C). St. Alphege sits in a chair on the left, vested in mitre and chasuble. He is attacked by Danes in helmets and chain mail (as in No. 1 above), brandishing swords and a battle-axe (one carries a lance with pennon). The saint's hands are extended in blessing towards a monk falling transfixed from behind with a sword and others already prostrate on the ground; the severed head of one is rendered in pink glass with ruby 'flash' for bloodstains. On the right another monk totters forward from a gateway beside a tree.

Reproduction: Williams, pl. 8. Colour Plate VIIIb

3. 'ST. ALPHEGE IS LED AWAY BY THE DANES TO THEIR SHIP' (C). Mitred and vested, he is being dragged by both wrists (not one only, as described by Dr. Mason) by a Dane in armour up a ladder with white siderails and ruby rungs into the ship; two other Danes, of whom one has his shield slung on his back, push him from behind and a fourth stands with lance erect in the stern. The ship, of which the sail is furled on the yard, has a dragon's head at the prow and a fish-tail at the stern, thus recalling the Viking ship from Oseberg in the University Museum, Oslo, and those represented in the Bayeux Tapestry (a ship of similar build, reduced to a symbol, is seen carved on a stone of the Bronze Age in the island of Gotland reproduced by Axel L. Romdahl, 'Bildstenar och Yxor', in *Fornvännen*, XLI, Stockholm, 1946, p. 7). The stays are painted in black on the blue glass of the background. The water is represented by wavy parallel bands of glass in three different colours; white glass painted with herbage in black indicates the shore, on the left.

Reproduction: Williams, pl. 7. Plate 32b

---

* Reproduced by the Rev. C. Woodforde, *Stained Glass in Somerset*, 1250–1830, London, 1946, pl. I.
† See M. Aubert, *Le Vitrail en France*, Paris, 1946, pl. XII.

§8 South Choir Aisle Triforium

THESE three windows are similar in disposition to the corresponding windows in the North Choir Aisle (see p. 69). They were restored about 1866 by Mr. Samuel Caldwell, Senior, by order of Dean Alford; in each window were inserted three medallions illustrating miracles of St. Thomas, from windows in the Trinity Chapel in which they have now been replaced. The Triforium windows have now been filled with medallions of which those in Windows I and III (in order from east to west) were originally in windows of the apse clerestory of the Trinity Chapel and are described on pp. 50, 51. The three medallions now in Window II, which are slightly smaller, are probably somewhat later in date, and may be assigned to the beginning of the thirteenth century. Window III retains its original border; those of Windows I and II, and the groundwork of all three windows, have been made up out of contemporary glass with rosettes and leafy scrollwork by Mr. Samuel Caldwell, Junior. The original location of the medallions is not known, but Mr. Caldwell plausibly conjectures that they were in one of the side chapels.

WINDOW I

1. THE DORMITION OF THE VIRGIN (see p. 51).

2. THE ASSUMPTION (see p. 51).

3. THE CORONATION OF THE VIRGIN (see p. 51).

WINDOW II

All these medallions are surrounded by borders of quatrefoil and inner borders of bead ornament.

1. THE CRUCIFIXION. The Virgin and St. John the Evangelist, standing on either side of the cross (green, with a painted diaper), are each accompanied by a second figure. Like the Crucified, these four figures are all to a large extent restored out of fragments of early glass. Plate 23b

2. THE RESURRECTION. Christ, fully draped and holding a small cross (without the banner which became customary in later medieval art) in His left hand, stands with right hand raised, upon grave-clothes, on the edge of the oblong tomb between two angels swinging censers; in front of the tomb is a soldier lying asleep, in chain mail with pointed helmet and oval shield ornamented with a rosette. Plate 24a

3. THE ASCENSION. Six Apostles, of whom three hold books, stand barefoot grouped round the central figure of the Virgin (who has white shoes) looking upward at the ascending Christ, of whom only the feet and the skirt of His robe are seen between two banks of clouds above. Plate 24b

WINDOW III

1. THE NATIVITY (see p. 50).

2. THE ADORATION OF THE MAGI (see p. 50).

3. THE PRESENTATION IN THE TEMPLE (see p. 50).

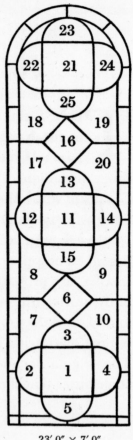

23′ 0″ × 7′ 0″

§9 East Window of Corona

THE theme of this window, occupying a position only second in dignity and importance to the eastern-most window behind the High Altar in the clerestory of the Trinity Chapel, may be regarded as summarising and carrying to their conclusion the series of twelve 'theological' windows in the aisles of the Choir (see p. 51). Like them, it contains 'types' and 'antitypes' from the Old and New Testament, some of the subjects being derived from the earliest Christian art, but it is confined to the culmination of the sequence in the Death, Resurrection and final Glorification in majesty of Our Lord; several of the subjects in the Choir windows are duplicated in this window, but not from identical designs. The window may be dated some time in the first quarter of the thirteenth century, but somewhat later than those of the Choir Aisles; the ornamental foliage with its coiling tufts of leaflets on fine stalks, which fills the intervals between the panels, shows a character of freedom and gracefulness, in the direction of what may be regarded as typical 'Early English' foliage and more advanced than the stately acanthus and palmette ornament still bearing the marks of Romanesque grandeur as seen notably in the windows of St. Denis, which is accessory to the pictorial panels in the Choir series. There are four modern medallions and a few other new insertions, chiefly in the lowest part of the window, made when the window was restored by George Austin about 1853. The window is divided by its armature into three great quatrefoils, composed each of a square surrounded by four semicircles, and between them two lozenges; in the intervals between these main divisions are smaller circular medallions against a groundwork of scrolled foliated stems. These lateral medallions are enclosed by bands of inscription describing their subjects and forming a commentary on their relevance to the subjects in the adjoining main divisions of the window. The sequence of the subjects is from the bottom of the window upwards to its arched top; the panels will

73

accordingly be numbered, as by Miss Williams and Canon Crum, in this order, the middle panel being taken first in each range and then the related surrounding panels in their order. The pictures in the panels all have a blue ground, as has also the border, of symmetrical foliage, mainly in amber and white, in two rows directed inward towards its middle and linked by zigzag strapwork; as a contrast, the ground of the intervening foliage ornament is ruby-red. The borders enclosing the large quatrefoil panels are white and ruby, those of the lozenges green and ruby, and of the circular medallions white and amber. The inscriptions are transcribed exactly as they stand; those parts which are misplaced or are interpolated from elsewhere to make good breakages are printed in italics.

Reproductions: Westlake, pl. LVIII (diagram), pl. LIX*a* (detail of construction), pl. LXIII*a* (border), pl. LXIV*c*, *d* (details of foliage); Lewis F. Day, *Windows* (3rd edition), London, 1909, fig. 99 (lower right corner); Nelson, pl. IV; L. B. Saint and Hugh Arnold, *Stained Glass of the Middle Ages in England and France*, London, 1913, pl. VI (scrollwork, in colours); C. J. Connick, *Adventures in Light and Colour*, London, 1937, pl. XL (in colours), p. 322 (lower part); A. van der Boom, *Ontwikkeling en Karakter der oude monumentale Glasschilderkunst*, Amsterdam, 1943, pl. 16.

(Upper Part) Plate 30

1. THE CRUCIFIXION. This panel is largely modern, though Westlake was so far deceived by it that in his book he chose it for the subject of two illustrations (plates LX, LXI) to exemplify thirteenth-century painting and glazing technique. He comments (p. 102) on the fact that 'the arms of Christ are cut to fit, and placed to the body without a lead division' (a feature shown clearly in his drawings but now no longer remaining, leads having been inserted presumably since Westlake saw the window); he does not seem to have realised that such an adjustment of two glass edges would have been almost impossible to achieve satisfactorily before the post-medieval substitution of the diamond cutter for the grozing-iron as an instrument for shaping the glass. 'The blue background is composed of ancient glass; so is the drapery about the body of the Crucified, and perhaps some parts of the other draperies' (M). Prior to Austin's restoration this position in the window was incongruously occupied by a figure of the Virgin, from the adjacent Tree of Jesse window (see p. 115), which had been placed here to fill the gap left when the original Crucifixion panel was destroyed by the Puritans. Nos. 2–5 are the corresponding 'types'.

2. MOSES STRIKING THE ROCK, 'type of the wounded Side of the Saviour' (C). Moses stands rod in hand on the left; at the foot of the rock, on the right, two men with bowls to catch the issuing water and two sheep drinking, clouds above. Inscribed: HAVSTVS SPIC PATITVR. LAPIS IS LATVS HIC APERITVR: EST AQVA CARNALI CRVOR AVTEM SPIRITVALI (Canon Mason points out that SPIC is an error for SIC) ('Just as this stone suffers the drawing [of water] so the side of this other is riven: water is for the carnal, but blood for the spiritual'). This subject occurs as a type of the Crucifixion in the earliest Christian art, as in a vault-painting of the second century in the Catacombs of St. Calixtus, near Rome.

Plate 29a

25

The Entombment
Early 13th CENTURY
CORONA
East Window

p. 75

26

(a)

(a) The Dormition of the
    Virgin

(b) The Assumption

    about 1200
    SOUTH CHOIR AISLE
    TRIFORIUM

    p. 51

(b)

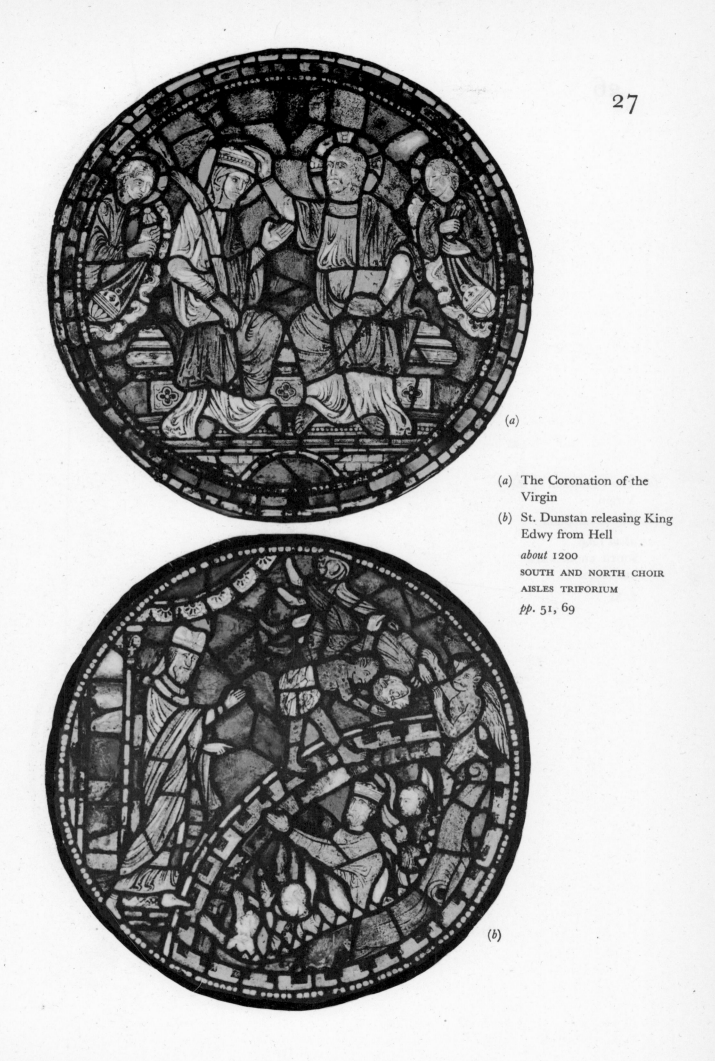

(a) The Coronation of the Virgin

(b) St. Dunstan releasing King Edwy from Hell

about 1200
SOUTH AND NORTH CHOIR AISLES TRIFORIUM

pp. 51, 69

28

(a) The Offering of Isaac

(b) The Grapes of Eshcol

Early 13th CENTURY
CORONA, *East Window*

p. 75

(a) Moses striking the Rock

(b) The Passover

(c) Daniel in Babylon

Early 13th CENTURY

CORONA, *East Window*

pp. 74–76

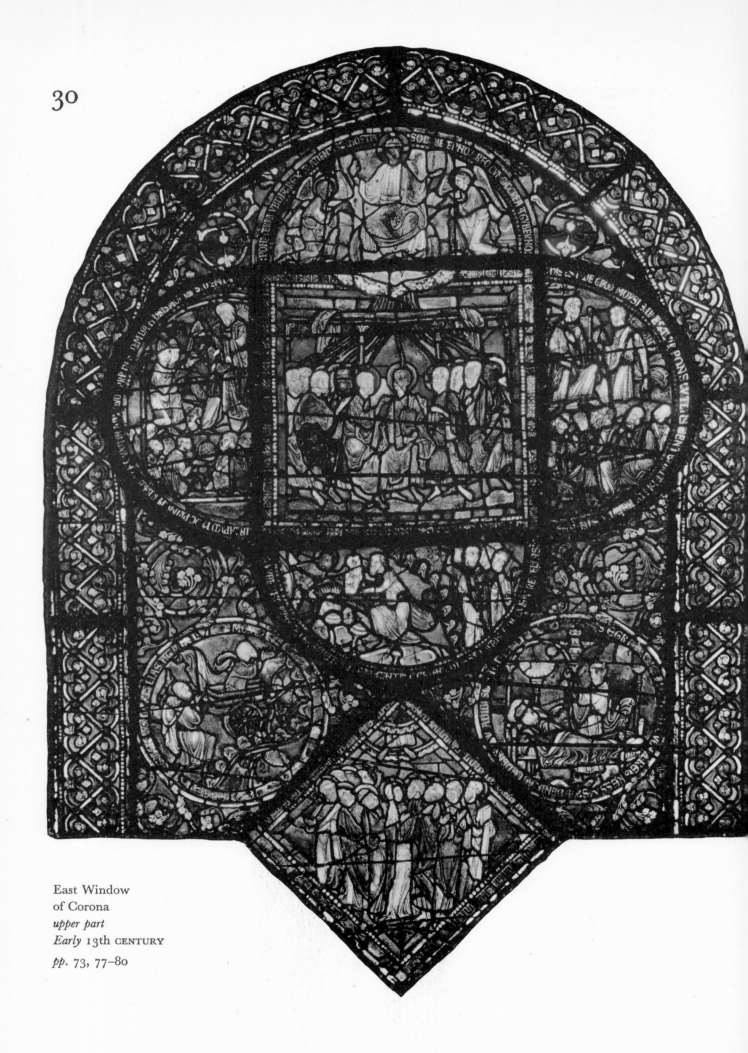

30

East Window
of Corona
upper part
Early 13th CENTURY

pp. 73, 77–80

(a)

(b)

(a) Christ and the Symbols of
the Evangelists
CORONA
South Window

(b) St. Martin and the Beggar

ST. MARTIN'S CHAPEL
First quarter of 13th CENTURY

pp. 112, 111

32

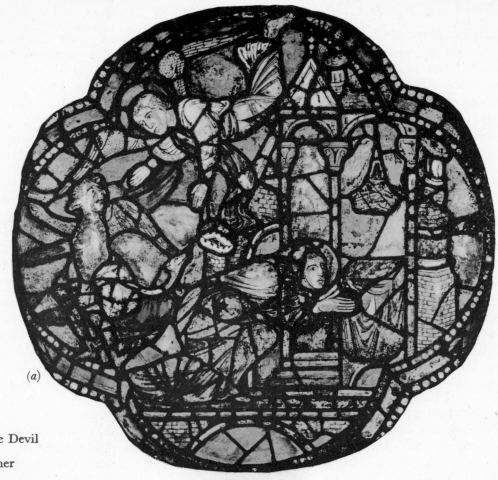

(a)

(*a*) St. Dunstan and the Devil

(*b*) St. Alphege a Prisoner

about 1200

NORTH CHOIR AISLE
TRIFORIUM

pp. 70, 71

(b)

3. THE OFFERING OF ISAAC. On the right, Isaac lies with face upturned on billets laid symbolically crosswise on the altar, of which the slab is white, the pedestal painted to simulate green marble; Abraham strides towards the altar with, in his left hand, a flaming torch to kindle the fire, and in his right an uplifted sword which is being arrested by the angel flying above a thicket in which the ram is seen. Border of geometrical motives derived from Arabic lettering (see p. 28*n*).

Described and reproduced in *C.C.C.*, No. 37, 1941, pp. 6, 7, pl. facing p. 7.

Plate 28a

4. THE PASSOVER. A bearded man holding a bowl in his left hand is marking with the sign T (*tau*), 'prophetic of the Cross', the lintel of a pedimented doorway; below, a younger man is striking the throat of a lamb whilst another holds a large basin with high foot to catch the blood. It is to be noticed that a touch of ruby 'flash' has been applied to represent blood at the tip of the knife, on the white glass employed for the knife and the forearm of the slaughterer. Inscribed: LABE CARENS NAT*VS*: ET AGNVS VT INMACVLATVS: PECCATVM FACT'. PECCATORVM PIE TACTVS. ('He that was born free from taint and as a spotless lamb was made the sin of sinners when smitten in piety'). The letters italicised appear to be an insertion to replace a breakage; FACT' appears to be rather a conscious abbreviation than 'a mistake for *factus*' as suggested by Dr. Mason. This subject formerly occurred also in Window IX of the 'Theological' series (see p. 51).

Reproduction: Westlake, Vol. I, pl. LIX*c*.

Plate 29b

5. THE GRAPES OF ESHCOL, 'type of Christ and Simon of Cyrene and of the vintage of the wine of the Eucharist' (C), giving 'the foretaste of the Promised Land won by the Passion' (M). Two of the returning spies carry on a staff between them 'a branch with one cluster of grapes'. Inscribed: BOTRVM RESPICERE NEGAT HIC. SITIT ISTE VIDERE: ISRAEL IGNORAT CHRISTVM: GENTILIS ADORAT ('This one refuses to look back at the cluster, the other thirsts to see it; Israel knows not Christ, the Gentile adores him'). 'The verses give a curious turn to the carrying of the grapes of Eshcol, the *Torrens botri* (*Numbers* XIII, 24)' (M). The two heads and parts of the drapery are modern restorations.

Described and reproduced in *F.C.C. Sixteenth Annual Report*, 1943, p. 31 and plate facing; reproduced also by Westlake, Vol. I, pl. LIX*e*, LIX*b* (detail).   Plate 28b

6. THE ENTOMBMENT. The body of Christ is being lowered by two bearded men into a marble sarcophagus which rests on a low arch; a third man, probably intended for St. Joseph of Arimathaea, is anointing the body out of a flask. The two Maries stand in the background. The sepulchre is shown as an arch of rock with a small tree growing on its summit. Geometrical border as in No. 3. Nos. 7–10 are the corresponding 'types'.

Reproduction: L. B. Saint and Hugh Arnold, *Stained Glass of the Middle Ages in England and France*, London, 1913, pl. 5 (in colours).   Plate 25

7. JOSEPH IN THE PIT. Joseph is half sunk in the pit (*cisterna* in the Vulgate), which two of his brethren appear to be filling in with mattocks; two others with mattocks shouldered stand by, whilst a fifth, on the left, holds Joseph's coat in his hand. The hand of God issues from a cloud above as an augury of deliverance. Inscribed: ARTAT TE C*PITVR PARVLVS* PVERVM LACVS IST *OR SIGNA* FICAT CRISTVM PVER . . . MVL*W* . . . ISTVM. The inscription has been mutilated

75

and portions have been intruded from elsewhere, the first of which—PITVR PAR—belongs to No. 9, as pointed out by Dr. Mason, who adds: 'the letters *riste tum*, which belong here, have been carried up to the same picture' (Jonah cast to the fish); he restores the entire inscription as: *Artat te Criste, tumulus, puerum lacus iste: significat cristum puer et tumulum lacus istum* ('The tomb confines thee, O Christ, this pool the boy: the boy signifies Christ and the pool this tomb').

Reproduction: *C.C.C.*, No. 36, 1940, pl. facing p. 5.

8. SAMSON AND DELILAH. They lie asleep, with a lamp above the bed, while a group of Philistines in helmets with nasal and chain mail look on from outside a door on the right. Dr. Mason speaks of a window, but between red-capped gold pillars is a foreshortened blue door painted with scrolled iron hinge-plates in black. Inscribed: ECCLESIE CAVSA *CHRIS*STI CARO MARMORE CLAVSA: VT SAMSON TIPICE CAVSA DORMIVIT AMICE: ('For the sake of the Church the flesh of Christ was shut in the marble, just as Samson typically slept for the sake of his beloved'). The same verses occurred in the picture in Window XII of the 'Theological' series, now lost (compare p. 51).

Described and reproduced in *C.C.C.*, No. 36, 1940, p. 5, pl. following p. 8.

9. JONAH CAST INTO THE SEA. The prophet is being lowered by a man out of the ship into the open mouth of the 'great fish', seen partly below the surface of the waves; the helmsman and two others in the prow look on. Inscribed: TENTVS ET EXTRVSVS. ABSORPTVS. PISCE RECLVSVS: HIC *RISTETVME* PITVR PARITER MORITVR SEPELITVR: except the second E, the italicised portion was brought from No. 7 (see above), and PITVR PAR is modern lettering by Austin, copying the original now inserted in No. 7. As Dr. Mason shows, the legend originally read: *hic cristus capitur pariter moritur sepelitur* ('He is held and thrust out, swallowed, shut up in the fish: here in like manner Christ is taken, dies and is buried'). The painting of the scene may be compared with that of St. Nicholas cast overboard, in a thirteenth-century medallion at Westminster Abbey, now in the Jerusalem Chamber. The same subject formerly occurred in Window XII of the 'Theological' series; it belongs, with other scenes from the story of Jonah, to the earliest Christian iconography, as in the second-century paintings in the Catacombs of St. Calixtus and on a marble sarcophagus of the third century in the Museo Pio-Lateranense, Rome.

Colour Plate IX

10. DANIEL IN BABYLON. The prophet, wearing a mitre, is seen half length looking out over the wall of a circular pit, with his name DANIEL written beside him; behind is a fortified city with the name BABILONIA above. Inscribed: CLAVSTRA LEO PATITVR DANIEL. CRIST SEPELITVR: HVNC LEO NON TANGIT NECIS ILLE REPAGVLA FRRANGIT (*sic*). Dr. Mason comments: 'In the first verse *claustra, leo*, are no doubt to be taken as without grammatical construction—as much so as the *Babilonia* in the sky—"Prison; lions; Daniel made to suffer. Christ buried"'; 'this man the lion does not touch, this other breaks the bars of death'. Like Nos. 2, 9 and 13 this subject derives from early Christian iconography, as in the paintings dating from the end of the first century in the Catacombs of St. Domitilla, near Rome.

Plate 29c

11. THE RESURRECTION. Christ stepping out of the tomb between two angels. Chiefly modern glass. Nos. 12–15 are the corresponding 'types'.

12. NOAH. Modern copy of No. 8 in Window III, North Choir Aisle (see p. 62), but with the title, NOE IN ARCHA, in the original glass inserted.

13. JONAH COMING TO LAND. He is seen stepping from the mouth of the fish on to the shore, with clouds above. To the right, a walled town. The prophet's drapery and the fish restored. Border similar to that of No. 3. The subject, which occurs in the paintings in the Catacombs (see No. 9), is treated in a closely similar manner in the *Nouvelle Alliance* window, of about the same date, at Bourges Cathedral and less resemblingly in the window illustrating the same theme at Chartres.

14. MICHAL AND DAVID (modern). Dr. Mason thus identified the subject, rather than as Rahab and the Spies.

15. MOSES AND THE BURNING BUSH. Moses is walking amongst hills, with three sheep in front of him, towards the flaming bush above which the bearded head of the Almighty (not 'an angel', as stated by Canon Crum) is seen issuing from a cloud. Border as in No. 3; it is separated from the armature by a band of blue glass, still remaining, which in other old panels has been eliminated in the course of re-leading and restoration of the window but has been introduced in the new panels such as Nos. 12 and 14.

Reproduction: *F.C.C. Fifteenth Annual Report*, March 1942, pl. facing p. 29.

16. THE ASCENSION. The Apostles stand in a group with the Virgin in their midst looking up at Our Lord, of whom only the feet and the skirt of His robe are visible, disappearing through a bank of cloud. There is one modern head (nearly in profile, next to the upward-pointing hand on the left).

The composition, as regards the grouping and treatment of the figures, closely resembles that of the same scene introduced in the nearly contemporary Crucifixion windows in Poitiers Cathedral. Nos. 17–20 are the corresponding types.   Plate 30

17. THE ENTRANCE OF THE HIGH PRIEST INTO THE HOLY OF HOLIES. Wearing a mitre and on one knee, he kneels swinging a censer, before the mercy-seat (which has an arcaded back); above it are two Cherubim kissing each other (in allusion to *Psalm* LXXXV 10, 'Righteousness and Peace have kissed each other'). Behind the High Priest hangs the veil of the Temple, outside which stands another priest. The inscription has interpolations and is mutilated beyond recovery: TVR-BAEOSSTAM . . . NTVAT . . . REDITHE. CRDEAMVS.

18. THE ASCENSION OF ELIJAH. He is shown kneeling with hands joined in a chariot drawn by horses (two appear to be indicated) which are half hidden in a cloud; his cloak is being wafted towards Elisha, who stands below. The naturalistic oak-leaves are an insertion of fourteenth-century glass. The inscription is defective, and difficult to decipher where still remaining : RAPT . . TEGMEN EO DAT HELIAS HOC HEL . . . MORTE . . . Dr. Mason comments: 'The legend appears to be *Rapto tegmen eo dat Helias hoc Heliseo*. The ablative absolute relating to the subject of the sentence would not be without parallel in this kind of Latin. The word *Morte* follows. Austin thought he could discern *Morte micrat* (no doubt it would be *migrat*) *victa deus*, which might well finish with something like *hic tellure relicta*.' The subject, treated in a somewhat similar manner, is amongst those carved on the wooden doors of Santa Sabina, Rome, of about A.D. 430.   Plate 30

19. THE SUNDIAL OF AHAZ (*Isaiah* XXXVIII 8). Isaiah stands by the sickbed of Hezekiah (who wears a crown). Above the king is the semicircular dial with spoke-like degrees, near which is the red globe of the sun. Inscribed: DENIS ACCEDENS GRADIB' SOL . . . TQ . . . S EGR . . . ILLVC [QV'?] REGRESSVS. Dr. Mason conjectures: 'The first half must have been *Denis accedens gradibus sol [a]tq[ue regressu]s*, but the letters in brackets are gone. Of the second half only *egri. . . illuc . . . a regressus* can be made out. It is possible that the *egri* was placed too early in the verse by the restorers, and is really the beginning of an *egressus* to balance the last word, though it may, of course, mean "of the sick man" .' Dr. Mason seems to be mistaken in reading . . . *a regressus;* the last word but one appears to be the enclitic *que*, abbreviated, nor does it seem quite clear that *egr* is followed by *i*. The sense seems to be: 'The sun going up by ten degrees and returning . . . returning thither'. Plate 30

20. THE TRANSLATION OF ENOCH. He is represented twice over—on the right on earth, prostrate in prayer, with his name ENOCH written beside him on a hill on which are two trees, on the left ascending towards a cloud in heaven. Inscribed: ENOCH SVBLATVS ET ADHVC IN CARNE MORATVS: HIC ASCENSVRVS FVIT HVC IVDEX RED[I] TVRVS ('Enoch was taken up and hitherto remained in the flesh: He (*i.e.*, Christ) was about to ascend, to return hither as judge'). Miss Williams entitles this medallion 'The Burial of Moses'.

21, 23. These two medallions are linked together. No. 23 at the summit of the window, of which the ancient glass has been replaced recently instead of Austin's restorations, shows CHRIST IN MAJESTY. He sits enthroned on a rainbow (as in *Revelation* IV 3; it is of yellow glass) between two angels who kneel in adoration on one knee; his right hand is raised in benediction and in his left he holds a book with cover divided into sixteen panels. From a cloud below his feet, in No. 21 (Dr. Mason is mistaken in mentioning a footstool), eleven crimson streams of fire pour down upon the heads of the seated Apostles, gathered on the day of PENTECOST out of doors (as shown by the grass beneath their bare feet) in front of a building with four pillars and curtains thrown over a beam. Those in the front row hold books. The youthful, beardless figure in the middle is perhaps intended for St. John; the mitred, bearded head on the left, if belonging to the panel and not introduced from elsewhere (possibly from one of the Becket windows of the Trinity Chapel), is perhaps St. Peter. The heads next to right and left of the central figure are of doubtful antiquity; the blue drapery on the shoulder of the front left figure is an insertion in fifteenth-century glass.

The upper panel has an inscription of which one half is defective and has insertions from elsewhere: PONT' (for *Pontus*) TERRA *VBDIAT REX TV ATIENTI SE HOSTIA*. SOL' (for *Solus*) AB ETERNO CREO CVNCTA CREATA GVBERNO ('Alone from eternity I create all things and govern creation').

No. 23 is discussed by the Author and reproduced in *F.C.C. Fifteenth Annual Report*, March 1942, p. 29. Attention is there drawn to the 'diadem recalling in form the mitre of the period' with which Our Lord is crowned, but further examination of the panel has convinced the Author that the two pieces of glass comprising the mitre and the face, though of thirteenth-century date, do not rightly belong in this place but have been interpolated from elsewhere, probably from one of the lost windows of the Becket series in the Trinity Chapel. The face has a sidelong glance, whereas in all traditional representations of Christ in Majesty such as those cited below he is shown

23′ 0″ × 7′ 0″

Plate IX

JONAH CAST INTO THE SEA; type of
the Entombment of Christ. Part of the East
Window of the Corona (9). About 1220. P. 76.

looking straight in front of him, as if at the congregation gathered in the church below.

Colour Plate X

Nos. 22, 24, 25 contain the types of Pentecost.

22. THE CONSECRATION OF AARON AND HIS SONS. Aaron kneels before Moses (with the name MOYSES), who is placing a mitre with *infulae* on his head; behind him sit two figures already mitred. Below the platform on which this ceremony takes place are the congregation; a bearded man in the middle holds a basket containing what appear to be small loaves, doubtless the unleavened bread of *Leviticus* VII 2, 26 Inscribed: IN CAPVD HOC PRIMV̇ PER BARBAM FLVXIT IN IMV̇. QVOD PRI̵' HIS *DAT I*D[?Q or O] EM DAT NOBIS MODO PLENIVS IDEM. Dr. Mason comments: 'The legend has reference to *Psalm* CXXXIII: *In capud hoc primum per barbam fluxit in imum* ("This first poured on his head flowed down over his beard"). The rest, however, is not so clear. Austin read *quod pri . . . his idem dat nobis modo*. The last few letters at present in the window appear to be a modern addition made by him. I should conjecture that the line originally ran something like *quod prius his, dat idem nobis modo plenius idem*. That makers of this kind of verse would not object to putting *idem* (neut.) as a rhyme to *idem* (masc.) may be concluded from a line formerly in Window VI (James, p. 20) *Sic omnes eadem vox hora cogit eadem*'. Miss Williams wrongly entitles this panel 'The Ordination of Deacons'.

Plate 30

24. MOSES AND JETHRO (*Exodus* XVIII 13–24). Moses sits on his judgment seat on a platform with the people beneath him; on his right stands Jethro, with his right hand raised in a gesture of admonition. Their names [*Moys*]ES, JETHRO, are written beside them. The surrounding inscription is defective and has been filled up with fragments from elsewhere: HIS EST DE CELO MOYSIS DA *EST DE PONS CVTENS GENTE IRIT' HIS DI ERGO AT SIN GNE*. The subject, 'which Miss Williams curiously calls "The First Council" ' (M) occurs also in Window III of the North Choir Aisle (see p 62).

Plate 30

25. MOSES RECEIVING THE TABLES OF THE LAW. He kneels on one knee on the tree-covered flaming mountain-top to receive the two tables from the Almighty (not 'an angel', as Canon Crum has it, p. 18), who issues from a cloud on the left; another band of cloud separates him from the Israelites behind him. Inscribed: NVBE TENEBRANTE LEX SPIRIŦ IGNE MICANTE CCELANS.HI EST DAŦ. HE COCC LAT REVELANS. Dr. Mason comments: 'The first line is made out to be: *Nube tenebrante lex spiritus igne micante*. The next word, *celans*, has been put too near to *micante* with another *c* before it. Austin thought that he could read *est dat hec celans hic occulat revelans*. Not recognising the Leonine character of the verse, he has shifted the letters about. I am not at all sure that all the pieces now in the inscription belong to it. The line might be reconstructed thus: *Lex est hec celans, datur hic occulta revelans*'. The lines as reconstructed by Dr. Mason may be rendered: 'In darkening cloud and flashing fire the law is the spirit. This law is one that conceals; here a law is given that reveals what is hidden.'

Colour Plate X

Whilst numerous examples could be cited from Romanesque and Early Gothic art of representations of Our Lord in Majesty showing a general similarity to that which forms the culminating subject of this window, the treatment here found is exceptional in one particular, that of its combination with Pentecost. In the great sculptured tympana of the French Cathedrals—Chartres, Le Mans, Bourges, Arles— Christ is represented in a closely similar pose, with right hand raised in blessing, but enclosed in a *mandorla* and surrounded by the Symbols of the Evangelists, as in the glass-painting recently recovered for Canterbury (see p. 112), and with the Apostles enthroned in a row beneath; nor in these instances is the throne formed, as here, of a rainbow—an attribute of the Last Judgment. In the tympanum over the Prior's Doorway at Ely Cathedral, dating from the earlier part of the twelfth century, we have the subject of Christ in Glory alone, in which the *mandorla* is flanked by angels but in an attitude as if starting away from the central figure; a similar tympanum at Water Stratford Church, Buckinghamshire, gives a much closer parallel to the Corona window in the kneeling gesture of the two Angels, whilst a small carving of the same subject over the North doorway of Little Barrington Church, Gloucestershire, comes still nearer to it, both as regards the kneeling angels and in the absence of a *mandorla*. The Ascension, with Christ enthroned between standing angels above the upward-gazing Virgin and Apostles, is carved as a tympanum at Anzy-le-Duc, Saône-et-Loire.*

In the Apocalypse window, slightly later in date, at Bourges Cathedral, a central medallion shows Christ seated on a rainbow with outstretched hands from which flames shoot down towards the Apostles, seated in two groups divided between the two adjacent medallions below; in respect of distribution over more than one medallion this Bourges Pentecost is comparable with that of the Corona, but the parallel ceases in the different rendering of the figure of Christ who, at Bourges, is not shown in the traditional gesture of Majesty and Benediction.

There are early precedents for the rainbow-throned Christ in English illuminated manuscripts, as for instance in the charter of the New Minster of Winchester, dated 966, and in the Shaftesbury Psalter, some fifty years older than our window†; in the latter case Our Lord's right hand is engaged not in blessing but in holding the orb of sovereignty, but the book, which in all other cases that have been cited is supported on the knee, is held upright, but open, in the left hand. A parallel in this latter respect is to be found at no great distance from Canterbury, in the Christ enthroned in Benediction of the Jesse window at Westwell Church, near Ashford.‡

Turning to the Pentecost panel (No. 21) we find interesting parallels in a late twelfth-century window at Le Champ (Isère) and in the SS. Peter and Paul window at Poitiers Cathedral dating from about 1200, both showing the streams of fire descending upon the Apostles. In the former,§ the subject occupies a medallion at the foot of the window, below two others showing respectively the Apostles looking up (as in No. 16 of the Corona window) towards a cloud in which their Lord has ascended, and Christ standing in Majesty between two angels; the Apostles are *seated*, not standing, and the pentecostal rays stream from an arc of a circle at the top of the medallion. In the Poitiers medallion,‖ St. Peter and five others—here again seated—do duty for the whole company of Apostles, and the rays descend upon them from the beak of the Holy Dove flying down from above.

---

* Reproduced by E. Mâle, *L'Art Religieux du XIIᵉ Siècle en France*, Paris, 1922, fig. 77.

† Both in the British Museum, and reproduced by O. Elfrida Saunders, *A History of English Art in the Middle Ages*, Oxford, 1932, figs. 10, 16.

‡ Reproduced by Westlake, Vol. I, pl. XLIVa.

§ Reproduced by J. L. Fischer, *Handbuch der Glasmalerei*, Leipzig, 1914, pl. 8.

‖ Reproduced by G. Heinersdorff, *Die Glasmalerei*, Berlin, 1914, pl. 12.

§10 Trinity Chapel Aisle Windows

('MIRACLE WINDOWS')

IN the aisles or ambulatory of the Trinity Chapel there are twelve windows, six on each side, which are likely all to have contained glass-paintings relevant to the sainted Archbishop whose shrine, until its destruction at the time of the Reformation, occupied the space enclosed between them. Only nine of these at the present day display ancient glass, and of these nine only seven retain some or all of the glass that originally belonged to them; the other two have been supplied in recent times with medallions made up of old glass which doubtless to a large extent belonged to the mutilated windows of the series. All twelve windows have their original thirteenth-century armatures, in themselves of great beauty, exhibiting different designs though with certain duplications on opposite sides of the chapel. The armatures were filled with pictorial medallions separated in most cases by foliage designs within ornamental borders, also based on stylised leaves and buds. All the pictures in the medallions remaining that can be identified depict subjects from the miracles recorded to have taken place in the years immediately following Becket's murder, and believed to have been due to the saint's intercessions or the healing virtue of his blood. Detailed accounts of these miracles were gathered together and set down within a short time of the martyrdom by two monks of Christ Church present in the priory when it occurred, Benedict, who was later to become Prior of Canterbury and eventually Abbot of Peterborough, and William.

These records compiled by Benedict and William, which in several cases deal with the same incidents and corroborate each other, were printed and published by J. C. Robertson as the second and first volumes respectively of *Materials for the History of Thomas Becket, Archbishop of Canterbury* (Master of the Rolls Series, No. 67, London, 1875–85). In some instances it has been found possible to identify the miracles depicted in the windows with those narrated by the two monks; in the descriptions which follow, references to such identifications are given in brackets as 'Benedict' and 'William', with page-references to the respective Volumes II and I of Robertson's book, on the authority of which it may here be pointed out incidentally that whilst priority in time seems to belong to Benedict, the narration of William was 'considered as the more important of the two, on account probably of its greater extent, and also of a kind of official authority which it derived from having been presented by the monks of Christ Church to King Henry II'.*

---

* Those desiring a critical examination of the miracle stories, with translations of portions of the Latin text, are referred to E. A. Abbott, *St. Thomas of Canterbury*, London, 1898.

Whilst the glass-paintings which survive relate only to incidents that occurred after Becket's death, it seems likely that those in the first one or perhaps two of the series of twelve windows illustrated his life and martyrdom; their disappearance would be sufficiently accounted for by the likelihood that they would have been marked out for destruction by the zealots to whom the cult of the saint was so obnoxious. If this conjecture is valid, the windows in question may have shown some resemblance to windows still extant at Sens and Chartres (dating from about 1190 and 1206 respectively) devoted to the career of St. Thomas himself.* The windows in the two cathedrals differ entirely in the distribution of the medallions, but correspondences in the details of some of these show them to be derived from a single original series of designs; the subjects at Chartres begin with the expulsion of Becket from England to exile at Sens, those at Sens with his reconciliation with Henry II and his return to Canterbury; both end with his murder and burial. There is also a third nearly contemporary Becket window, at Coutances Cathedral.

Eugène Chartrain, writing of the Sens window,† suggests that there may have been a second window in that cathedral giving the earlier portion of the saint's history; he also expresses the opinion that the existing window may be based on a cartoon made for Canterbury, but this would seem to involve a somewhat earlier date than is likely for the first or second window in the Trinity Chapel (assuming these to have been filled with scenes from Becket's life).

It has often been remarked that the windows of the Trinity Chapel display, in the design of their armatures and in their borders and accessory decorations, a close similarity to those of Sens and Chartres; in evidence of the intimate relations subsisting between the latter city and Canterbury it is pertinent to recall that Becket's secretary, John, Archdeacon of Salisbury, became Bishop of Chartres, where he died in 1180.

These 'Miracle Windows', as they are often conveniently called, which date from about the second or third decade of the thirteenth century,‡ are of value not only for their beauty of design and colour, but also as pictures not of more-or-less idealised scriptural or legendary scenes but of incidents of contemporary life. As such they may be taken to give a reliable record of costume, both ecclesiastical and secular, and of church furniture, lamps, flasks, glass vessels, tools, weapons and other accessories of the daily life of the period. They are also of great interest as showing the structure both of the tomb of the saint in the Crypt and of the shrine to which his body was translated in the year 1220 and which was destroyed in 1538. The tomb appears in many of the

---

* See Tancred Borenius, *St. Thomas Becket in Art*, London, 1932, pp. 45–47, where the upper part of the Chartres window is reproduced (pl. xiv). The lower part of the Sens window is finely reproduced in colours in Marcel Aubert, *Vitraux des Cathédrales de France*, Paris, 1937, pl.vii.

† *La Cathédrale de Sens*, Paris, 1926, p. 85.

‡ As indicated by the representations of the saint's shrine; see pp. 17, 91, 106.

23′ 0″ × 7′ 0″

Plate X

CHRIST IN MAJESTY: PENTECOST:
MOSES RECEIVING THE TABLES OF
THE LAW. Three upper panels (21, 23, 25) of
the East Window of the Corona, illustrating antitypes in the New Testament with their Old Testament types. About 1220. Pp. 78, 79.

medallions; with the oval openings in its sides for the insertion of the hands of pilgrims wishing to derive healing benefit by touching it, its nearly contemporary counterpart is still extant on the south side of the nave of Salisbury Cathedral; this is what is known as Lord Stourton's Tomb, actually part of the Shrine of St. Osmund.*
The shrine resembling in shape and decoration the Limoges enamel reliquaries of the period, is depicted in Window V, 1,† and again in Window XII, 21 and 22. In most of the windows that survive the medallions have descriptive legends, now mostly mutilated, in Lombardic lettering reserved on a ground of black enamel; as a rule, but not in every case, these inscriptions are in rhyming Leonine hexameter verse.

Gostling, writing of these windows, says that their designer, 'to show the luxuriance of his fancy, formed his historical pieces in small panels fitted to their iron framing, of such various patterns that no two windows were alike: but the variety and elegance of the Mosaic grounds and borders, and the richness of the colouring are more admired by the curious, and make the loss of what has been destroyed the more regretted'. Dr. Mason (p. 28) points out that Gostling's statement is not entirely correct, inasmuch as there are three correspondences of design between the north and south sides, namely between Nos. II, III and IV and Nos. XI, XII and IX respectively; thus there are only two cases of identity between facing windows.

In the descriptions of the windows which here follow italic capitals are used to indicate all those portions of the explanatory Latin inscriptions which are out of place and have been inserted from other medallions.

WINDOW I

This window retains its original border, of exceptionally wide proportions, composed of repeating acanthus scrolls pointing outwards, with a square enclosing radial foliage at each lower angle. The rest of the window has been partly filled by Mr. Caldwell at various times since 1919, with glass of the thirteenth century recovered from amongst material removed from various windows at the time of earlier rearrangements and restorations.‡ Before this rearrangement the portion within the border was filled with plain quarries; on one of these, which has been preserved, the following inscription has been scratched with a diamond by the glazier:

Sepr 22nd
Kings Crownation [sic]
William Baker
GLAZIER
1789

---

* 'Originally the pedestal of a shrine. Without doubt . . . all that is left of the shrine of St. Osmund' (Gleeson White, *The Cathedral Church of Salisbury*, 4th ed., London, 1921, p. 46).

† Copied in R. Scarlet's MS.; see p. 21, also Plate B(d).

‡ See Mason, p. 28; *F.C.C. Seventh Annual Report* (1934), pp. 29, 30; *C.C.C.*, No. 31 (October, 1938), pp. 13, 14.

(George III was crowned on September 22, 1761.) The window now displays, within its border, four medallions (Nos. 1–4) from one of the windows illustrating the miracles of Becket, set one above another in the middle, and beneath the lowest of these, a panel showing the Archbishop himself enthroned under a canopy (No. 6); on the left of the Archbishop, in the lower angle, is a half medallion (No. 5) also containing a miracle subject. The medallions and half medallion have borders of 'mock Arabic' or 'crown' ornament between two rows of beads. The remaining spaces of the window are filled with plain white glass.

1. AN OFFERING AT THE TOMB OF ST. THOMAS. To the left, a man stooping to lay a coil of wire on the tomb, on which stands a candle in a candlestick; behind him to the left, a lectern, and a bearded man wearing a close cap (perhaps a priest) who points towards two youths on the right, one of whom holds a stick whilst the other points to a passage in a book which he is opening, on a second lectern. No inscription.

2. AN UNIDENTIFIED SCENE. A bearded man, perhaps a pilgrim who has fainted on the way, lies on his back in the foreground whilst six others stand round pointing upwards with vigorous gesticulations. A cloud above indicates that the scene is in the open air. Inscribed: POPV . . . . ETC . . . *DE* . . . . ; the last two letters are introduced from elsewhere; the deficiencies are filled in with 'mock Arabic' ornament.

3, 4. VICTORY IN A JUDICIAL COMBAT (Benedict, p. 247). (3), Two young men, wearing tunics and cross-gartered hose, each armed with a shield, are fighting with cudgels. The judge, in a long cloak, stands by on the left with a short staff in his hand; two other men, one of whom kneels, look on from the right. Clouds above. Inscribed: PVGNANT PVGILES MAG . . . The missing part of the legend has been replaced with 'mock Arabic' ornament; Mr. William Urry, who identified the subject and contributed a note on these two medallions ('The Thirteenth-Century Miracle Glass: an Identification') to *C.C.C.*, No. 31 (October, 1938), p. 13, conjectures that when complete it may have run: *Pugnant pugiles mag*[*no cum furore*] ('The fighters fight with main and might'). (4). The stronger is lifting his opponent on his back, to dash him heavily to the ground; the opponent stretches out his arms in supplication to St. Thomas. Discarded shields and cudgels lie on the ground. The judge advances with staff uplifted on the left, whilst the two onlookers cower glancing back over their shoulders on the right. Inscribed: MINOR.DESPERATVS SC̄M.TH.INVOCAT ('The smaller man in despair called upon St. Thomas'). Reproduction: *F.C.C. Seventh Annual Report*, 1934, facing p. 39. Plate 36c, d

5. A CRIPPLE AT THE TOMB OF ST. THOMAS. Beside the tomb, on which is a candle, stands a man with a crippled child on his back in the presence of a gesticulating priest; the child wears a tight bonnet. Of the inscription only LVMP (the last letter uncertain) remains; the deficiency is supplied with 'mock Arabic' ornament. Plate 36b

6. ST. THOMAS OF CANTERBURY. He is seated on a bench under a round arch with turrets and battlements above springing from the foliated capitals of columns; he points upwards with his right forefinger and holds a book in his left hand. He is vested in mitre, chasuble, pall, dalmatic and alb. Behind his head his name: S. THOMA . . E (for *Episcopus*).

This panel had its place originally in the triforium of one of the East Transepts, as shown by the original armatures of those windows, in which Mr Caldwell found it to fit exactly; he discovered it cut into three pieces, inserted in the background of the windows of the North Choir Aisle Triforium (see p 68; compare Mason, p 28).

Plate 36a

WINDOW III

The window is divided into four large lozenge-shaped panels separated by pairs of medallions nearly in the form of three-quarters of a circle, the whole surrounded by a border of interlaced bands with foliage in white, green, pale murrey and gold on a blue ground. The ground of the panels and medallions is blue, that of the interspaces ruby. Panels 4 and 7 were removed by Dean Powys in 1792 to the South Window of the South-West Transept (at M4, 5; see p. 142) and reinstated where they now are in 1920.

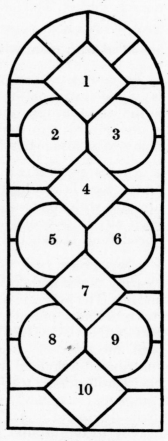

19′ 0″ × 5′ 0″

1, 2, 3. A RIDING ACCIDENT. Dr. Mason suggests this may be 'the story of Baldric . . . . who was injured by a fall from his horse' (William, p. 375).* (1). A man on the left seizing the bridle of a restive horse, whilst another on the right comes to the help of the rider, who lies with eyes closed in the foreground; a tree and clouds above indicate open country. Inscription (too defective for conjectural restoration): . . . PRODEAS . . . ADE . . . DCI:. (3). 'His wife urges him to invoke St. Thomas who appears' (M), crook in hand (as in Window IV, No. 8, which is based on the same cartoon), at his bedside as he lies asleep. Of the inscription, only FEN remains, and this, like the miscellaneous fragments that fill out the line, may have been inserted from elsewhere. (2). He gives thanks at the tomb of the saint. A priest on the right blesses him whilst he stoops, barelegged, with joined hands over the tomb; his shoes are on the ground at the base of the panel, a discarded garment behind him. In the background his wife and another man stand gesticulating. Only fragments of inscription remain below (MINIMIS and ECCL, not both from the same legend).

4. STEPHEN OF HOYLAND DELIVERED FROM NIGHTMARES (Benedict, p. 44). He lies awake in bed, with a demon at his head and another at his feet clutching at the coverlet, whilst a veiled woman stoops over him between them soothing him with her hand; a third demon with red face floats down from above behind her. The inscription is almost obliterated (VEXAT . . . . . EIONIO).

5, 6, 7. UNIDENTIFIED PILGRIMAGE SCENES. (5). Pilgrims on their way to the tomb, four on horseback, four behind on foot, in front a cripple on crutches; the nearest rider seems to be taking a ring off the little finger of his right hand, perhaps to

---

* For these references to William of Canterbury and Benedict of Peterborough, see above, p. 81.

85

give it to the cripple who is looking back towards him. The inscription is almost entirely obliterated; ... EN .. can be read. (6). Five pilgrims (two men, two women and a youth) at St. Thomas's well (the *Fons Thomae*), with a priest who sits in attendance, with what is perhaps a money-bag in his left hand and a cup in his right; another cup stands on a shelf above the well. One woman drinks from a cup, other pilgrims carrying embroidered bags. Dr. Mason comments: 'They may represent an ordinary pilgrimage, but possibly it may be, as Miss Williams says, that of the pilgrims to Compostella who were saved from shipwreck by St. Thomas (Benedict, p. 112)'. In this case it may be that the bags contain 'the Crosses destined for S. James' which 'were presented to the shrine of the "liberator", S. Thomas' (W). A mock Arabic inscription below. (7). In the middle, a tomb (in which the openings generally shown in representations of the tomb of St. Thomas are not visible); behind it are two men engaged in debate, one holding a short staff. Other figures are grouped to left and right, and seated below in front of the tomb.   Plate 33a, b

8. A VISION BY NIGHT. A young man, pointing with his right forefinger, standing by the bedside of a bearded man who looks up at him; between them is a scroll on which the inscription is now mostly undecipherable: .... TV ... *TV* SANGVINIS ST'VALE (..... *sanguinis sancti, vale*). Dr. Mason reads only the last word— mistakenly, as *vestes*; he comments: 'The sufferer ... might be William Patrick ... one of the earliest miracles—who, when nearly mad with toothache, was visited in bed by a graceful youth, who directed his attention to the martyr, and healed him by the touch of the hem of the martyr's cloak' (Benedict, p. 47). Miss Williams, followed by Dr. Nelson, wrongly interprets the subject as 'a King resting upon a bed ... possibly Henry II relating his vision to Benedict, who is standing by holding a scroll with an inscription'. She is also mistaken in saying that 'the head of the King is of a later date'; it is treated in the same manner, notably in the curled ending of the eyebrows, as heads in other medallions of this window. 'Mock Arabic' inscription below, interrupted by a stylised bush which springs from the foot of the medallion, in front of an inner border.

9. WILLIAM THE PRIEST OF LONDON (Benedict, p. 42), who 'was cured of paralysis by drinking a drop of St. Thomas's blood, being the first to be healed by that manner of application. Standing over the tomb he holds a cup, into which one monk' (with cowl partly drawn over his head) 'puts the precious drop' (taking it with a long spoon out of a bottle), 'while another pours upon it a flask of hallowed water' (M). At either end of the tomb a tall candle in a candlestick. Appended to the figures and separated by their heads are the words: SANG (*Sang[uis]*) DIS(*dis[tillatus?]*)*EOIN* AQVA; the italicised portion, to right of the head of the patient, is largely effaced and is an insertion, being painted on pinkish glass (like that of the heads), whereas the other legends are on white glass. Below, the title: LLELMVS SACERDOS LVNDON' ([*Wil*]*lelmus sacerdos Lundon[ensis]*), 'William the priest of London').   Plate 40c

10. AN UNIDENTIFIED CURE. Dr. Mason describes it as follows: 'The lowest diamond gives a scene of healings at the tomb. A blind young man is brought by his mother, as it would seem. A monk in a yellow cap touches his eyes. Behind the mother sits a man suffering with pains in the head, waiting his turn. A woman in a yellow cloak stands near the monk pressing her hand against her cheek. As in most pictures of the tomb, a box lies on the slab, no doubt containing relics of the saint; and

(a)

(b)

(a) Pilgrims on the way to Canterbury

(b) Pilgrims at St. Thomas's Well

about 1220–1225

TRINITY CHAPEL

Window III

pp. 85, 86

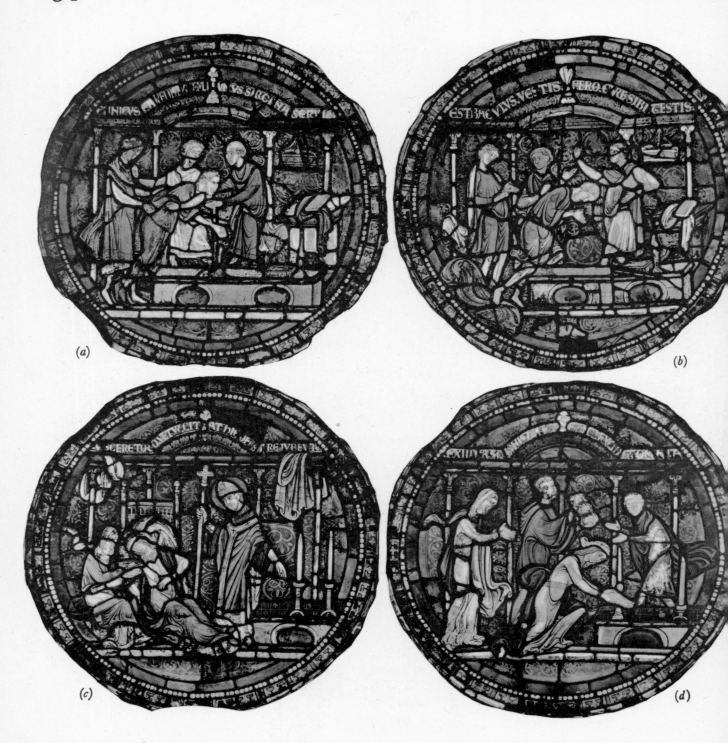

34

(a)

(b)

(c)

(d)

(a, b) Robert of Cricklade
(c, d) Cure of a Woman

about 1220–1225

TRINITY CHAPEL

Window IV

pp. 89, 90

(a)

(b)

(c)

(a, b, c, d) Eilward of
Westoning

about 1220–1225

TRINITY CHAPEL
Window V

pp. 94, 95

36

(a)

(b)

(a)　St. Thomas of
　　　Canterbury

(b)　A cripple at the tomb of
　　　St. Thomas

(c)

(d)

(c, d) Combat Scenes

Early 13th CENTURY TRINITY CHAPEL *Window I pp.* 84, 85

(a)

(b)

(a) Petronilla of Polesworth
(b) Audrey of Canterbury

about 1220–1225

TRINITY CHAPEL
Window IV

pp. 88, 90

38

(a)

(b)   (c)

(d)

(a, c) The Plague in the House
        of Sir Jordan Fitz-eisulf

(b, d) Richard Sunieve

(e)   Robert of Rochester

        about 1220–1225

        TRINITY CHAPEL
        Window VI

        pp. 100, 97, 98

(e)

(a)

(b)

(a) Richard Sunieve
(b) Robert of Rochester
about 1220–1225
TRINITY CHAPEL
Window VI
pp. 97, 98

39

(*a*, *b*) Women visiting the
    Tomb

(*c*)   Willaim the Priest of
    London

about 1220–1225

TRINITY CHAPEL

Windows V, III

pp. 93, 86

by the tomb stands a desk with a book laid on a white cloth. Perhaps the scene is typical rather than special.' Below is a fragment only of the descriptive legend . . . . VNT.V.

WINDOW IV

The window consists of sixteen medallions (circular except for the two uppermost, which are cut into by the curve of the pointed arch) with figure-subjects, in pairs, separated by smaller circles or semicircles filled with symmetrical branching stems with small leaves surrounding a central rosette. The outer border is composed of palmette ornament springing outward. The medallions are enclosed by bead-ornament within a ring of 'crown' ornament (see page 28*n*); they are noteworthy for the splendid diapers, varying in composition, of foliage and berries on coiled stems painted in reserve on the blue glass of the ground, which distinguish this window from all others in the Cathedral. Parallels to this use of diaper, at Lincoln and Strasburg, are referred to on p. 20 above.

23' 0" × 7' 0"

1. PILGRIMS WITH WATER OF ST. THOMAS. A man is hurrying forward to meet two others, one of whom is pouring the healing water with its mixture of blood (represented, as Mr. Caldwell has pointed out, by pink glass flashed with ruby), from a bottle into a bowl held by the second with outstretched hands. Inscribed *SVBTPESHRE VESTIS: PERO EST BACVLS*. The inscription, which does not belong to the medallion, is defective, and appears to be a duplication, with words transposed, of that on No. 10 (below, *q.v.*); the fragmentary lettering before VESTIS is in a different script. Miss Williams and Dr. Nelson wrongly interpret this as an offering at the Tomb. Dr. Mason mistakenly describes the bottle as 'a small round box presumably containing Canterbury water or other relic of the Saint'; Canon Crum better describes the subject: 'Pilgrims with phial of holy water visit a sick man'.

2. ST. THOMAS VISITING A SICK MAN. The Saint, with his cross supported against his left shoulder, lays his right hand on the forehead and his left on the pulse of the man, who lies in bed half naked under a green coverlet; a gown is thrown over what appears to be a high-backed chair to the right, and a curtain over a beam.

Inscribed: QVA DOLET HAC PLANAT DOLET HIS TRIB' ET TRIA SANAT (*Qua dolet hac planat, dolet his tribus et tria sanat*, 'Where the pain is, there he smooths; the pain is in these three places and he heals the three'.) HAC has been mistakenly read as HIC (W., M.); Dr. Nelson correctly reads HAC. It appears to have escaped notice hitherto that to the right of the Archbishop's cross, immediately below one beam, is a strip of inscription 'in reserve' on a black ground; most of this has been obliterated and only the final T between two stops is legible. It may be conjectured that T was preceded by S and that the initials (for *Sanctus Thomas*) were intended as a label to establish the identity of the figure beside which it is placed, as in several of the scriptural subjects in the windows of the North Choir Aisle (see pp. 55, 63).

3, 4. THE HEALING OF PETRONILLA, A NUN OF POLESWORTH (William, p. 163). This conjectured identification was first made by Dr. Mason and is accepted by Canon Crum. (3). Petronilla in a fit of epilepsy, supported by two women and followed by two others, is being brought to her abbess. Inscribed on the arch above: CONVALET EGRO *EFVNCT* (*Convalet, aegro*[*tat*], 'She grows better, she is sick . . .'). The concluding portion, in a different script, has been introduced from elsewhere. Dr. Mason erroneously reads: [*no*]*n valet stare.* The figures are in part restored (the face of the abbess and the hand of the woman on the left are modern). Below the subject a band of cresting, perhaps a later insertion. (4). Her feet are being bathed by an attendant in a basin near the tomb, on which stand two lighted candles (one partly missing) in candlesticks; a 'towel' (W, N) is not to be seen. Behind the tomb, a monk (his cowl over his head) with a spoon and bowl and a man pouring holy water from a bottle into a bowl held by a woman. The beam above swathed in curtains. On the arch, the inscription (very defective, with one insertion in a different script): S:DE*MIMPHATV*NONGINCHOTA; [*l*] *ympha* refers to the healing water.

Plate 37a

5, 6, 7. Modern.

8. THE DREAM OF KING LOUIS VII OF FRANCE. The subject of this medallion, recently restored to the Cathedral, was at first conjectured to be St. Thomas appearing to King Henry II of England,* though there seems to be no record of such an apparition. The later interpretation, which may undoubtedly be accepted, was suggested to the Author by Mr. W. P. Blore, who quotes Benedict of Peterborough's *Gesta Regis Henrici Secundi*†: it is there reported that St. Thomas appeared at night three times to King Louis, warning him with threats to make a pilgrimage to the tomb at Canterbury if he wished his son to recover from the infirmity with which he was stricken. In the sequel Louis visited the saint's tomb, in 1179, and made many presents to the church, including a gold cup and the famous jewel, the *régale* of France. The saint, holding in his left hand a pastoral staff (instead of the more usual archiepiscopal cross)‡ stands by the bedside of the sleeping king; his right hand is raised in warning gesture. It will be noted that the king wears his crown in bed, to mark his identity (like the sleeping Magi in the North Aisle of the Choir, p. 88). The inscription on the arch above is defective and partly inserted from elsewhere; at the right hand end it has been replaced by lengths of ornament derived from Arabic inscription in three different stages of development (see p. 28*n*); what remains reads: ELLAM *MRADI* VARIAN (?)SFV. The blue diapered background has been in part replaced (on the right) by foliage ornament of the fifteenth century. The medallion is based on the same cartoon as Window III, 3.

Colour Plate XI

---

* *F.C.C. Eighteenth Annual Report* (June, 1945), p. 31.

† Rolls Series, ed. Bishop Stubbs, Vol. I, p. 240.

‡ Other pre-Reformation instances of this substitution, in a thirteenth-century painting at Tarassa in Catalonia and in a North German statue of Becket from Skepptuna in Sweden, may be seen in the illustrations of Professor T. Borenius, *op. cit.*

9, 10. THE HEALING OF ROBERT OF CRICKLADE, Prior of St. Frideswide's, Oxford (Benedict, p. 97).* 'He suffered from swollen feet, so that he could not put on a shoe, nor stand to preach or to minister' (M) (9). He totters towards the tomb, supported by two attendants and received by a priest at the altar, on which is a book; above it hangs a 'crown' for lamps; on the tomb, a green money-box with slit in the lid. Inscribed: CLINICVS EN [or ENT] *REDDEVCEMI* VNVS SARCINA SERVIS (*Clinicus en . . . . . . unus sarcina servis*, 'The physician . . . . . the bundle to the servants'). Dr. Mason reads: '*Unicus en*, then some intruded words, *unus sarcina servis*'; but the letter preceding the first N has not the V form which is universal for the vowel *U* in these inscriptions; the L with a shortened I above its horizontal stroke is paralleled in EXILIT in the legend of No. 12 (below). The medallion is based on the same cartoon as No. 14 below. (10). Robert bows bare-legged over the tomb in thanksgiving, whilst the attendants and priest stand by with gestures of astonishment; his stick (on the tomb), boots and green cloak are cast off as witnesses of his cure. Inscribed: EST BACVLVS VESTIS PERO CVRE SIBI TESTIS (*Est baculus, vestis, pero, curae sibi testis*, 'His stick, his garment, his boot, are witnesses to his cure'). Miss Williams (followed by Dr. Nelson) is in error in reading: *cunctis ibi* for CVRE SIBI, also in saying that 'the right leg is diseased, the other has a red stocking and yellow shoe'; both legs are bare, the stockinged leg being that of an attendant. The composition is in part based on the same cartoon as No. 13 below. A grotesquely inaccurate woodcut of this medallion is given in the illustration of W. J. Loftie's 'Notes' in the *Archaeological Journal*, Vol. XXXIII (1876), where it is wrongly described as the '22nd subject in third window, Trinity Chapel', and said to depict the cure of a physician of Périgord and to show 'relics' on the tomb (compare p. 96 below). Plate 34a, b

11, 12. THE CURE OF A WOMAN, PERHAPS JULIANA PUINTEL (Benedict, p. 92; the identification is Dr. Mason's).† (11). Whilst she is propped up in her high-backed chair (W—rather than 'bed', as Dr. Mason has it), 'attended by another woman who holds a basin for her, St. Thomas appears to her and points her to his tomb, on which are two stout tapers. The yellow curtain seen over the tomb, corresponding to the one over the lady's head, and one bed post [*sic*] at the foot, shows that the tomb is only seen in a dream or vision' (M). Attention may be drawn to the jewelling on the head and staff of the Archbishop's cross. Inscribed: VISCERE TORQVAETVR CITAT HIC OFFERRE IVBEVTR (*Viscere torquetur, citat hic, offerre jubetur*, 'She is tormented in her bowels, he summons her, she is bidden make an offering'). The form TORQVAETVR, with a ligature like the cross-stroke of A connecting V and T, seems to be quite clear; it will also be noticed that V in *jubetur* is placed before the final ligatured T R. Old glass has been restored to this medallion by Mr. Caldwell in place of the new portions mentioned by Miss Williams; these included the head of 'a priest' (W) now replaced by the mitred head of St. Thomas (12). The sufferer kneels, placing a coil of wire on the tomb, on which are two lighted candles. 'Her maid stands praying behind her, while a man gives a coffer to the custodian of the tomb' (it is to be questioned whether this is not rather a book than a coffer). Inscribed: EXILIT A SOMNIS OFFERT DOLOR EXCIDIT OMN-

---

* This identification is due to Miss Williams; but Dr. Mason seems to have confused this Robert of Cricklade, the Prior, with another Robert, '*Canonicus ecclesiae Sanctae Frideswithae*' who is the subject of the immediately preceding narrative in Benedict's *Miracula*.

† The identification seems doubtful; in Benedict's account the offering made is that of a *candle*, not a coil of wire.

ITV (*Exilit a somnis, offert, dolor excidit omn* [*is*], 'She leaps up from her sleep and makes an offering; all the pain falls away'). The three final letters are an insertion in a different script.   Plate 34c, d

13, 14. CURE OF A MANIAC. Canon Crum accepts Dr. Mason's tentative identification with Henry of Fordwich (Benedict, p. 66), 'a dangerous lunatic, who was brought to the saint with his hands tied behind his back, protesting and struggling' (M). (13). He is being thrust towards the tomb, with his hands bound behind his back, by two men who belabour him with birchrods; a priest standing by a lectern to the right turns towards them; on the tomb, a money-box and two coils of wire leaning against candlesticks. Inscribed: AMENS ACCEDIT (*Amens accedit*, 'He approaches demented'); it will be noted that these words combine with the legend of the next medallion to make a single hexameter verse. The composition is in part based on the same cartoon as No. 10 above. (14). The cured sufferer kneels before the tomb on which are a candlestick and a money-box; his attendants stand behind, and a priest before a lectern on the right, with gestures of thanksgiving or surprise; the cord and birchrods of chastisement lie on the ground in front. Inscribed: ORAT SANVSQ' RECEDIT (*Orat sanusque recedit*, 'He prays and goes back healed'). Based on the same cartoon as No. 9 above.

15, 16. AUDREY (ATHELDRIDA) OF CANTERBURY cured of quartan fever (Benedict, p. 54). (15). She is seen beside the tomb about to drink from a bowl offered by a priest who stands to the right; a man (head modern) pointing upwards and a woman look on from the left. On the tomb (as in No. 16 also) are a money-box and a candle with a coil of wire resting against the candlestick. Three of the figures are repeated (from the same cartoon with slight variations) in No. 16 below. Inscribed: ARVIT EXANGVIS REDIT HVASTO SANGVINE SANGVIS (*Aruit exsanguis, redit hausto sanguine sanguis*, 'She was dried up, bloodless; when the blood (of the Saint) had been imbibed, her blood came back'). The ligatured vowels in HAVSTO are transposed. (16). Audrey advances to the tomb with her companion behind her, to receive the bowl in which the priest on the right is mixing a draught with a spoon, whilst between them is a man holding up a flask. Inscribed: CESSANT QVARTANE VIS FORMA SVBIT QVASI SANE (*Cessant quartanae, vis, forma, subit quasi sanae*, 'The quartan fevers depart, her strength, her figure, come back as if in health'). Dr. Mason comments: 'it is not easy to see why there should be two separate pictures of the miracle . . . . . . Perhaps the man in the right-hand picture is explaining to the tomb-keeper that Ethelreda cannot drink the blood of the martyr unless mixed with water'. Compare No. 15 above.   Plate 37b

WINDOW V

The main division of the window is into four circles one above another, with smaller half-circles at a tangent between them, the whole enclosed within a wide border. Within each major circle is inscribed a quatrefoil of which each quarter forms a separate pictorial panel; similar pictures are also contained within the half-circles. The outer border exhibits a straight green stem from which spring leaf-buds in pairs of two alternating designs, in blue, yellow, green, and murrey, the larger pairs being enclosed each within a white circle traversed by the stem; the ground of the border is ruby within the circles, blue outside them. The medallions have a blue background.

23′ 0″ × 7′ 0″

Plate XI

ST. THOMAS OF CANTERBURY AP-
PEARING IN A DREAM TO KING
LOUIS VII OF FRANCE. Medallion (8) in
Window IV of the series illustrating the miracles of
St. Thomas, in the aisles of the Trinity Chapel.
About 1220. P. 88.

The ground between the main divisions is decorated with a rectangular diaper on a blue ground with small ruby flowers at the intersections. The large circles have green borders painted with quatrefoils; the interspaces between the panels are filled with leafy scrolls on a ruby ground. Where the descriptive legends occupy two lines these are in some instances the one of white, the other of yellow glass. The representation of St. Thomas's shrine in the first panel points to a date about 1220.*

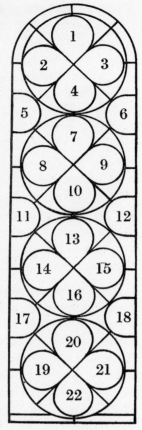

23′ 0″ × 7′ 0″

1. ST. THOMAS APPEARING above a monk asleep in bed. The saint, in mitre and vestments, his archiepiscopal cross in his right hand, is represented issuing from the end of his shrine, which is 'without its removable cover' and resting on 'a slab supported by two arches' (M). Inscribed: INC*ARCT*-MERETRO . . . . . . N . . . O . . RE FERETRO. As Dr. Mason remarks, apart from *feretro* only a few letters are now legible; some have been wrongly inserted. The saint's gesture is not that of benediction, as Dr. Mason seems to imply—a gesture performed with the *right* hand—but rather of exposition or dictation, as if to the historian of his miracles. The shrine has its original form, with a finial at each end of the gable (a third was added in the middle by Prior Henry of Eastry in 1315 (M)); it has a pattern of foliage in semicircles on the roof and rosettes in quatrefoils and semicircles on the side, closely resembling that of many Limoges enamel shrines and reliquaries of the period. It is represented again in Window XII, 21, 22 (see p. 111). The head and vestments of the saint, in old glass, have in recent years been substituted for modern glass inserted by Austen. It has been assumed by Miss Williams and Dr. Nelson that the sleeping monk is Benedict of Peterborough, but as Dr. Mason points out 'the historian may be either William or Benedict', as both men had similar visitations (compare William, p. 138; Benedict, p. 27). It may be pointed out however that although Benedict speaks of the saint appearing in mass vestments (*in vestibus et ornamentis pontificalibus . . . quasi missarum celebraturus mysteria*), neither writer speaks of him as emerging from his shrine.

Reproduction: Westlake, Vol. I, pl. LXIIc.   Colour Plate XII

2. Perhaps ROGER OF VALOGNES cured of a swollen foot at the tomb of the saint. (William, p. 538 (M).) He sits by the tomb barelegged, whilst a kneeling 'friend or servant' is bathing his foot in a bowl and two 'ministers of the tomb' (M) approach hurriedly, bringing another bowl and a towel. Branches of foliage trail across the arches behind. Inscribed: + DETVMET IN VOTO LAVACRO . . . . . SANG-VINE . . . Dr. Mason reads: *Detumet in voto, lavacro, [prece], sanguine [poto]* ('As he makes his vow, washes, prays, and drinks the blood, the swelling goes down'), commenting that 'the words in brackets are no longer legible'.   Colour Plate XII

3. A WOMAN AT THE TOMB. She stoops over it with outstretched arms, her gown drawn up so as to reveal her left leg in a green stocking (not bare, as Miss Williams

* See p. 82

and Dr. Nelson state). 'She appears to have sprung out of the arms of a woman behind her' (M), seated. 'A man beyond her carries a tall taper. Another taper stands on the tomb.' Facing them, two monks, one in the act of benediction, the other (restored) holding a book. The roof-beam is ornamented with two dragons. Inscribed: + MAGNIFICAT *GVNTA* RATVM LETVM MEDICVM MEDICATVS (*Magnificat gratum laetum medicum medicatus*, 'the healed sufferer glorifies the joyful healer'). The verse appears to be complete apart from the letters VNTA inserted in a different script, in which case the lines must originally have been filled out with ornament. In view of the gender of *medicatus*, which does not seem to accord with the subject of the cure shown in the picture, it may perhaps be questioned whether this inscription rightly belongs in this place and may not rather belong to one of the other, now missing, original panels in the window (7, 8, or 9). It will be noticed that the inscription is preceded by a cross between four dots as in No. 2. Miss Williams's conjectured restoration (adopted by Dr. Nelson)—*Magnificat sanctum, satiat medicamine planctum*—is wholly inadmissible; the word MAGNIFICAT is clearly followed by a G *on the same strip of glass.*   Colour Plate XII, Plate 50c

4. GODWIN OF BOXGROVE (?). A man, naked except for a cloth round his waist, is pressing forward to receive from another a shirt diagonally cross-striped; behind the former is a chair over the high back of which a third man with a wand in his right hand is watching the scene. For the remainder a note by the Author in *C.C.C.*, No. 42 (October 1947), p. 21, may be quoted: 'The right-hand portion of the picture . . . poses a question which remains unanswered. Beyond the crimson-framed doorway, for such it appears to be, out of which the bestower of the shirt is emerging, is seen, only in part, the tomb of St. Thomas with a priest behind it, standing by a lectern; on the lectern lies an open book at which he is pointing. The figure of the priest . . . is repeated with only slight modifications in two other compartments of the same window . . . an instance of the practice common at all stages in the history of glass-painting . . . of making a single cartoon serve for the composition of more than one subject. This part of the panel seems to bear no obvious relation to the remainder, although the priest looking backward over his shoulder might be supposed to be watching the actions of the figures behind him; there is no parallel, in the many scenes in which the saint's tomb is depicted in the "Miracle" windows, to the representation of only a part of it, with only one of the familiar openings, two on each of its sides. This gives rise to a doubt whether this part of the panel . . . may be the result of a patching at some stage of restoration; it is necessary to point out, however, that if such is the case, the column with its capital and the spring of an arch above are part of the original composition, since they correspond exactly with similar features on the left flank of the picture.' The inscription cannot belong, and may have related to one of the medallions now missing and replaced with modern glass: GVSTAT DISTENTA CVTE FIT GVSTV ME . . . TV . . (*Gustat distenta cute, fit gustu me-[dica]tu[s]*, 'His skin distended, he tastes, by the tasting he is cured'); Dr. Mason reads only *Gustat* or *gustato*, and *cute fit*. The lower line of the inscription is too much decayed to be wholly legible. The reference seems to be to a cure of dropsy or leprosy, effected by tasting the Water of St. Thomas, of which the charitable act in the picture may be the sequel.

Miss Williams suggested the identification with Godwin of Boxgrove (William, p. 339), 'who distributed all his clothes that he might be an example of voluntary poverty'; this may be accepted, as it is by Dr. Mason, as a probable explanation of the picture. The story relates that Godwin in a dream saw St. Thomas taking off his robe and mantle, and that, supposing this vision to be a divine warning that he should himself give away his garments and display humanity towards the poor, in a moment of charitable insight he gave one of his two shirts (not 'all his clothes', as Miss Williams has it) to a pauper, retaining the other because he himself was poor. If the figure on the extreme right is to be accepted as being in its proper place, it may be conjectured that the priest is pointing to the passage in St. Matthew's Gospel (XXV, 36) referring to the clothing of the naked as one of the 'Corporal Works of Mercy'. The head of the figure on the left is a recent reinstatement in place of a mitre which had been incongruously inserted, as if balanced on the back of the chair.

The chair, with its turned uprights, is interesting as exhibiting a widely distributed form which originated probably in the period of the Germanic Migrations and of which the earliest representations are in the miniatures of Carolingian illuminated manuscripts. It survived as peasant furniture in Scandinavia and Germany almost to modern times; a typical Norwegian example from Hedemarken, perhaps of the fifteenth century, is in the Kunstindustrimuseum at Oslo.

The relevant passage in the story as related by William of Canterbury is somewhat obscure in its meaning and may therefore be here cited: *Videns per somnum quod beatus Thomas sibi togam et pelliciam detraheret, credensque quod erogationis vestimentorum suorum et humanitatis pauperibus exhibendae divinitus admoneretur, alteram tunicarum suarum caritatis intuitu pauperi dedit, alteram, quia ipse pauper erat, retinuit.* A parallel to this scene of clothing the naked is provided in the Cathedral by the contemporary medallion depicting St. Martin sharing his cloak with a beggar (see p. 111).

Reproduction: *C.C.C.*, No. 42 (October 1947), facing p. 24.   Colour Plate XII

5. 6. VISIT TO THE TOMB OF A WOMAN 'all swollen with dropsy'. In the left picture she is seen approaching a building, walking with a crutch and supported behind by her companion; in the right, they are leaving the building, which is here shown reversed, looking back at it as they go. Inscribed: (5) QVE VENIT EGROTA TVRGESCIT YDROPICA TOTA (*Quae venit aegrota turgescit hydropica tota*, 'She who comes sick is all swollen with dropsy'). (6). GREM*D*ITFLATA*RE* . . . . VENERAT-ATENVATA. This verse as it stands presents difficulties. The right extremity of the upper line is of plain inserted glass. The fourth letter is uncertain, being partly hidden by a repairing lead; the eighth and ninth are also hardly decipherable. The spacing does not seem to justify the conjecture that portions of the two lines have changed places and that the inscription originally ran: *Venerat inflata gremium . . . . redit a[t]tenuata,* ('She had come with bosom swollen, she returns attenuated'), though the nature of the dropsical swelling ('*inflata gremium*') is borne out by the left-hand picture. Miss Williams saw in these pictures 'a blind lady and her blind attendant feeling their way to the tomb', and then 'turning round to take one more look', their 'bandages . . removed, the staff left behind'. Dr. Mason pointed out her mistake, noting that 'no such story appears to be told in William or Benedict', though himself mistaken in reading '*Hydrope*' as the word in the inscription (the only one quoted by him) 'suggesting a different complaint'. Canon Crum merely describes it as 'women helping one another to the tomb and going away healed'.   Plate 40a, b

7, 8, 9. Modern.

10, 11, 12. THE LAME DAUGHTERS OF GODBOLD OF BOXLEY (Benedict, p. 170). (11). The sisters, lame from birth, approaching the Cathedral on crutches, clouds above them. Inscribed: NATE SORTE PARI' PEREG RE VENIVNT MEDICAR.

(*Natae sorte pari peregre veniunt medicar*[*i*], 'The sisters born with an equal lot come on pilgrimage to be healed'); the last letter has been replaced by plain yellow glass. (10). The elder is visited at night by St. Thomas while reclining asleep by the tomb (on which are a candlestick and a green money-box), the younger leaning on her crutches over it, a priest with open book and an attendant standing by. Inscribed: DESAN*STAN* . . GA SOROR . . . ANXIA . . ESE. This legend is defective and contains intruding lettering in a different script; Canon Mason reads *Soror anxia sese*, but there is an upstroke clearly visible after the second A of *anxia* which precludes an S as the last letter but three. (12). The saint appearing on the second night to the younger sister as she sits weeping whilst the elder stands giving thanks (the face and vestments of the saint are restored). Inscribed: SANAT MAIORE OX PRI . . . MA SEDA' MINOREM (*Sanat maiorem nox prima, secunda minorem*, 'The first night brings health to the elder, the second night to the younger', referring to the fact that the elder sister was healed on the first night and the younger only when St. Thomas appeared in answer to her complaints, on the second). Part of the final letter of *maiorem* and the entire N of *nox* are missing, the lettering having been closed up and the blank supplied with later glass inserted at the end of the line. The figure of St. Thomas is modern. According to Benedict, the younger sister framed her appeal to St. Thomas in the words of Esau to his father: 'Hast thou but one blessing, my father? Bless me, even me also'.

13–18. EILWARD OF WESTONING (Bedfordshire) and his quarrel with Fulk, from whom he stole a pair of ditcher's gloves and a whetstone to make good an undischarged debt (Benedict, p. 173). (4). Eilward brought by two men, bound, before the magistrate in a columned building. Inscribed: PIGNVS IAM*MO* DICIVM VM CENSETVR INIQVVM. The inscription is out of order and defective, MO being apparently an interpolation from elsewhere. It may be restored conjecturally as follows: *Pignus i*(*ud*)*icium* (*d*)*am*(*n*)*um censetur iniquum*, 'He is sentenced to a pledge, judgment and an unjust penalty'. *Pignus* may perhaps refer to the ordeal by water he was made to undergo. Reproduction (with part of border from Window II in the North Choir Aisle) in colours: Warner, pl. following p. 116. (15). His punishment, as he lies with a plank on his chest, by blinding and mutilation at the hands of two executioners in the presence of the seated magistrate and several onlookers—out of doors, as shown by clouds and a tree. Inscribed: *VDVNTVR* ECTA SVNT LVMINA MEMBRA RESECTA (. . . . *ecta sunt lumina, membra resecta*, 'His eyes are cut out, his members amputated'); the first seven letters are an interpolation. (17). Eilward in bed being healed by St. Thomas, who 'makes the sign of the cross upon his forehead and the sockets of his eyes with the end of his pastoral staff' (M) (the—contemporary—piece of glass behind the saint's head is perhaps an insertion, where the head of the staff would be expected to appear). Inscribed: REDDITA SVCCRE *FVRTVM* . *BE* SENSIMQ' RECRESCVNT (*Reddita succre* [*scunt*] . . . . *sensimque recrescunt*, ' . . . . are restored and swell up and gradually grow again'). The lost word, which has been replaced by FVRTVM . BE in a different script, may be conjectured to have referred to the gradual (*sensim*) healing of Eilward's mutilation rather than to his restored sight. (16). Eilward pointing to his eyes whilst 'rich pilgrims' (C), one of whom has a money-bag, offer him silver coins, and he gives a gold coin with his left hand to a cripple on the right; the cripple has a beggar's bowl and supports himself with his hands on iron clogs. Inscribed: . . . . AM NSTOR*T*EM VA SINISTRA. This inscription is damaged beyond recovery. Miss Williams reads: *Dat ille stipes pauperibus*, but, as Dr. Mason comments, where she 'got

(a)

(b)

(*a, b*) Plague in the House of
Sir Jordan Fitz-eisulf

about 1220–1225

TRINITY CHAPEL
Window VI

pp. 99, 100

42

(a)

(a, b) William of Kellett
       about 1220–1225
       TRINITY CHAPEL
       Window VII
       pp. 101, 102

(b)

43

FVRENT IE RG GITN PPEOR AT IN SEOVEIS IS

(a)

A LWEI S I EUIEM SA SUME PARIS FAC

(b)

(a) Adam the Forester
(b) William of Kellett
about 1220–1225
TRINITY CHAPEL
Window VII
pp. 101, 102

44

(a)

(b)

(a, b) John of Roxburgh
about 1220–1225
TRINITY CHAPEL
Window XI
pp. 103, 104

the inscription from is unexplained'. The last word doubtless refers to the alms given by Eilward with his left hand. (18). Eilward gives thanks at the tomb of the Saint (this panel is not 'new', as stated by Miss Williams, although largely restored). Inscribed: ASTAT NARRANTI POPVLVS MAGNALIA SANCTI (*Astat narranti populus magnalia sancti*, 'The people stand by as he narrates the mighty works of the saint'). Dr. Mason could read only the last word, and that wrongly, as *sancte;* the Author is indebted to Mr. W. P. Blore for supplying the indistinct word *magnalia*. (13). This panel has been taken by Miss Williams to be the first scene of this story ('he is riding out of the city'), by Canon Crum, following an alternative suggestion of Dr. Mason, as the last ('Eilward leaving Canterbury giving thanks'); but the inscription, with its reference to leprosy, makes it extremely doubtful whether the panel belongs to the Eilward story at all, and should not rather take the place of the modern panel No. 7 as part of an entirely different narrative. The story of Eilward, at present beginning at its crisis, requires an intro-ductory scene which would have occupied this portion in the window. Inscribed: SPE RECREANTE PR *LVΩN* T ADEVNTI' LEPRA RECEDIT. The reversed letters are an insertion in a different script. The lettering is difficult to make out in places. The following conjectural restoration is suggested: *Spe recreante precat adeunti lepra recedit*, 'Hope creating him afresh, he prays; as he approaches the leprosy abates'. Against this however is the circumstance that the rider is seen leaving and not approach-ing (*adiens*) the gateway which, on the analogy of the similar structure in Nos. 5 and 6, may be taken to be that of Canterbury or of the Cathedral. Of the many cures of leprosy recorded by William and Benedict there are two that may possibly be in question as being those of soldiers or knights (it will be observed that the rider in the picture wears spurs), those of Gerald, a Knight of 'Porta Clausa' (William, p. 437) and Walter of Lisors (Benedict, p. 203).

The story of Fulk and Eilward is related at length, on the lines of Benedict's narrative, by W. J. Loftie in the *Archaeological Journal*, Vol. XXXIII (1876), pp. 4, 5. He comments: 'As the ordeal was condemned by the Council of the Lateran in 1214, this story may be dated in the early years of the century'; this does not of course imply that the representation of it may not have been painted at a later date.   Plate 35

19, 20, 21. THE CELLARER HUGH OF JERVAULX (Benedict, p. 159). (19). 'The Abbot of Jervaulx administering extreme unction to his dying monk' (M) as he lies in bed; to the right, an attendant with what Miss Williams conjectures to be a wafer-box* upon an altar. Reproduction: Westlake, Vol. I, pl. LXII*b*. Inscribed: DES. ERANT MEDICI PATER 7 FRATRES 7 AMICI (*Desperant medici, pater et fratres et amici*, 'The physician, his father and brothers and friends are in despair'). The words 7 FRATRES have been reinstated since Dr. Mason wrote his account of the window; as he points out, Miss Williams has made the mistake of interchanging the legends belonging to Nos. 19 and 20; her transcription of this legend (repeated by Nelson) is moreover incorrect. (20). The Abbot giving a draught of water from the holy well to the monk, who now sits up in bed; Dr. Mason comments that 'an atten-dant in white, at the head of the bed, holds what appears to be the vessel from which

---

* The drawing of this object given on p. 34 of her book shows an extension on the right which has been misunderstood; this is actually the left hand of the attendant, with fingers closed on the rim of the object. On the glass (which is broken and repaired) the jewelled border, shown distinctly in her draw-ing, is now almost effaced. Also, what Miss Williams describes as an altar has rather the appearance of a lectern.

the miraculous water was drawn', but the vessel, the left half of which is missing and replaced by old glass from elsewhere, appears to be the same shown in No. 19 and described as a wafer-box. Inscribed: SPES DESPERANTI SVPEREST IN SAN-GVUINE SANCTI *IME* (*Spes desperanti superest in sanguine sancti*, 'Hope remains for the hopeless in the blood of the saint'); IME inserted in a different script. (21). Hugh is cured by 'a copious discharge of blood' (M) from his nostrils; the abbot with crosier and two monks holding books look on, also a man wearing a skull-cap, perhaps a lay physician. Inscribed: . . . . SC BIBIT HIC CVIS SANGVINE SANAT. This inscription has been in part rearranged and is so defective that it has defeated conjectural restoration.

Loftie (*loc. cit.*, p. 5), followed by Miss Williams, interprets these panels as giving the story of Peter, a physician of Périgord (William, p. 261), but Dr. Mason comments: 'There is nothing in his history corresponding to the somewhat repulsive scene she describes as "dying" '; he identifies the subject as that of Hugh of Jervaulx. The woodcut facing p. 1 of Loftie's article is wrongly described in the title as illustrating the Périgord physician's cure, although it actually reproduces No. 10 in Window IV (*q.v.*).

22. Modern.

WINDOW VI

The design consists of four panels one above another (three square, the uppermost truncated by the curve of the arched top of the window), from the corners of which radiate almond-shaped panels dividing the large circle which encloses each square in such a manner that the intervening compartments are of hatchet-shaped outline; the medallions, which are each surrounded by a broad ruby ring bordered with white, have blue backgrounds, as have also the interspaces between them. The outer border of the window is filled with foliage in murrey, white, yellow and green forming loops, the ground being blue within these, ruby outside them.

Reproduction (lowest portion only): Nelson, pl. VII.

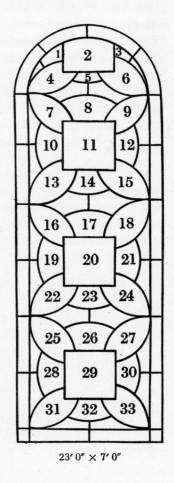

23' 0" × 7' 0"

1, 2, 3. HEALING OF JULIANA OF ROCHESTER. Dr. Mason's tentative identification of her as the blind Juliana 'led by her father Gerard' (Benedict, p. 204) may be accepted as certain. (1). Led by her left wrist in his right hand, she walks behind her father, her right hand on his shoulder, her eyes closed; clouds above. Inscribed: . . . AT *EGRVM E* TRAHITVR PEREGRE SINE LVCE; this may perhaps be restored as *A patre trahitur . . . . peregre sine luce*, 'She is led on her pilgrimage by her father, without light (in her eyes)'. Dr. Mason mistakenly reads . . . *trahitur peregrina*. (2). Supported by her father behind her, she leans over the tomb whilst a priest touches her eyes with water from a bowl in his left hand, an attendant with staff behind him; on the altar a candle; two glass lamps hang from the arches above. Inscribed: HIC CRVOR EST TACTVS S' NONDVM . . . . ANGVOR ABA*MA* (*Hic cruor est tactus s[ed] nondum languor aba[ctus]*). The latinity seems dubious, but the meaning appears undoubtedly to be: 'Here the blood is applied, but the weakness is not yet removed'; this would confirm Dr. Mason's conjecture that we have here 'the apparently vain application of St. Thomas's blood to her eyes'. MA has been inserted in place of the last four letters. (3). Sitting on a bench in a building beside her father, she points to her eyes, now seeing. Inscribed: SANA DOMI FACTA LVX REDDITA CVRA PERACTA (*Sana domi facta lux reddita cura peracta*, 'At home she is made whole, the light is given back (to her eyes), the cure is completed'). This inscription has been completed since Dr. Mason read *sanando . . cura*. Miss Williams gives the inscription now attached to No. 4.

4–9. RICHARD SUNIEVE OF 'EGEWERDE' (Edgeworth, in Cheshire or Gloucester-shire?), cured of leprosy (Benedict, p. 245); the identification is Dr. Mason's. (4). Richard driving out to pasture the four horses of his master, Richard Fitzhenry. He holds in his right hand a staff, in his left a short post and cord for tethering the horses. The nearest horse has a dappled coat. Inscribed: PASTOR ALENDORVM CVRAM PVER EGIT EQVORVM (*Pastor alendorum curam puer egit equorum*, 'The boy herdsman performed the task of feeding the horses'). This inscription is quoted by Miss Williams as being over panel No. 1. Reproduction: *C.C.C.*, No. 28 (October 1937), facing p. 5. (5). He reclines asleep beneath a bush, to awake a leper, whilst the horses browse at large; the tethering cord is wound like a girth round the nearest. Inscribed: SANVS SOPITVR LEPRA SVRGENS OPERITVR (*Sanus sopitur, lepra surgens operitur*, 'He falls asleep healthy, when he rises he is covered with leprosy'). Dr. Mason thus correctly reads the legend wrongly transcribed by Miss Williams as: *Sanctus sopitur lepras* $\begin{Bmatrix} vulnusque \\ ulcuçque \end{Bmatrix}$ *aperitur* (of which she gives an incorrect translation having no reference to the scene depicted). She connects the panel with 'the story of an Irish soldier, Walter', related by William, p. 545. Reproduction: *C.C.C.*, No. 28 (October 1937), facing p. 5. (6). In a room with double arcade reminiscent of that on the East Transept turrets of the Cathedral, he sits up in bed to receive food (a bowl and a platter or perhaps a flat loaf, mistaken by Miss Williams for clothes) offered on a tray at arm's length by his mother, whose mouth is muffled as a precau-tion against infection; he reaches with his right hand for a ewer which stands on a low table beside the bed. Inscribed: OMNIB; ABIECTVS VIX SIC A MATRE RE-FECTVS (*Omnibus abjectus vix sic a matre refectus*, 'Cast out by all he is thus scarcely fed even by his mother'). Reproduction: *C.C.C.*, No. 28 (October 1937), facing p. 7. (7). Recovered from the disease, Richard prostrates himself before the tomb, on which stands a candlestick with lighted candle; 'with his left arm stretched upon the tomb, he feels with his right hand for something which seemed to have fallen from his face' (M). A priest stands by with a bowl into which he is dropping blood of the saint (represented by a piece of ruby glass) from a rod; his mother and a third man look on. Inscribed: LANGVIDVS ERIGITVR VENIT ORAT POTAT ABIVIT (*Languidus erigitur venit orat potat abivit*, 'He rises languid, he comes, prays, drinks, goes away'). Dr. Mason omits the last three words of this inscription and erroneously reads '*ad*' after the first three. Reproduction: *C.C.C.*, No. 28 (October 1937), facing p. 7. (8). Walking with a staff, followed by his mother, 'he shows his face, now healed, to his master and mistress' (M). This scene is interpreted by Miss Williams: 'Two men (*sic*) address a knight and lady'. Inscribed: FIT CARO QVE PRIDEM COLOR 7 VIGOR 7 STATVS IDEM (*Fit caro quae pridem color et vigor et status idem*, 'His flesh becomes as it was before, his complexion and strength and carriage are the same'). This legend has not been quoted by previous writers. The initial F is partly lost by the flaking of the glass. Reproduction: *C.C.C.*, No. 28 (October 1937), facing p. 8. (9). In the presence of his master, who brings a candle, his mistress, his mother and a fourth onlooker ('his whole household'), Robert pours out an offering of money on the tomb. Inscribed: AMAT*ER* DOM*VS* SVA TOTA. The beginning of this inscription, not given by previous writers, is lost, and the middle part too much corroded to give a clear reading; only the termination seems to be distinct: *domus sua tota*, 'his whole household'. Reproduction: *C.C.C.*, No. 28 (October 1937), facing p. 8.   Plates 38b, d, 39a

10, 11, 12. Modern. Miss Williams's claim that the woman in No. 12 is original holds good only of a small portion of the drapery (in ruby glass).

13, 14, 15. ROBERT OF ROCHESTER (Rodbertulus, 'Bobby'), the boy drowned in the Medway whilst stoning frogs (Benedict, p. 226). (13). Six boys throwing stones at frogs, three of which are seen leaping out of the sedge-bordered river, whilst Robert falls into it, face forward; two of his companions carry a supply of stones in the skirts of their long tunics. There seems little reason for the uncertainty expressed by Dr. Mason and Canon Crum as to the nature of the victims of their sport, nor do the boys, intent upon it, and all apparently older than Robert, whose age is recorded as eight, show any signs of 'shouting that Robert has slipped in the river', as Miss Williams describes it. Dr. Mason comments that 'the frogs . . . . . are borrowed from the similar story of Philip Scot (William, p. 200; Benedict, p. 238)'. Inscribed: DVM RVIT *SN* FVNVS RANARVM: CORRVIT VNVS (*Dum ruit* [*ad*] *funus ranarum corruit unus*, 'As he rushes to the death of the frogs one boy falls headlong in'); there is an extraneous interpolation after RVIT. (Dr. Mason has only ' . . . . . *corruit undis* or *unus*'.) (14). Two boys with breathless gestures, telling the news of the accident to Robert's parents, who rush out of their house, the mother supported by her husband. Inscribed: *ERIT HISN*: *HIC F* NT MERSI COMITE . . CA REVERSI (. . . . . *tn mersi comite*[*s*] . . . . *ca reversi*, '. . . the comrades of the drowned boy'). The first twelve letters are an extraneous insertion; something is missing after HICF and after COMITE, the words having been closed up. Dr. Mason comments: 'The lettering below has been wrongly arranged: the words *hic immersi comites* can be made out'; but NT is quite clear immediately before MERSI. (15). The rescue. Robert drawn up out of mud after the ebb of the tide by a man wading with his tunic girt up round his waist; the two messengers look on, and the mother, with the father behind her, stretches out her arms to receive the body of her child. Inscribed: DEFVNCTVM FLENTES PISCANTVR IN AMNE PENTES (*Defunctum flentes piscantur in amne parentes*, 'Weeping, the parents fish for the dead (boy) in the river'). This inscription has been restored to the window since the publication of Dr. Mason's book. Plates 38e, 39b

16, 17, 18. Modern.

19, 20, 21. THE HEALING OF A MANIAC. Miss Williams's conjecture that it is a murderess, Matilda of Cologne (Benedict, p. 208), may probably be accepted. (19). Two men belabouring her with rods—'perhaps on the approach to Canterbury' (M), as shown by the pillared building in the background. The instruments of chastisement, in this as in other similar scenes, are bundles of twigs or rods (as Dr. Nelson has it) rather than cudgels or sticks, as elsewhere described. Inscribed: ALTERNAT GESTVM: NVNC VM N SA . . CQ' MOLESTVM. Portions of the inscription have changed places, and some of the letters are difficult to make out or

23′ 0″ × 7′ 0″
Plate XII

MIRACLES OF ST. THOMAS OF
CANTERBURY. (1) The saint emerging from
his shrine in an apparition to a sleeping monk.
(2) Perhaps Roger of Valognes cured of a swollen
foot. (3) A woman at the tomb of the saint. (4) Perhaps Godwin of Boxgrove distributing his clothes
to the poor. Upper portion of Window V in the
Trinity Chapel. About 1220. Pp. 91–93.

completely effaced, though the first three words and the last one, the only ones read by Dr. Mason, are quite legible. The suggested reading is: *Alternat gestum nunc sa[n]um n[un]cque molestum,* but *sanum* is somewhat uncertain. ('She alternates her bearing, now sane, now troublesome.') Miss Williams's conjecture—*Alternant mentem, gestum quoque vincla furentem* (adopted in part by Dr. Nelson)—is proved incorrect by the fact that ALTERNAT G is all included on a single length of glass, without intervening lead. (20). The woman collapsing beside the tomb of St. Thomas beneath the blows of one of her attendants (his head is restored), whilst the other stands with rod uplifted addressing a third man who leans on a staff; a monk sits reading from a book on the right. Miss Williams and Dr. Mason have both slightly misinterpreted this scene; the second attendant is not 'addressing the priest who is reading' (W), nor is he 'leaning upon his (cudgel), whilst he explains the case to an attendant carrying a candle' (M). A curtain is draped over a beam in front of the arcade behind. Inscribed: STAT MODO IOCVNDA . MODO LAPSA IACET MORIBVNDA (*Stat modo iocunda, modo lapsa jacet moribunda,* 'Now she stands gleefully, now she collapses and lies as if dying'). (Not *iucunda,* as Miss Williams and Dr. Mason have it: Dr. Nelson reads correctly *iocunda,* but omits *modo,* for which Miss Williams wrongly supplies *quae.*) (21). The victim, healed, 'is prostrate in thanksgiving at the tomb, while the keepers stand with their cudgels at rest' (M). A priest with cowl over his head and book in his right hand, stands receiving a candle (N), which he is putting into a candlestick on the tomb. Inscribed: AMEN CLAMAT AREDIT ADSVASA. The legend is defective; as in the corresponding panel, it was originally continued in a second line now filled with diaper. There are gaps to fill after the second word and at the end: *Amen clamat[ur?] . . . . a redit ad sua sa[na* or *lva?],* ' "Amen" is the cry, [she] returns sane (*or* safe) to her own affairs'. Dr. Nelson alone among previous writers quotes it, as: EXCLAMAT AREDIT AD SVAS A.

22, 23, 24. Modern.

25–33. THE PLAGUE IN THE HOUSE OF SIR JORDAN FITZ-EISULF of Pontefract, who had known Becket in his lifetime. The narrative, which follows the longer version given by Benedict (p. 229), not that of William (p. 160), starts with the lowest left-hand corner. (31). The funeral of the first victim, the nurse Britonis, who died in August; the coffin, covered with a pall, carried on a bier by four men, a priest walking in front with a book in one hand, a holy-water sprinkler in the other; beyond can be seen the heads of four other followers one of whom holds with both hands what has been, perhaps wrongly, taken by Miss Williams and Dr. Mason to be 'a huge lighted taper'. The priest wears an embroidered stole. Inscribed: NVTRICIS FVNVS RELIQVIS SVA FLAGRA MINATVR. (*Nutricis funus reliquis sua flagra minatur,* 'The funeral of the nurse threatens the survivors with each his own scourge'); Miss Williams's *sui,* followed by Dr. Nelson, is corrected by Dr. Mason. (32). Death of Sir Jordan's son William, aged ten, who died ten days after the nurse. The child laid on a bier, his parents stooping over him, and a priest with a book in his left hand sprinkling him with holy water (as Miss Williams and Dr. Mason point out, as against Dr. Nelson, who sees in this Extreme Unction—'anointing with holy oil'; Miss Williams also refers to the Host or Viaticum placed on the forehead of the child, but this is not now discernible). Inscribed: PERCVTITVR PVER Z MORITVR PLANCTVS GEMINATVR (*Percutitur puer et moritur, planctus geminatur,* 'The boy is smitten and dies, the lamentations are redoubled'). Thus Dr. Mason correctly, where Miss Williams and Dr. Nelson have *Perculitur puer moritur planetus geminatur.*

(33). Pilgrims arriving with water of St. Thomas. The child's mother lifting his head while Jordan pours water into his mouth; two pilgrims with water in jars, one with a staff, at the foot of the bier. Inscribed: VOX PATRIS VIS MARTIRIS VT RESTI-TVATVR (*Vox patris, vis martiris, ut restituatur*, 'The voice of the father, the power of the saint (plead) that he may be restored'). 'The glass painter seems not to have copied the verse correctly' (M); there are scrolls flanked by dots after the second and fourth words. Reproduction: *F.C.C., Seventh Annual Report* (1934), facing p. 32. (25). Jordan receiving from his wife coins she has brought in a bowl and about to place 'two in each hand of the child' lying on the bier, 'to be presented to the saint at Mid Lent' (M). Inscription (releaded since 1939): PROFERT AD F . . NS *S*VOTIVVM CVN PRECE MVN' (*Profert ad funus votivum cum prece munus*, 'He brings to the corpse a votive gift with a prayer'). This inscription and the next two are omitted by Miss Williams and Dr. Nelson; Dr. Mason comments that 'the verse is imperfect, and it has been pieced out: the word *votivum* can be seen in it: the first words seem to be '*vir opera credens*'. CVN is a painter's error for CVM. (26). The child, now on a bed, sitting up and feeding himself, whilst his parents sit facing one another at the bed-ends with hands outstretched in thanksgiving. Inscribed: HIC PVER ERIGITVR SANVS NEC MARTIR ADITVR. (*Hic puer erigitur sanus nec martir aditur*, 'Here the boy sits up healed, but no approach is made to the martyr'). Dr. Mason is mistaken in reading *Ut puer erigitur sanus;* he omits the remainder. (27). 'A blind and lame leper named Gimp was thrice visited by the martyr, and bidden to warn Jordan of what would happen if he failed to perform his vow' (M); St. Thomas, mitred and cross in hand, appearing to Gimp as he lies asleep (naked under the coverlet, after the mediæval manner) in bed. It will be noticed that the leper's disease is not here indicated (as usually, and in the next following scene) with spots on his skin. Inscribed: . . RO . . . ANDATVR VOTI REVS VT NON EATVR. (. . . . [*M*]*andatur voti reus ut non eatur*, 'Bound by his vow, he is commanded that the journey should not be made'). Dr. Mason is in error in reading *soluatur* for *non eatur*. (28). The parents come to Gimp, who rises up in bed to give his message; 'The knight's wife points with her right hand towards the place of pilgrimage' (M). Inscribed: . . EDVLVS ACCEDIT VOT*AMVNDVM R* EC OBED *N*AR ([*Cr*]*edulus accedit vot*[*i meminit n*]*ec obed*[*it*], 'He approaches believingly, he remembers his vow and does not obey'). This is the convincing restoration of the inscription by Dr. Mason, who points out that 'some letters have been wrongly introduced'; Miss Williams and Dr. Nelson read: *Credutis accedis vot fert nec obedit.* Reproduction: *C.C.C.*, No. 33 (July 1939), facing p. 34. (29). The leper's message having been ignored, an elder son of Jordan now dies; St. Thomas appears armed with a sword above a corpse surrounded by 'three of the servants in grievous pain' (Canon Crum takes them to be brothers who 'hug their heads with distracted hands') and 'Jordan and his wife too ill to rise' (M) from the high-backed chairs in which they sit at head and foot of the bed. Inscribed: VINDICTE MOLES DOMVS EGRA ⁊ MORTVA PROLES. (*Vindictae moles domus aegra et mortua proles*, 'The piling up of vengeance, a sick house and offspring dead'). (30). The accomplishment of the vow. Jordan empties on the tomb 'a large bowl full of gold and silver pieces' (M)—in white and yellow glass—whilst his wife follows leading their boy by the hand (both hold pilgrim's staves), and an attendant looks on. The original inscription has been lost and replaced by fragments on which can be read: IT . . . . OMRAT . EMIT . . . IS . Reproduction: *C.C.C.*, No. 33 (July 1939), facing p. 34.   Plates 38a, c, 41a, b

WINDOW VII

The window is filled with sixteen circular medallions set one above another in pairs, within a border of foliage in white, gold, murrey and green on a blue ground; the interspaces between the medallions are filled with foliage on a ruby ground. The upper medallions (1–8) were made up out of miscellaneous fragments of glass by Samuel Caldwell, Senior, in 1893. Nos. 9–14 were brought from the windows of the South Choir Aisle Triforium (see p. 72), and Nos. 15 and 16 from the North Choir Aisle Triforium (see p. 69) in 1920; the order of these lower medallions has been altered since Dr. Mason wrote his account of the window. The inscriptions are in prose.

1. A man in bed with a priest stooping over him and three other figures. Inscribed: ELO SIC . . . SLEC . . .

2. A woman kneeling, placing an offering on the tomb of St. Thomas in the presence of three other figures. Fragment of inscription: HO . . .

3. Similar to No. 2. Fragment of inscription: ATES.

4. Similar to No. 2. No inscription.

5. A monk and three other figures standing beside the tomb. Inscribed: . . . ERBA DEI. Dr. Mason suggests that this fragment of inscription (*verba Dei*, 'The words of God') may have come from Window VI in the Theological series (see p. 53).

6. A figure kneeling in the act of washing the feet of another beside the tomb, with two other figures. No inscription.

7. A figure kneeling beside the tomb in the presence of two others. Fragment of inscription: RVIT.

8. A man sitting up in bed drinking from a flask whilst four others stand by, one of whom, holding a crook, bends over him. Fragment of inscription: TIC.

9–12. WILLIAM OF KELLETT (near Lancaster), the carpenter, who had been remiss in the performance of a vow of pilgrimage (William, p. 273). These panels were removed to their present position from the South Choir Triforium in 1920. (9). His axe has slipped and he is cutting his left shin as he works 'at his open-air bench' (C) (as shown by the fringe of cloud above, not 'in a shop', as Dr. Mason has it); five other men look on with animated gestures; on the ground, a pool of blood. Inscribed: DM . OPATVR *NTV* AMSEC*N*ET . EGROT . . T. (*Dum operatur [sur]am sec[at e]t aegrot[a]t,* 'Whilst at work he cuts his shin and sickens'); there are two insertions from elsewhere. Dr. Mason's *moratur* cannot be accepted, in view of the stop between the M and O, and because a close inspection shows the third letter to be **P** not R; of his *secat* only the first three letters remain. Reproductions: (tracing), Williams, pl. 9; Nelson, fig. 9; Read, pl. 8. (10). St. Thomas appears to him in a dream. He lies asleep in bed with his back turned towards the Archbishop, who stands behind the bed in mitre and mass vestments with arms outstretched holding a pastoral staff in his left hand. Inscribed: *ΛLVЯƎN* ED NEM . SA HOME *PARIS . FAC.* We have here parts of two different inscriptions combined, and although the two do not conform as regards the size of the lettering, the content seems to show that the smaller relates to the medallion itself (perhaps [*sangui*]*nem Sa*[*ncti T*]*home*, 'the blood of St. Thomas'), the italicised portion, in which the inverted fragment is probably [*vul*] *neratus*, 'wounded', is similar in scale to the inscriptions on other medallions in the window and could relate to the story of Kellett; it has to be remembered that the window may originally have comprised other medallions illustrating this story besides those which still remain intact. The medallion is from the same cartoon as that of the Dream of King Louis in Window IV (No. 8, p. 88). (11). A woman removes the bandage from his leg as he sits up on his bed, 'showing scarcely a sign of his terrible wound' (C). Inscribed: LIGATVRAM SOLVIT ⁊ VVLNVS NON REPPIT (*Ligaturam solvit et vulnus non repperit*, 'She loosened the bandage and found no wound'). (12). He leaves the city gate of Canterbury exultant, for the open country (indicated by a tree to the right), carrying an axe in his left hand and with two more tucked in his girdle. Inscribed: EGRESSVS . AD OPA S *ESORAS . . . OMENDA* (*Egressus ad opera s . . .*, 'Going forth to work . . . '); not, as Dr. Mason has it, beginning 'with something about *ecclesia*', followed by '*adorat* or *adorans . . .* and then part of the word *oneris* or *onerare* from another place'. Colour Plate VIb, Plates 42a, b, 43b

13–16. ADAM THE FORESTER shot by a poacher (William, p. 342). (13). On the left Adam is seen tottering, arm in arm with a companion (who carries an axe by the blade in his left hand), his throat transfixed by an arrow which has been shot by the gamekeeper facing him, whose quiver hangs from his belt; on the extreme right a second poacher walks away with a deer slung on his back from a staff. In the middle are two trees. The string of the bow is painted in black on the blue background. Inscribed: FVR FVGIENS GVTTVR ꝔFORAT INSEQVENTIS (*Fur fugiens guttur perforat insequentis*, 'The thief as he flees pierces the throat of his pursuer'). Dr. Mason points out that the inscription 'begins as if it were going to be a verse, but then desists'; it may be remarked that in the text of William *two* companions of Adam and three poachers are mentioned. Reproduction: (tracing), Williams, pl. 5. (14). A man sitting up in bed drinking the water of St. Thomas out of a glass flask; a man and woman stand watching him at the foot of the bed. Inscribed: BIBENS AQVAM S. TH. SANVS EFFIC *MO* VA (*Bibens aquam Sancti Thomae sanus effic*[*itur aq*]*ua*, 'Drinking the water of St. Thomas he is made whole by the water'). 'The story of the carpenter makes no mention of this, so the picture may represent some other cure' (M); Canon Crum takes this scene to belong to the story of Adam the Forester. (15). A sick man sitting up in bed with three bearded friends gathered round; a green high-backed chair in the background. The mutilated inscription (DESPERANT M *ON MBRI* ITER ERES AMICI) refers to friends and despair. Whether this medallion has any part in the story of Adam is doubtful. (16). Adam's thank-offering at the tomb, over which he stoops in the presence of a companion leaning on a stick behind him and an attendant with staff standing on the right; a lamp-ring hangs under the arcade behind. Inscribed: SIM MELOR MEDICO PRECES ⁊ MVNERA (. . . . *medico preces et munera*, '. . . to the physician prayers and gifts'; the first part is mutilated). Dr. Mason reads erroneously *reges et munera* and comments that 'the legend is made up, and seems to have nothing to do with the picture'. All three heads are restored. Plate 43a

WINDOW IX

This window was composed of two tiers of circular medallions containing figure-subjects, with smaller roundels and half-roundels between them, the interspaces being filled with small seven- or eight-petalled flowers painted in reserve in black on

(a)

(b)

(c)

45

(a) John of Roxburgh
(b) Gilbert le Brun(?)
(c) A dying man healed
about 1220–1225
TRINITY CHAPEL
Window XI
pp. 104, 106

46

(a)

(b)

(a) A girl restored to life

(b) A funeral

about 1220–1225

TRINITY CHAPEL
Window XI
pp. 105, 106

(a)   (b)

(c)   (d)

47

(a)   James, son of the
Earl of Clare

(b, c, d)   Geoffrey of
Winchester

about 1220–1225

TRINITY CHAPEL
Window XII
pp. 108, 107

48

(a)   A leprous monk
(b, c, d) William of
      Gloucester

      about 1220–1225

      TRINITY CHAPEL
      Window XII

      pp. 109, 110

white glass set in a ruby ground. The two medallions at the foot of the window were reinstated by Mr. Caldwell in 1929, together with borders up to the same height which consist of paired leaf-buds forming heart-shaped motives on a ruby ground.

1. PILGRIMS ON THE ROAD TO CANTERBURY. A bearded man on a white horse, riding towards the left, heads the company, followed by a young man, a woman and a third man with a staff, all on foot; a cloud above, a tree to the left.
Reproductions: *C.C.C.*, No. 2 (April, 1929), facing p. 8; Babington, p. 129.

2. AN OFFERING AT THE TOMB. Two men stoop forward over the tomb on the left whilst a priest standing on the right looks back at them over his shoulder. Two arches above, under one of which hangs a lamp.

WINDOW XI

This window was filled with ancient glass previously in the hands of Samuel Caldwell, Senior, by Canon Edward Moore, D.D., as a memorial to Anne Moore, his second wife, who died December 27, 1906. It is composed of a column of six circular medallions, with semicircular medallions at a tangent to them based on the border, which is filled with foliage in green, mauve, gold and white on a blue ground; the medallions have blue borders and the ground of the interspaces between them is ruby. 'One or two changes were made in the window in 1920—chiefly by reintroducing pieces which were shown by their conformation and by their pale blue edging to have belonged originally to it'; the principal of these were Nos. 1 and 4, 'the two fine roundels at the top of the window' (M), which were until 1920 in the windows of the South Choir Aisle Triforium, as was also No. 13. The medallion No. 16, as well as the half-medallions 2 and 3, 8 and 9, 11 and 12, 14 and 15, combined together in pairs to make complete roundels, had previously been in Window VII and are so described by Miss Williams. The remaining medallions were made up out of old glass by Caldwell. Since the publication of the books of Dr. Mason and Canon Crum Nos. 8 and 11 have changed places.

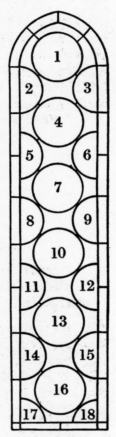

22' 0" × 4' 9"

1–4. JOHN, THE GROOM OF ROXBURGH, rescued from drowning (the subject identified by Miss Williams); three of these panels were for a time in the triforium of the South Choir Aisle. The story is told by both William (p. 296) and Benedict (p. 266); the incidents depicted coincide more nearly with the narrative of the latter (1) His horse, over its fetlocks in the Tweed into which the groom (out of sight below the surface) has been thrown, is being pulled by the bridle out of the water by a man on the left, whilst another hurries up on the right. Inscribed: HVC SE *ON* . . . *O* SAP (?)EQ'—A PLEBE REDVCTVS (*Huc se . . . . sap(?)equus (or equusque(?))a plebe reductus,* '. . . his horse brought back by the people'). Dr. Mason comments: 'The writing below ends with *eductus*, a word which William uses in his narrative; but it is doubtful how much of the inscription properly belongs to the picture'; only ON . . O however appears to be inserted. His further suggested reading of the middle of the text—*O sancte Thoma*—is inadmissible. (2). Having been rescued by St. Thomas, the groom crawls on hands and knees along a bridge over the river, with water gushing from his mouth. Inscribed: EXTEN(?) IT IN . . RT . S . . . . O̅TE . REPT'; the inscription is largely defective or obliterated: the last words are perhaps *ponte repentem*, 'crawling on the bridge'. This panel and No. 3 'were formerly soldered together to form one circle in Window VII, and were divided and transferred to this one in 1920' (M); they are described by Dr. Mason as being in the position of Nos. 5 and 6, and *vice versa*. (3). Two of his friends in a boat (with fish-tail prow) 'search the river-bed for him with poles' (C); clouds above. Inscribed: MERSV̅ PISCANTVR ME . . . . NTVR (*Mersum piscantur* . . . . , 'They fish for the drowned man'). Plate 45a. (4). He is laid on his back 'on a white blanket in front of a blazing fire' of logs laid in a grate with foliated finials, with dense smoke above, 'in the house of the toll-gate keeper' (M) at the bridge; a woman kneels at his head, lifting up his right arm, whilst another stoops over his feet; two small lighted lamps hanging from arches show it is night; part of his body is missing, replaced by fifteenth-century glass; the smoke is a modern restoration. Inscribed: +IGNIB' ADMOTV' REPARATVR CORPORE TOT' (*Ignibus admotus reparatur corpore totus*, 'Being laid by a fire he is restored in his whole body'); the first two words are not easily decipherable and are omitted by Dr. Mason, who makes *toto* the last word of the verse.   Plates 44a, b, 45a.

5. PILGRIMS. A man with staff and wallet walking in front of a pedimented doorway. The inscription below has been replaced by a band of mock Arabic inscription. Canon Crum suggests that this and the next following may depict 'pilgrims at the gate of Canterbury', but Dr. Mason writes, perhaps more aptly, of a 'door'—there is no indication of a town wall or battlements.

6. A YOUNG MAN KNEELING beneath an arch over which drapery is thrown, with arms outstretched towards a door similar to that in No. 5; the inscription has here been replaced as in No. 5.

7. A DYING MAN HEALED. An elderly man lying naked in bed with eyes shut, 'apparently dying or dead' (M); a woman and a young man, perhaps his wife and son, stand by, the latter holding what appears to be a jar with 'the life-giving water' (M); at the bed-foot stands a priest with open book (not the men with the water, as Dr. Mason has it). Inscription replaced by mock Arabic lettering.   Plate 45c.

8. Two men in a building holding between them what appears to be a rope with which they are perhaps about to raise, or lower into a tomb, a green coffin with a mauve pall thrown over it. Inscribed: . . LLV̅ MERENTES THOME VOVERE PARENTES (*I(?)llum maerentes Thomae vovere parentes*, 'The mourning parents dedicated him to Thomas'). The first letter has been lost and replaced by what appears to be a colon. Dr. Mason (followed by Canon Crum) seems to have misunderstood this panel, which he describes (as No. 11) as follows (without any reference to an inscription): 'A sick or dying man, perhaps a leper, in his bed. A priest is ministering to him'; he appears not to have noticed the feet *of both figures* visible below the 'bed'. It seems possible that this panel may relate to No. 15, in which there is a coffin covered with a similar pall, and should find a place next to it, instead of No. 14.

9. A PILGRIMAGE. A little lame boy, barefoot, leaning on a stick, is being led by his mother, who takes him by the arm with her right hand and holds a staff in her left; his father walks behind, to the right is a bush. They are 'presumably on pilgrimage'. Dr. Mason conjectures this may be a scene in the story of Henry of Beche (Benedict, p. 88), 'nine years of age, who had been unable so much as to stand, but after being put to lie in the Martyrdom, walked away with these helps'. Fragments of inscription remain: ... VAM ... FFERI ... CH ...

10. AN OFFERING. A bearded man laying wire on the tomb, on which is a candlestick, in the presence of a second man and two priests, one of whom is reading in a book on a desk, another desk to the left; drapery thrown over the arcade above. The inscription replaced by mock Arabic lettering. Dr. Mason and Canon Crum are in error in describing the pilgrim as a woman ('possibly the girl who was shown above sitting up in bed'). The former also comments: 'As nowhere else, there are two prayer desks, at the two ends of the tomb'; but this is seen again in Window XII, 1.

11. AN UNCERTAIN INCIDENT. A man lying on the ground, partly covered with a yellow coverlet, leaning up against a green cloth; to the right, a priest stands looking towards him, to the left, a woman laying her hand on the priest's shoulder. The inscription has been mutilated: E(?)VENVMDV M .. LVGEN A(?)VERVM MORIETVR *E*. This medallion is described (as No. 8) incorrectly by Dr. Mason and Canon Crum as showing a girl sitting up.

12. AN OFFERING. A young man stooping to lay a coil of wire on the tomb on which is a candle in a candlestick; a priest stands by on the right. Inscribed: FIT THOME GRAT' DAT VOT$\bar{V}$ LETIFICAT' (*Fit Thomae gratus, dat votum laetificatus*, 'He becomes grateful to Thomas, he is made glad and gives his offering'). Dr. Mason reads: *Fit Thome . . . ad votum letificatus.*

13. A YOUNG GIRL RESTORED TO LIFE. She sits up on a bier with a woman leaning over her from behind and two bearded men approaching with gestures of gladness; one holds out a length of drapery. Inscribed: D(?)ATVRSI CIN$\stackrel{\circ}{\text{C}}S\bar{\text{C}}$S VENIVNT IN GAVDIA PLA(?)NCT' (*Datur si cinctus sanctus veniunt in gaudia planctus*, 'If the hallowed girdle is given, lamentations turn into rejoicings'). Dr. Mason describes the scene: 'On the removal of the cloth which covered her face, she sits up, to the joy of her mother behind her, and of her father at the foot of the bier;' he suggests that the story is that of Cicely, daughter of Jordan of Plumstead, Norfolk (Benedict, p. 235, William, p. 190). He comments: 'The inscription is made up: it begins with—*batur* (or—*patur*) *sic* (or the beginning of *signum*) and ends with *veniunt in gaudia pl[ena?]*'. But the reading given above can be made out without much difficulty except the first letter, which seems to be a D cramped by the narrowing of the band, and the A of *planctus* obscured by a repairing lead: it is true that *datur* ('is given') violates the requirement of a long syllable at the beginning of a hexameter, but this may perhaps be held to be paralleled by the occurrence in medieval hexameters of a short syllable before the cæsura in the third foot, of which the inscription in Window XII, 1, is an instance. It is surmised that the cloth held by the foremost man is a girdle or waist-wrapping that has been 'sanctified' by dipping in the healing water; and this interpretation, rather than that of a covering that has been removed from the girl's face, seems to be favoured by her gaze, which appears to be directed at something which is being brought to her. Miss Williams's ingenious transcription, accepted by Dr. Nelson (*Dat vires sanctus vertunt in gaudia planctus*)

certainly does not accord with the text; she describes the child as 'a boy sitting upon a bed, resting on a bier covered by a pall', and conjectures the story to be that of 'Philip Scot . . . drowned while stoning a frog'. Plate 46a

14, 15. A BOY RESTORED TO LIFE. Dr. Mason says this is probably the story of Gilbert, son of William le Brun, who had been given up for dead (Benedict, p. 257). (14). A boy sitting up in bed embraces his father, who stoops over him with cloak flowing out behind whilst his mother stands by. Inscribed: ARRID? FLENTI PVER ASSVRGIT VENIENTI (*Arridet flenti puer, assurgit venienti*: 'The boy smiles at his tears and rises towards him as he comes'. (15). Accompanied by his mother and his father, who lays his hand on his head, the boy stoops to place a coil of wire as an offering on the tomb. Inscribed: DONA REDONATO RED . . . NTVR DEBITA NATO (*Dona redonato red[du]ntur debita nato* (not *Vota redonato etc.*, as Dr. Mason has it), 'Her son having been given back to her the due offerings are given'). Plate 45b

16. A FUNERAL SCENE. To the left a bishop (or priest with a mitre-like cap) at the head 'of the little bier', on which is a coffin covered with a mauve pall, 'recites the prayers for the dead from a book; a clerk with bucket and brush sprinkles the dead with holy water' (M). Behind him are another priest with a book and a group of four mourners. The coffin has cruciform finials at the corners. Inscribed: DEFVNCTV PLORAT PLEBS P Q'PR . . BITER ORAT (*Defunctum plorat plebs pro quo pr[es]byter orat*, 'The congregation mourn for the dead for whom the priest prays'). The small coffin is that of a child; it seems possible that this panel relates to the same story as Nos. 14 and 15. Plate 46b

17, 18. SCENES AT THE TOMB. (17). A man and two women kneeling by the tomb; a white draped altar at one side, a lantern above. The inscription appears to be made up of various fragments of lettering and is beyond interpretation: ORAB ITA SOLA FRA ISFERE SEQVNTV *FRATER*. (18). Three men standing and a woman with a coil of wire kneeling at the tomb. Fragments of lettering (. . . ITM EC . . . ES) have been put together with Arabic script ornament in the band below.

WINDOW XII

The design of the window consists of a tier of interwoven fan-shaped compartments each divided vertically to form two panels and having a foliated ornament at its base. The panels have each a wide ruby border edged with white. The general border of the window is filled with foliage in green, yellow and murrey on interlaced white stems against a blue ground. The general tonality of the window as a whole is strongly blue. The base of each pictorial panel is supported on a 'bridge' of two arches; many of the panels are heavily restored with modern glass.*

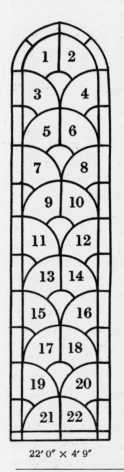

22′ 0″ × 4′ 9″

---

* The pictures of the shrine in Nos. 21, 22 denote a date for the window about 1220 at the earliest.

52′ 0″ × 24′ 0″

Plate XIII

DAVID. This panel, of which the original location is unknown, was in 1920 inserted in the South Window of the South-West Transept (M.4); the diaper background was made up by Mr. Samuel Caldwell Junior out of thirteenth-century fragments. About 1200. Pp. 68, 148.

1–6. THE CHILD GEOFFREY OF WINCHESTER (William, p. 206). (1). He lies nearly dying of fever in a cradle or cot supported on a low table, whilst his grandmother bends over him and St. Thomas appears behind her, his right hand uplifted to bless, a book in his left hand; on the left, the mother stands with hands clasped in prayer, looking back over her shoulder, a lamp hanging above her. Inscribed: THOME VIRTVTE VIS FEBRIS CEDTT ACVTE (*Thomae virtute vis febris cedit acutae*, 'By the virtue of Thomas the violence of an acute fever is reduced'); it will be noticed that in the third foot of the hexameter, where normally a long vowel is required, there is the short final *e* of *virtute*, just as in Window XI, 13, the verse begins with a short vowel; also that the glass-painter has written CEDTT (with two different forms of T) by mistake for CEDIT. Reproductions: (tracing), Williams, pl. 12; Nelson, fig. 30. (2). The child makes an offering to St. Thomas. He stands naked, supported by his mother, who with her right hand helps him to stretch out his arm, apparently to drop a coin in a money-box held by a bearded priest wearing a tall fur cap; the grandmother stands behind the priest. 'Immediately under the child's feet are the swaddling clothes, or perhaps the winding sheet in which he had been wrapped. He appears to be standing on a low wooden stage' (M). Dr. Mason is surely in error (followed by Canon Crum) in taking this scene to represent the measuring of the child for a coil of wire to be given to St. Thomas; he perhaps mistook for a measuring-rod what is actually one of the columns (red with green capital) of the building in which the scene is enacted; the money-box appears to have escaped his observation. Inscribed: .... EM PIETAS FERRO S: NON SINIT ETAS (.... *em pietas ferro s[ed] non sinit etas*). Dr. Mason comments: 'I do not know where Miss Williams found the good leonine verse which she gives in her letterpress [*Auxilium pietas fert quod sibi non sinit aetas*, adopted also by Dr. Nelson]. It does not agree with her drawing, nor with the window as it stands, which gives . . . *pietas ferro si non sinit etas*. It seems likely that S: should be expanded as *sed* rather than *si* [". . . . but his age forbids"].' It is evident that the boy was a younger infant than he appears to be in the picture, but in this respect the rendering is in conformity with innumerable paintings of the Madonna with her infant Child. Reproduction: (tracing), Williams, pl. 13. (3). The collapse owing to a gale of the wall of the house on the child's cradle soon after his recovery; his mother and grandmother, one standing, one on the right seated, 'look on with terror' (M); portions of embattled coping and shingled roof can be discerned among the debris. Inscribed: ECCE REPENTINA PREMITVR PVER IPSE RVINA (*Ecce repentina premitur puer ipse ruina*, 'Lo, the child himself is crushed by a sudden downfall'). Reproduction: (tracing), Williams, pl. 14. (4). The two women (one kneeling, one standing) pray, whilst the child's father sits distracted, his head on his hand, among the ruins. This medallion is largely modern; the inscription has been lost and replaced by a band of mock Arabic lettering. (6). 'The mother, after invoking St. Thomas, falls fainting to the ground. One of the servants throws water over her' out of a bowl he holds in his left hand; 'another with a pickaxe clears away the debris, while the grandmother looks on' (M). Inscribed: ... ANABA℈ PRIVS T(?)VNC SERVARE ROGATVR. This does not yield a satisfactory versification or sense; ... *prius hunc servare rogatur* may be the intended termination, with *tunc* written by a painter's error (of which other examples have already been recorded) for *hunc*. Dr. Mason, the first to attempt decipherment, reads only: ... *prius* ... *servare rogatur*. In the tracing of the panel, reproduced in Miss Williams's illustration, the line appears to begin with Q or O; if Q is accepted, the defective words may be conjectured to be *Quem sanabatur* or *laniabatur* (the terminal abbreviation sign is for VR; as against the second alternative it must be admitted that the ligature of N and A seems to be clear, ruling out an intervening I). The sense would be: 'He (St. Thomas) is asked to save him who was before being healed' (or 'who was being mangled'); the latinity of the relative *quem* attracted to the accusative case of the implied antecedent is unusual but not without precedent. This inscription would belong more fitly to the 4th panel. Reproduction: (tracing), Williams, pl. 15. (5). The child is found unhurt among the ruins; his mother stoops over him, the servant with the pickaxe points towards him, the other, with felling-axe over his shoulder, beckons to the grandmother and a bearded man who stands on the right. Inscribed: MOLES DIRIPIT . . . . S REPERITVR. Dr. Mason restores as follows: *Moles diripit[ur puer incolumi]s reperitur*, suggesting *arridens* as an alternative to *incolumis*. ('The mass of wreckage is torn apart; the child is found unhurt' or 'smiling.') Reproduction: (tracing), Williams, pl. 16.   Plate 47b, c, d

7–8. JAMES, INFANT SON OF ROGER, EARL OF CLARE, cured of hernia (William, p. 228; Benedict, p. 255). This interpretation of the scene, suggested by Dr. Mason, may certainly be accepted, as it is by Canon Crum, as an alternative to that of Miss Williams, who takes these pictures to be in continuation of Nos. 1–6. (7). This panel is for the most part modern. The child 'is laid on a bier as dead. The mother demands a miracle of St. Thomas though the Countess of Warwick and others dissuade her' (C); three women gathered round the bier, a border of 'crown' ornament in place of the inscription below. (8). 'The child is healed with a rag of St. Thomas's hair-shirt' (C). He 'stands on a stool at the end of the tomb'; his mother holds him up while 'the water of St. Thomas is applied to the seat of the disease' by another woman out of a basin on a high stem (her drapery is shaded on the *outer* side of the glass). His father, standing on the left with staff in his left hand, 'points to the place' (M). Inscribed: VENTRI INTESTI MONVMENTVM FIT MEDICINA (*Ventri intesti[na] monumentum fit medicina*); the last letters of *intestina* are omitted ın the legend, which is intact apart from slight breakage at the end. Dr. Mason comments: 'I should take' the inscription 'to mean that the internal cure was a proof of the saint's efficacy'. Miss Williams's reading, repeated by Dr. Nelson, though giving a satisfactory meaning, does not accord with the text: *Ventri intestinam monumentum dat medicinam*. Reproductions: (tracing), Williams, pl. 17; Babington, p. 130.   Plate 47a

9, 10. HEALING OF A LAME YOUNG MAN. (9). Supported on crutches, with arms outstretched, and followed by a woman, perhaps his mother, with hands clasped in prayer, he approaches the tomb, on which is a money-box; his cloak lies on the ground behind him; a man, perhaps a priest, with *left* hand raised in benediction stands by, with a book on a lectern beside him. The inscription has been lost and replaced by 'crown' ornament, except for the fragmentary words . . . GVIN . . . . SANGV . . . , referring to 'blood', of which the first is certainly out of place. (10). Stooping forward, the young man offers a basin of coins at the tomb, on which is a candle in a candlestick; the woman stands behind him, holding his crutches, whilst a priest holding a book looks on from the right. The figures are to a large extent restored. Inscribed: SVPPLEX IMPLO . . . . *VIƆV* PRONVS ADORAT (*Supplex implo[rat] . . . . pronus adorat*, 'The suppliant implores . . . he stoops in adoration'). This inscription seems to apply more fitly to No. 9, in place of the fragmentary lettering there inserted. Miss Williams's suggestion that the subject might be Eilwin of Berkhamstead (Benedict,

124) is rejected by Dr. Mason on the plea that 'he would doubtless have been represented with his crutches'; but Dr. Mason (followed by Canon Crum) has needlessly reversed the order of the panels. He has overlooked the crutches held by the woman in what is surely the later panel in the sequence, and describes No. 9 as representing the sufferer rising to his feet, healed, whereas he is leaning forward supported on his crutches. In favour of Eilwin as the subject are the crutches swathed with cloth to obviate soreness of the armpits, and the ferrules to strengthen their lower ends which can be made out in the painting, both of which conform with Benedict's text (*Involutis tam corio quam pannis baculorum suorum summitatibus, ne sibi vel decoriarentur vel laederentur ascellae ... Ne baculi usu assiduo prorsus attererentur, ferro contexerat extremitates*); on the other hand, Eilwin's companion Walter, mentioned by Benedict as being present, is not shown in the panels, whilst the chronicler has no mention of a woman as here depicted. Reproductions: Williams, (tracing), pl. 18; Babington, *Canterbury Cathedral*, Nelson, fig. 31; p. 131.

11. A LEPROUS MONK meeting two pilgrims who carry flasks with holy water. This may be an incident in the story of Elias of Reading (compare No. 12 below); the panel is however to a large extent modern.

12. TENDING OF A LEPROUS PRIEST, whose disease is indicated by spots on his skin. Canon Crum describes this: 'Another monk, a leper (?), is washed. An Abbot looks on.' Dr. Mason discusses the subject as follows: 'In the picture to the right, a monk, perhaps suffering from leprosy, is sitting in a stool with bared arms and legs. Two friends apply to him the water of St. Thomas, and one of them discusses the case with his abbot, who stands beside an altar or a shrine. As the cure of Elias of Reading, to which Miss Williams refers, was done far from Reading, without the knowledge of the abbot (Benedict, p. 242; William, p. 416), we should probably look elsewhere for the interpretation. Is it John of Croxton (Benedict, p. 217)? There is no inscription to guide us.' But Dr. Mason has not observed that the head of the abbot with his crozier is level with that of the sufferer, and that the 'altar or shrine' is therefore the chair on which he is seated, whilst the gestures of the 'two friends' are those of a clinical examination. One is pointing to the condition shown by the patient's bare arm, whilst the other, with a flask held up to the light, is making a uroscopic examination.

Benedict's account of the cure of the leper Elias mentions watering eyes ('*oculi lacrymosi atque fluentes*') as one of the symptoms of his disease, a trouble which seems to be indicated by the gesture of the patient holding his left hand to his face; and the companion panel (No. 11), though inverting the sequence of events, may well represent his meeting with 'returning pilgrims' (according to William) or a 'knight whom he loved' ('*miles quem diligebat*', according to Benedict), who dissuaded him from continuing his journey to Canterbury and cured him by giving him water of St. Thomas to drink and wash his face with. As against Robert (miscalled John) of Croxton,* who had a swollen eye healed, it must be pointed out that Benedict says nothing of his being a leper, a disease clearly indicated in this panel and No. 11 above.

The panel is of interest as a document in the history of medicine. The earliest parallel that can be cited is in an initial letter with a figure of Galen similarly holding up a bottle† in a Salerno MS. (now in Breslau) 'De pulsibus et urinis', written about

---

* The name is Robertus in Benedict's text; John is a marginal error in the Rolls edition.

† Reproduced by Th. Meyer-Steineg and Karl Sudhoff, *Geschichte der Medizin im Ueberblick*, 2 ed., Jena, 1922, fig. 94.

1160–70, therefore about half a century before the painting of the Canterbury window. The best-known example is perhaps the carved relief of Medicine among the series of Arts on the Campanile ('Giotto's Tower') at Florence, strangely misinterpreted by Ruskin (*Mornings in Florence*, VI, 134) as a potter in his workshop, symbolising the ceramic art. A French example ('Le Médecin et la Mort') in a MS of the fifteenth century in the Bibliothèque Nationale, Paris, is reproduced by Prof. Laignet Lavastine, *Histoire Générale de la Médecine*, Paris, 1938, Vol. 2, p. 104, where a late parallel is given (p. 217) in a Dutch painting by Ostade, dated 1665. The only parallel in glass-painting known to the Author is in a tracery-light of a window at Minster Lovell, Oxfordshire, dating from about 1450, where one or other of the two physician martyrs, SS. Cosmas and Damian, is represented in doctor's scarlet gown and skull-cap holding up a glass phial in his right hand for examination.* Reproduction: (tracing), Williams, pl. 19.   Plate 48a

13–18. WILLIAM OF GLOUCESTER (Benedict, p. 261; William, p. 253), a workman employed by Roger of Pont l'Évêque, Archbishop of York (an opponent of Becket), who was buried by a fall of earth when laying water-pipes on the archbishop's estate at Churchdown. (13). A mound of earth on which trees and herbage are growing collapses on the back of William, who is seen digging waist-deep in a hole. Two companions walking by on the right with spades in their hands look back at the accident. Below, parts of a band with berries on a continuous stem scratched through a black ground. (14). The eye-witnesses, still carrying their spades, bring news of the mishap to the bearded priest who stands, with a man and woman behind him, at the door of his house. The inscription is too defective to be intelligible: . . . NT REFO(?)A . . VMES . . NTVRM . . (15). 'A woman of the village telling her son and another man next morning that she knows by a vision that William is still alive' (M); the figures are standing in a house with pillars. Inscription defective, with mock Arabic lettering to fill the gaps: OME . EX . . . . TIVN . . . INSP . . . This medallion is mostly a modern restoration. (16). The bailiff of the estate, who was out riding his horse, 'his ear to the ground, hears William's groans'. (C). Meanwhile another man, towards whom the bailiff is looking up, holds his horse by the reins. A tree in the background. Inscribed: . . . ACCIDIT ⁊ CERT . . . *SIBI* VM *SVO* (VM perhaps belongs after CERT, *Accidit et certum* . . .). (17). The priest addressing a crowd of his parishioners (almost entirely modern glass). Mock Arabic lettering alternates below with fragments of inscription (. . . ARVIT . . . IXAN . . .). (18). 'The bailiff rides once more to the priest's house to tell him' (M). He is shown on his horse followed by his companion (head modern), barefooted, with a staff; he gesticulates to the bearded priest and a woman who are coming out of a doorway. Inscribed: MIRATVR MVLTVM POPVLVS SPIRARE SEPVLTVM ('The people marvel greatly that the buried man breathes'). (19). The parishioners with shouldered mattocks and axe go to the spot, directed by the bailiff who follows them riding out of a gateway. Mock Arabic fills gaps in the disordered inscription: GVIS . . . . REDIT . . . HVASTOR (*for haustor*). (20). William is exhumed. Four men with spades are digging him out; he is seen set free, from the waist up. To the left stands the bailiff giving directions and holding his horse. Inscribed: . . . MAM QVEM DICIT EREPTOREM BENEDICIT ([*Tho*] *mam quem dicit ereptorem benedicit,*

---

* See E. A. Greening Lamborn, 'The Lovel Tomb at Minster', p. 18, in *Oxfordshire Archaeological Society, No. 83, Report for the year 1937.*

(a) (b)

(c) (d)

(a, b, c, d) William of
Gloucester

TRINITY CHAPEL
Window XII

pp. 110, 111

(a)

50

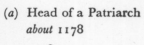

(a) Head of a Patriarch
   about 1178
   p. 46

(b) Head of Christ
   Early 13th CENTURY
   p. 115

(c) Detail
   about 1220–1225
   TRINITY CHAPEL
   Window V
   p. 92

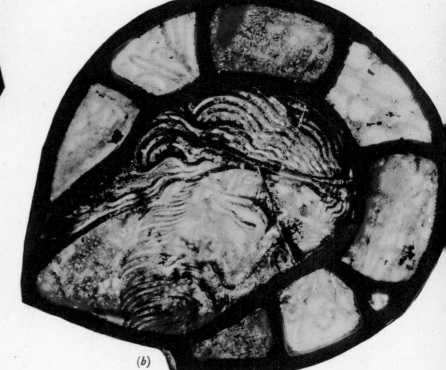

(b)

(c)

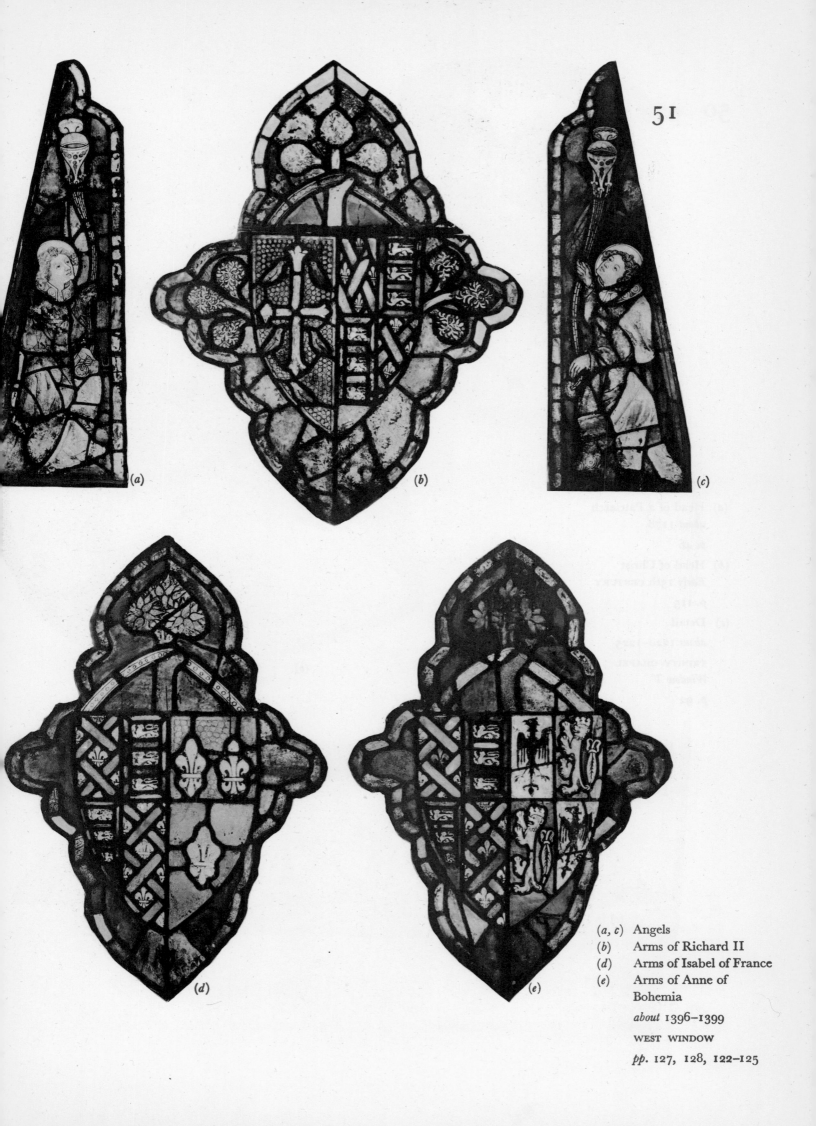

(*a*, *c*) Angels
(*b*) Arms of Richard II
(*d*) Arms of Isabel of France
(*e*) Arms of Anne of
        Bohemia
about 1396–1399
WEST WINDOW
pp. 127, 128, 122–125

52

(*a*) St. John the Evangelist
(*b*) St. Philip
(*c*) Apostle, unidentified
(*d*) St. James the Greater

about 1396–1399

WEST WINDOW

pp. 127, 125, 126

'Thomas whom he calls his rescuer he blesses'). Reproductions: (tracings), Williams,
pl. 20–25.   Plates 48b, c, d, 49a, b, c

21. AN OFFERING AT THE SHRINE. A lady kneels to lay a coil of wire (not 'alms
in a bowl' as Dr. Mason has it, followed by Canon Crum). 'She appears to be praying
for the lady behind, who presses her right hand against her cheek. Probably this
second lady is the one who is giving thanks in the right-hand picture' (M). Two men
stand behind on the right. Inscription mutilated, with mock Arabic in the intervals:
.. ITVR(?) EC .. ƎꟻꟻƎ ... LES. Reproductions: (tracing), Williams, pl. 26;
Nelson, fig. 32.

22. A lady kneeling in prayer at the shrine, perhaps the same woman as in No. 21.
Behind her are a man stooping and a woman standing with hands joined in prayer.
From the arches above hang a crown of lamps and a single lamp. Inscribed: ORABIT
SOLA FRATRIS FER .. F *EQVNTV* FRATER. The sense cannot be conjectured.
This medallion and No. 21 'are of special interest, because they alone of all that now
remain depict offerings at the shrine, as distinct from the tomb, of St. Thomas ...
The end of the shrine is in each case seen above the altar which was placed at the
west end of it. The shrine rests upon a slab supported on red columns, but in reality it
must have stood much higher than as here shown. Erasmus says that a ladder would
be needed for the purpose of looking into it' (M). This comment overlooks the fact that
the shrine is represented also in Window V, 1 (see p. 91 above). Reproductions:
(tracing), Williams, pl. 27; Warner, *Canterbury Cathedral*, p. 58 (part only, reversed).
                                                                              Plate 49d

§11 North-East Transept, St. Martin's Chapel

THE window in St. Martin's Chapel, on the east side of the Transept, contains a
tier of five roundels, alternately large and small, set in a groundwork of ornament within a wide border. Of the roundels, only the lower small one, described below, is ancient, and may be attributed to the first quarter of the thirteenth
century. The border and the groundwork in the interspaces between the roundels are
mostly of old glass, contemporary with the ancient roundel. The border consists of
leaves alternately green and mauve on a white stem against a blue ground. The
roundels have borders composed of tufts of leaves, three in each, alternately purple
and yellow on a blue ground. The intervals are filled with foliage in green, purple,
yellow and white on a ruby ground.

ST. MARTIN AND THE BEGGAR. The saint, on horseback, turns backward,
dividing his cloak with his sword to give a portion of it to a beggar behind him,
naked except for a loin-cloth. In the background to the right is a tree, on the left a
building with battlements. Round the edge of the medallion is a modern inscription:
NOS MVLTI VNVM CORPVS SVMVS IN CHRISTO SINGVLI AVTEM
ALTER ALTERVIS (*sic*) MEMBRA ('We being many are one body in Christ, but

every one members one of another', *Romans*, XII 5). The saint's name, S MARTHMVS (*sic*), is written above him. 'Large parts of the beggar's figure and of the drapery of St. Martin are modern, as well as the head and hind quarters of the horse' (M., p. 53).   Plate 31b

§12 Miscellaneous Early Glass

UNDER this heading have been gathered various panels recently acquired and reinstated in the Cathedral, a fragment for which a location has not yet been assigned, and a fourteenth-century tracery-light.

SOUTH WINDOW OF CORONA

The panel described below, inserted in the window adjacent to the East Window of the Corona, was purchased in 1938 at St. Alban's Court, Nonington, together with the panel now replaced in the head of the East Window of the Crypt (cf. p. 65). That it originally belonged to the Cathedral there is little reason to doubt, but there is no evidence to show from which window it came. It may be dated on stylistic grounds early in the thirteenth century.

CHRIST IN MAJESTY. His figure, seated on a stone bench with right hand raised in benediction and left hand on a book which rests on His knee, is enclosed within a vesica-shaped aureole with ruby background and green border interrupted at intervals by yellow squares with painted quatrefoils; He is clothed in a white robe under a green-lined mauve mantle, His feet bare. The aureole is surrounded by the Emblems of the Evangelists, on a blue ground studded with rosette-like stars, the whole panel being enclosed within a border of green flowers set on a ruby band. The emblematic figures have each a label inscribed with the appropriate name—the angel, in green and white drapery, MATTHEVS, the lion, golden with green wings, MARCVS, the ruby golden-winged bull, LVCAS, and the murrey eagle IOHANNES; they hold scrolls with the respective legends: BINI; SIBIS; *UN*IT; FONT (the italicised letters are a modern restoration).

The design is in general arrangement closely similar to that of a page in a late twelfth-century psalter from Westminster Abbey in the British Museum (Royal MS. 2A XXII, f. 14), in which, however, the emblematic figures carry no scrolls, the angel lacks a name-label, and Christ is shown seated not on a throne but on a rainbow; according to E. Mâle (*L'Art Religieux du XIIe Siècle en France*, Paris, 1922, p. 4), this throne derives from the commentary on the Apocalypse of the Spanish Abbot Beatus, of Liebana; his conception was illustrated in Spanish illuminated MSS. from the tenth century onwards and formed the basis of many French tympanum-sculptures beginning with that of Moissac (early twelfth century) and of such minor works as covers in Limoges enamel for books of the Gospels.

Reproduction: *F.C.C. Twelfth Annual Report* (1939), frontispiece.   Plate 31a

EAST WINDOW OF CRYPT

UNIDENTIFIED SUBJECT. A man in a cloak thrown over a long robe followed by a veiled woman, probably his wife, is emerging from a house on the right to meet two young messengers who approach with lively gesticulations; one of them carries a short staff in his left hand, the other is pointing behind him with outstretched right arm. To left is a tree, clouds above. At the foot, a defective inscription: . . . CAVIT . . . CLESIA . . . DICI, with a scrolled stem to the right.

The grouping of the figures is similar to that of a scene in the story of Robert of Rochester (Trinity Chapel, Window VI, 14, p. 98). The panel may be part of an otherwise missing series illustrating another miracle of St. Thomas, but its dimensions have not been found to be compatible with any of the windows in the Trinity Chapel.

WATER TOWER

WINDOW I

This window retains its original form, not having been reconstructed in the fifteenth century like the four of the remaining six windows which were not blocked by the construction of the Prior's Chapel (see p. 137). It has been filled recently with a new composition made up by Mr. Caldwell out of early thirteenth-century glass orginally in other parts of the building. Within a border of symmetrical leaf-ornament are three medallions separated by foliage on coiled and branching stems. The upper and lower medallions are filled with radial arrangements of foliage; the middle medallion, which is larger than these, contains the subject of:

CHRIST APPEARING TO ST. MARY MAGDALENE. She approaches Him, veiled and bowing towards Him, from a gateway on the right; He faces her with left hand raised. The garden is indicated by small trees and herbage.

Reproduction: Babington, p. 127. Frontispiece (in colours)

PANELS FROM THE NAVE

The panels described below, now inserted in the East Window of the Crypt and two windows of the Water Tower, are believed by Mr. Caldwell originally to have occupied places in the windows of the Nave, before it was rebuilt in the fourteenth century. They evidently form parts of a series in which Patriarchs, Prophets and Apostles were represented standing in pairs confronting one another under arched tabernacles; the Apostles are distinguishable by being barefoot from the Old Testament figures, which are shod. All the figures hold inscribed scrolls some of which are damaged and difficult to interpret; the names still in some instances remaining at their feet suggest that all the panels were originally so inscribed. The glass is of early thirteenth-century date.

I. PANELS IN EAST WINDOW OF THE CRYPT

1. JACOB AND ISAAC. They stand beneath a trefoil arch flanked by turrets; the

113

scrolls in their hands are inscribed respectively: [*Ex*]IVIT SONVS EORVM ('Their sound went into all the earth', *Rom.* X, 18); DICENT: OFERENTÊ (*Benedicent offerentes* or *offerentem*). Names inscribed below: IACOBAS, ISAAC.

Thanks are due to the late Mr. W. P. Blore for the identification and suggested emendation of the texts. Plate 21C

2. ISAIAH AND JEREMIAH. Standing under a low arch with two quatrefoil windowed structures above. The inscriptions on their scrolls are hardly legible; that of Isaiah appears to read: PPREPERO DIC VE, but has been convincingly interpreted by Prof. Claude Jenkins as *Praepropere dic ve* ('With all haste cry woe!'). The defective legend on Jeremiah's scroll appears to be: .. S .. SERVAT .. BE. Names inscribed below: ISAIAS, IEREMIAS. Plate 21C

II. PANELS IN THE WATER TOWER

These panels were inserted here when the Water Tower windows were re-arranged by Mr. Samuel Caldwell, Junior, in 1900. In all four panels the Saints stand under a semicircular arch with battlements above.

Window III, upper half. Both lights have a border of lozenge-shaped quatrefoils, and a diaper made up of small rosettes and pointed leaves to fill the space above the figure panels, all in thirteenth-century glass.

1. ST. BARTHOLOMEW AND ST. SIMON. The legends on the scrolls held by the Apostles have been completely obliterated and replaced by fragments from elsewhere. St. Simon holds also, in his left hand, what appears to be a spear with a small square banner attached. Names inscribed below: S: BA. MAEVS, S: SIMON. For the banner carried by St. Simon comparison may be made with the fifteenth-century figure in the West Window (see p. 127); no other parallels in the iconography of this Apostle are known to the Author; his usual attribute in later medieval art is either a saw or a boat.

2. ST. JOHN THE EVANGELIST AND AN UNIDENTIFIED APOSTLE, perhaps St. James the Less. The inscriptions on their scrolls are entirely obliterated. They hold in their right hands, St. John a chalice, his companion what may be a club and therefore identify him as St. James the Less. Their names have been replaced by quatrefoils.
Plate 21b

Window V, upper half. In both lights there is a diaper border of pointed leaves and small rosettes and a filling above the figure panel, consisting of a foliated scroll, all in thirteenth-century glass.

1. ST. JAMES THE GREATER AND ST. MATTHIAS, the former holding a scroll inscribed CONIVGATVS; of the inscription on the scroll of the latter all that remains is ... VS EOR ..., showing that it was originally the same as that accompanying the patriarch Jacob, *Ivit sonus eorum* (see p. 113). Beneath their feet are their names Sᶜ. IACOBVS, Sᶜ. MATHIAS. The significance of the word *conjugatus*, 'yoked together', is not apparent. Plate 21a

2. TWO APOSTLES, unidentified, holding scrolls inscribed respectively: CONIVGATVS and IVIT SONVS EORVM, as in No. 1 above. The left-hand figure has a blue-bladed short sword in his left hand; the second figure has a book in the right hand. The names have been entirely lost but for a single S. The figure with the sword may perhaps be St. Paul.

50′ 0″ × 25′ 0″

Plate XIV

PROPHET, unidentified. In a tracery light (C.5)
of the West Window. About 1396–1399. P. 126.

PANEL, UNPLACED

ST. DUNSTAN. The saint, vested in mitre, pallium and murrey dalmatic, sits in a white chair with ruby and green seat, writing in a book on a desk. The desk is covered with a white cloth and has a green supporting stem. The book is inscribed: OBSCVLTA O FIL PRECEPTA MAGISTRI. The panel, insofar as it is ancient, may be dated about the beginning of the thirteenth century, and was perhaps originally in a window near the shrine of St. Dunstan in the Choir (compare p. 69 above); the upper part, including the blue background, the head and hands of the saint, and the book with its inscription, is a modern restoration (probably the work of George Austin), based on an illuminated MS. of Smaragdus on the Rule of St. Benedict, of about 1200, in the British Museum (*Roy.* 10A, XIII, f. 2 v°). The panel came to the Dean and Chapter Minet as a gift from Miss Susan in 1944, and is reputed to have been purchased at Canterbury. Its future location has not yet been determined.

FRAGMENT, UNPLACED

HEAD OF THE DEAD CHRIST, of early thirteenth-century date. The face pale mauve; the halo has a cross of white glass (painted with foliage and probably obtained, to fill gaps, from thirteenth-century quarry panes) against a ruby ground with very thin 'flash'. The head, with eyes closed, is probably from a Crucifixion, and is considerably larger in scale than that in the restored Crucifixion of the East Window in the Corona (see p. 74). The inclination of the head is to the spectator's right, not to the left (as is usual in early medieval Crucifixion paintings); it is possible that the fragment belonged to a Descent from the Cross,* where also however normal practice required the reverse inclination. The treatment is strikingly similar to that in a fragmentary thirteenth-century wall-painting of the Crucifixion in the choir of Ulcombe Church, Kent; it may also be compared with that in a window at Rheims Cathedral.† Plate 50b

EARLY FOURTEENTH-CENTURY GLASS

PANEL from a tracery light. In the shape of a quatrefoil with lobed, acutely-pointed leaves of white glass; three of these have their original painting of three oak-leaves; on the glass replacing the fourth is a maple-leaf. The centre of the light is of yellow glass painted with a six-petalled flower. The original location of the panel is unknown; it probably belonged to some part of the cathedral buildings no longer surviving—no still extant fourteenth-century window has tracery from which it could have come. Plate 58c

---

* Compare a window at Chartres reproduced in E. Mâle, *L'Art Religieux du XIIe Siècle en France*, Paris, 1922, fig. 92.

† Reproduced in M. Aubert, *Le Vitrail en France*, Paris, 1946, pl. XVI.

§13 'Jesse' Window

The window in the Corona next on the north to the East Window is filled with a design by George Austin of the type known as the Tree of Jesse, representing, in the form of a schematised genealogical tree, the descent of Christ from Jesse, based on the prophecy of *Isaiah* XI, 1–3. This scheme, of which the origin and evolution are fully described in *The Early Iconography of the Tree of Jesse* (Oxford, 1934), by Dr. Arthur Watson, received its standard formula for glass-painting in a window in the Lady Chapel of the abbey church of St. Denis, near Paris, made at the instance of Abbot Suger in 1144; small portions of the original glass were incorporated with modern work when the window was restored in 1848.* The Canterbury window in its general disposition follows the scheme of St. Denis: a vine springing from the recumbent figure of Jesse forms a middle tier of compartments enclosing figures which culminate at the top in those of the Virgin Mary and Our Lord; each compartment is flanked by two half-compartments containing figures of Prophets who foretold His coming.

Although there seems to be no written record of the fact, it appears that Austin in designing his window was guided by some remnants of a 'Jesse' in glass of the thirteenth century, which presumably at one time occupied this same window. Evidence of this is provided by an anonymous coloured tracing dated 1848, in the Victoria and Albert Museum,† of a figure of the Virgin from a Jesse window in Canterbury Cathedral (Plate B(*b*)). The Virgin sits, crowned, on a throne enclosed between branches of a conventional vine which she grasps with both hands outstretched; her name SCA MARIA is inscribed on a label above her shoulders (the M and A being ligatured). Above, separating the panel from the next that would have come above it, is a horizontal band with motives consisting of four small leaves springing diagonally from a small central flower; lengths of this same ornament, doubtless belonging originally to this Jesse window, have been employed by Mr. Caldwell to fill out the small panels of thirteenth-century glass, with pairs of standing figures, which he has inserted in the East Window of the Crypt and in the windows of the Water Tower (see pp. 67, 137). In the disposition of the figure and in the style of the palmette-flowers which spring from the branches of the vine this panel follows so closely the formula set at St. Denis as to show that its designer was consciously following that model—as is also the case with the great Jesse Window at Chartres‡

---

* See Watson, *op. cit.*, pp. 112–120, pl. XXIV, XXV.
† E.I.D. 4154–1.
‡ Reproduced by Watson, *loc. cit.*, pl. XXVI.

slightly later in date than that of St. Denis, and the single figure which is all that is left of a Jesse at York Minster.*

The present whereabouts of this panel is not known. The panel was known to Charles Winston; Westlake † writes 'Winston, lecturing at a meeting of the Archæological Institute in 1848, says some of the oldest glass in this country is part of a Jesse Window in Canterbury Cathedral, and part of another in York Minster: all this glass is of the last half of the twelfth century'. In a footnote signed N.H.J.W. (relating to the Canterbury example) he adds: 'I cannot find this window'.

Mention may be made here of a fragmentary thirteenth-century 'Jesse' now in a window of Nackington Church, near Canterbury, with figures of David, Solomon and the Virgin, which is reputed to have come from the Cathedral.‡

There is no satisfactory evidence in support of the assertion, which appears to be based on mere conjecture; the dimensions of the Nackington Jesse do not fit with any window in the Cathedral, nor does it seem likely that there would have been more than one Jesse window in the Cathedral or elsewhere in the Priory buildings (for instance, in the Prior's Chapel).   Plate B(b) facing p. 13

---

* Typical figures from St. Denis and Chartres are reproduced together with the York figure by Westlake, Vol. I, p.28.

† Vol. I, p. 41.

‡ See K. H. J., 'Thirteenth Century Glass at Nackington Church near Canterbury', *Archæologia Cantiana,* Vol. L (1939), p. 161.

CHAPTER II

LATE GOTHIC GLASS

§1 West Window

THE West Window of the Nave was constructed shortly before the end of the fourteenth century. It is divided by transoms into three main ranges of lights, seven in each range, and three ranges of small tracery lights above, with smaller 'eyes' at the apex. The period when the glazing was begun is shown, by the inclusion of shields with the arms of Richard II and both his Queens, to be between the years of his second marriage and his death, 1396–1399. Of the original glass only a portion remains, notably the fillings of most of the tracery lights, of the upper main range, and of the middle light of the middle range, this last having been reassembled and reinstated by Mr. Samuel Caldwell, Junior, in the present century. It seems possible that at first only the tracery was filled with coloured glass, and that the main ranges were glazed either with some simple pattern or with plain glass quarries pending the completion of the window. It is usually assumed that the twenty-one main lights were occupied by a series of figures of the Kings of England. The inscriptions below them are no longer in existence (except for the fragment with the word *Rex* reproduced in Plate 64b), but Gostling (2nd ed., 1779)* records that 'each had his name under him *in the old black letter*: of which there are very little remains. These seven† are Canute, under whom remains *Can*. Edward the Confessor holding a book, under him remains *Ed*. Then Harold. William I holding his sceptre in his right hand, and resting it transversely on his left shoulder, under him remains . . . *mus Cŏquestor Rex*. Then William II, Henry I, Stephen. The tops of the canopies are all that is left of the fourteen niches of which the two next stages consist: if these were filled in the same manner, the series of Kings would finish with Richard III'.

---

* In the 1st (1774) edition it is stated that the names 'are lost, except that under the fourth is . . . mus Conquestor'.

† That is, the seven in the upper range; the eighth figure, lately inserted, was not known to Gostling.

(*a, b, c*)   Prophets, unidentified
(*d*)   St. Simon (?)
(*e*)   Apostle, unidentified
(*f*)   St. James the Less

about 1396–1399

WEST WINDOW

pp. 124–127

54

(a)

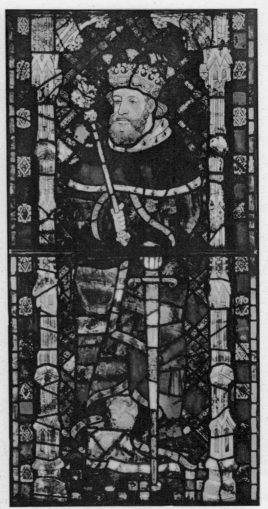

(b)

(c)

(d)

(a, b, c, d) Kings of England

about 1396-1399
(or later)

WEST WINDOW

pp. 129, 132

(a)

(b)

55

(a) Arms of John,
    Duke of Bedford(?)
    and Bokyngham

(b) Arms of Bradwardine
    and Chichele
    First half of
    15th CENTURY
    WEST WINDOW
    pp. 130, 131

(a)

(b)

(a) Two Saints, unidentified
15th CENTURY

(b) Tracery Light
about 1396–1399
WEST WINDOW
pp. 131, 126

Gostling's conjecture has hitherto been accepted without comment by other writers, including the author of this book.* On close examination, however, it will be found to be seriously open to question. That the main lights should have been designed so late as the reign of Richard III—and this is the only possible conclusion if we are to suppose that the series of royal portraits ended with that sovereign— seems quite inadmissible, on grounds of style; a comparison with the Royal Window (p. 155) given by Richard's brother, Edward IV, shows how unlikely such a dating must be. Evidence for dating can be found elsewhere. Whilst it is possible, as suggested above, that the tracery lights are somewhat older than the main lights, it would be rash to decide too readily that this must be the case; a comparison of the head of the full-faced king in the second light of the upper range (E2) with that, for example, of St. Philip (C2) shows that contemporaneity need not be excluded. Certain details in the painting of the tracery figures, such as the shoes with 'cusping' at the junction of the sole and upper, suggest that there may be some relationship with the few remaining figures from the windows of Winchester College Chapel, a point discussed more fully on p. 122; it must be granted that there is a greater divergence between the Canterbury kings (in the main lights) and those from the Jesse Window at Winchester (Plate B(c)),† but here again there is a surprising correspondence in the crowns of two of the kings (E5, I4), which in their schematic form, with a row of frond-like finials, resemble the crowns at Winchester and are notably unlike those of the Kings in the upper range with their yellow-stained details and, in some cases, a suggestion of the *repoussé* handling of actual goldsmith's work. The loose beardless head (possibly that of Richard II) described on p. 135 has also a 'Winchester' crown. It is interesting to compare this series of Kings of England with another, of nine, ranging from Constantine to Henry VI, about a century later in date, in the great window of St. Mary's Hall, Coventry.‡

The glazing of Winchester College Chapel is believed to have been begun in 1393 and to be the work of Thomas of Dadyngton (or Deddington), a glazier earlier employed on St. Stephen's Chapel, Westminster. § The Author has argued on internal evidence that some at least of the Winchester windows may have been painted after the death of Richard II (1399), although in the lifetime of William of Wykeham (d.

* *F.C.C. Sixteenth Annual Report* (1943), 'The Great West Window', p. 30.

† A single one of these is in the Victoria and Albert Museum (reproduced in the Museum's *Review of the Principal Acquisitions during the Year*, 1921, fig. 21). Five others are in a private collection in Jersey City, U.S.A.; part of a seventh has in recent years been restored to the College. Mention should also be made of the kings in the Jesse window in the choir of York Minster, of which the close similarity to the Winchester Jesse is discussed by J. A. Knowles in *The York School of Glass-painting*, London, 1936, pp. 109–111; one of the kings with crown like those at Canterbury here discussed is reproduced in *Treasures of Art: Stained Glass at York Minster*, by Canon F. Harrison, London, n.d., pl. 6.

‡ See *The Nineteenth Volume of the Walpole Society*, 1930–31, Oxford, pp. 89–110, Bernard Rackham, 'The Glass-paintings of Coventry and its Neighbourhood'.

§ See J. D. Le Couteur, *Ancient Glass in Winchester*, London, 1920, pp. 18–20.

1404)*. That there should be some relationship between the Winchester and Canterbury windows is therefore by no means surprising; architectural connections between the two cities have been discussed elsewhere (p. 21); it accords with probabilities that a window which, from the Royal shields introduced in its composition, may be assumed to have been given by or perhaps in memory of the King, should have been furnished by the King's glazier at Westminster. But on stylistic grounds a date more advanced in the fifteenth century seems to be required for the main lights. The shafts of the canopies, with sculptured falcons and greyhounds introduced in bracketed niches, find a parallel which can approximately be dated in a window, with similarly enriched canopies, given probably by Nicholas Blackburn, Junior, to the church of All Saints, North Street, York;† Blackburn was in 1429, like his father before him, Lord Mayor of the city,‡ and a date shortly after that event may be postulated for the York window. A more cogent argument for dating the Canterbury window later than the reign of Richard II is afforded by comparing the main lights with the windows erected in the Beauchamp Chapel at Warwick, by contract dated 1447 between the executors of Richard Beauchamp, Earl of Warwick, and John Prudde, of Westminster, King's glazier (Plate B(*a*)); the figures that occupy the main lights of these windows are set against a trellis of intersecting bands with ornaments or emblems in the interspaces, quite unlike the 'seaweed' or feathery leaf diaper which is the commonplace background of the fifteenth century. The resemblance is striking between this trelliswork and the varied diapers which fill the canopies behind the figures in the Canterbury windows, and the conclusion is obvious, that these latter were also designed in the royal workshop. Whether the Canterbury glass can be accepted as an early manifestation of a type of ornament still in favour when the Beauchamp Chapel was glazed, or the two examples may be taken to be contemporaneous, might be regarded as an open question if it were not for the evidences pointing back towards Winchester and York, which seem to favour the first alternative. Comparison with the North Transept Window (of the reign of Edward IV) makes it incredible that this West Window could be later than it, even if only by a few years; a window designed under Richard III would surely have shown the background of curtains or hangings, usual in windows of such importance, which will be discussed on a later page (p. 60).

There remains another grave objection to the series of twenty-one Kings, ending with Richard III, assumed by Gostling—it would entail the inclusion of a portrait of his nephew and victim Edward V. This surmise being rejected, it becomes necessary

---

* *Journal of the British Society of Master Glass-painters*, No. 4 (April 1926), p. 23; also *Victoria and Albert Museum Guide to the Collections of Stained Glass*, 1936, p. 50.

† Reproduced by G. Benson, *The Ancient Painted Glass Windows in the Minster and Churches of the City of York*, York, 1915, figs. 50, 51; Read, pl. 23.

‡ See J. A. Knowles, *op. cit.*, p. 43; Benson (*op. cit.*) gives 1429 as the date of a second mayoralty of the father. Both father and son are described in the dedication on the window as: *quondam major civitatis Ebor.*

to ask who were the occupants of the lights now filled with twelfth-century figures from the Choir Clerestory. We have seen that an eighth king, unknown to Gostling, has recently been reinstated in the centre position of the middle range, for which however his pose, fronting half-right (from the spectator's point of view) does not seem to be suited—the alternate odd-number places in the upper range being taken by full-front figures; that he occupied the first or fifth place in a second series of seven is a reasonable assumption which would yield a series of fourteen kings in all. They would conclude with Edward III, grandfather of Richard II, the putative donor of the window, and such a conclusion can only be regarded as entirely fitting; the objection that, on stylistic grounds, what is still extant of the main lights of the window can hardly be dated so early as Richard's reign, can be met by the argument that the window was begun and its design laid down in principle in his time, and its lower portion completed only some years after his death, on the lines originally intended but with such alterations in details of the design—the sculpture-enriched canopy shafts and the trellis-diaper backgrounds—as have been discussed above. It may be pointed out, moreover, that on dynastic grounds a series of portraits ending with Edward III would be not less acceptable to the Lancastrian sovereigns than to Richard II whom they supplanted on the throne. If it is asked who, then, were the occupants of the lowest range of lights, it has to be confessed that there is no answer that will be readily acceptable; a series of archbishops would not have been quite inappropriate, or seven non-biblical saints whose disappearance could be accounted for by their offensiveness to Puritan susceptibilities. But it must be admitted that no evidence in the shape of fragmentary remains of such figures has been discovered to support these surmises; it is, however, perhaps relevant to mention that in the MS. notes, dated 1599, of R. Scarlet (compare p. 21 above), there is mention of two figures of an archbishop as being in the West Window of the Chapter House, which appears to have contained standing figures similar to those of the window here under discussion.

Of the general colour effect of the window as originally designed, a good impression can be obtained by viewing it from the entrance to the Corona, at the east end of the Cathedral, from which position the extraneous glass in the lower parts of the window is hidden from sight by the openwork straining-arch under the central tower. The general tonality will be seen to be very different from that of the thirteenth-century windows, in which blue is dominant, with much ruby and golden yellow; here, dark neutral tones—tawny brown, deep green, purplish mauve, with not so much ruby and still less blue, the whole in a setting of shimmering white. The window is also markedly less rich in bright colours than the Royal Window in the North-West Transept to which it is closely akin in the architectural construction of the stonework.

The window has to some extent been restored since the beginning of the nineteenth century. Repairs by Austin in 1854 to the lowest range of lights, including figures from the Choir Clerestory, are mentioned on p. 26 above. A volume of accounts for 1874–93, in the Chapter Library, contains the following entry, in a report for the year 1879–80: 'To taking out, restoring, reglazing and refixing eleven lights of painted glass in large west window, also taking out, restoring, reglazing three lights which are not yet fixed about 114 feet superficial' (no figures are given of the cost). It was perhaps at this time (if not earlier) that the fragmentary names inscribed under some of the kings were taken out, and the existing uninscribed pedestals substituted; the white glass in the latter appears to be largely modern, but ancient blue and ruby 'pot-metal' has been used to fill the openings in the architectural designs. The strange disparity, both in design and in technique, of the royal crowns will not escape the observant, and may perhaps be accounted for by these restorations; the character of some of the kings' faces is also such as to raise the question of a similar possibility. It is significant that an album of drawings by Austin includes a tracing of the head of the first of the Kings (E1) which might have been used in the painting of a new head.

Reproduction (the entire window): *F.C.C. Sixteenth Annual Report* (1943), pl. facing p. 30.

TRACERY LIGHTS

These, below the topmost openings with the Royal shield, seem to have contained originally sixteen Prophets distributed between the uppermost range (B), where they were flanked by the shields of the Queens, and the middle range (C), and the Apostles with, on either side, an angel in the lowest range (D). Of the Prophets, only eleven now remain, whilst the number of the Apostles is augmented, by duplication of several, to seventeen. Among the figures originally belonging to the tracery there are doubtless some which have been displaced, but in the opinion of Mr. Caldwell the six Prophets in the upper range still occupy their original stations.

Whether any of these interpolated figures came, as stated by Miss Williams, about 1799 from the West Window of the Chapter House seems questionable, in view of their dissimiliarity to the figures lower down in the window (range H); in any case, as Dr. Mason points out, she is wrong in describing them as 'Saints and Bishops'.

A1. ARMS OF RICHARD II, Azure a cross paty and five martlets or (St. Edward the Confessor), impaling Quarterly, 1 and 4, Azure semée of fleurs-de-lis or (France Ancient), 2 and 3, Gules three lions passant gardant or (England). The ground of the dexter half of the shield is painted with a fish-roe diaper; the French quarterings have each four lilies in yellow glass leaded in a trellis of blue. The shield is hung by its blue strap from the white branches of a tree bearing three tufts of foliage (above and on either side of the shield) and springing from a green stock at the base of the light; background murrey.

Richard II of out his great veneration for St. Edward adopted his traditional shield as an impalement with his own Royal coat; in the Wilton Diptych in the National Gallery the Confessor is one of the three saints by whom the King is being presented to the Virgin. The impaled arms are painted on the back of the

50' 0" × 25' 0"

Plate XV

KING, presumed to be Canute, the first of a
series of Kings of England. In one of the main lights
(E.1) of the upper range in the West Window.
About 1396–1399 or perhaps somewhat later.
P. 128.

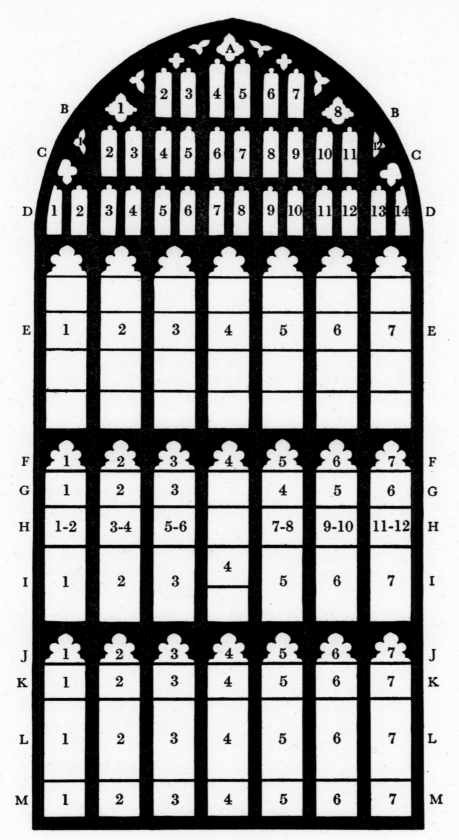

Height 50 feet, width 25 feet

DIAGRAM OF WEST WINDOW

diptych, together with the crest of a lion statant gardant and Richard's badge of a white hart lodged (probably derived from the hind badge of his mother, the Fair Maid of Kend, compare p. 151 below). A contemporary example in stained glass is to be found in the North Aisle of Westwell Church, near Ashford, where Richard's arms as here emblazoned are impaled with those of his first wife, Anne of Bohemia. M. V. Clarke (*Fourteenth-century Studies*, Oxford 1937, 'The Wilton Diptych', pp. 274–276) quotes Froissart and the St. Albans author of the *Annales Ricardi Secundi* as her authority for the view that the Confessor's arms thus impaled with those of France and England had perhaps been used by Richard for special purposes as early as 1394, before being publicly assumed by him in the winter of 1397–8. The Westwell shields are discussed, with reproductions, in the light of Miss Clarke's essay (which had previously been published in the *Burlington Magazine*), by Ralph Griffin in *Archæologia Cantiana*, Vol. XLVII (1935), pp. 170–174.

Reproduction: *C.C.C.*, No. 41 (1945), pl. facing p. 16. Plate 51b

B1. ARMS OF ISABELLA OF FRANCE, second Queen of Richard II (m. 1396), France Ancient quartering England (as in A1), impaling Azure three fleurs-de-lis or (France Modern). The arrangement is similar to that of A1 but with altered colouring; the strap is blue, the tree entirely green, and the background ruby. This shield is an interesting illustration of the retention by the English Kings (until 1405, under Henry IV) of the old blazoning of the French arms, with a powdering of lilies, which had in France itself been abandoned, in favour of three lilies only, by Charles V about 1375.

Reproduction: *C.C.C.*, No. 41 (1945), pl. facing p. 17. Plate 51d

B2–7 contain figures of PROPHETS (unidentifiable) standing on pedestals in the form of a finial branching out into a pair of large cusped leaves (more elaborate in the two middle lights); above the head of each, in the upper foliation of the light, is a five-petalled rose. The colours of draperies and background vary. Gostling speaks merely of 'six small figures'.

2. Holding a scroll outstretched in front of him with both hands. Dark green robe with pattern of discs, blue mantle, brown tippet, pointed dark green cap with edge turned up, dark grey shoes. Background dark murrey, rose white.

3. Right hand raised, a scroll in the left hand; ruby robe with seeded pattern and border of rosettes, dark blackish-purple mantle, deep murrey tippet and shoes, brown flat cap. Background dark green, rose white. Plate 64e (head only)

4. Left hand raised, holding a scroll, right arm swathed in mantle, which is blue; golden yellow robe patterned with foliage on coiled stems against a cross-hatched ground, round green cap with upturned brim, dark green shoes. Pedestal yellow-stained and higher than in B2, 3, with finials at the angles of its base. Background ruby, rose white.

5. He holds a staff in his right and a scroll in his left hand; pointed ruby cap, olive-brown robe with seeded pattern, murrey mantle, ruby shoes. The pedestal similar to that of B4. Blue background, golden rose. Plate 53c

6. Holding a book with both hands. Dark blue robe, dark green mantle, light brown cap similar in shape to that of B2, dark purple shoes. Background purple, rose white. Plate 64d (head only)

7. Right hand laid on breast, left holding a long pendant scroll. Robe amber, figured with zones of quatrefoils and mock inscription alternately, belt of square links, mantle blue, ruby tippet, baggy purple cap, background dark green, rose white.

Plate 53a

8. ARMS OF ANNE OF BOHEMIA, first Queen of Richard II (m. 1381, d. 1394), France Ancient quartering England (as in A1), impaling Or an eagle displayed sable quartering Gules a lion rampant with forked tail argent crowned or (Bohemia). The gold crown of the Bohemian lions is rendered by painting in yellow stain on the white glass of the figure. The arrangement and colour of the setting are identical with those of B1. Gostling wrongly describes the eagles as having 'two heads'. The Queen's arms as here emblazoned (but with eagles having two heads) are seen impaled with those of King Richard in the window at Westwell referred to under A1 above.

Plate 51e

C1. A whorl of three olive-green leaves springing from a blue disc on a ruby ground.

C2–11 appear originally to have contained ten figures of Prophets (Gostling is certainly mistaken in calling them 'ten saints'); they stand on high pedestals branching out at the top into large leaves, like those of the topmost range. Their places have now in five cases been taken by Apostles, of which one (C6) was originally in the lowest row of tracery lights and the remainder (C2, 3, 10, 11) were brought from elsewhere (perhaps the West Window of the Chapter House, but it is possible that all five were not originally in the same window); these interpolated figures can readily be distinguished by their pedestals, in which there is a chequered pavement for them to stand on, above the supporting foliated pedestal.

2. ST. PHILIP, holding three round barley loaves (*John* VI, 5–9). He is clothed in a dark green robe under a deep purplish-ruby cloak, brown shoes; brownish halo; background blue, rose white. Philip is depicted holding loaves on the fifteenth-century screen at Cawston Church, Norfolk.* The tall, fluted, cake-like loaves recall those in a fifteenth-century glass-painting of the Last Supper at Great Malvern Priory.†

Plate 52b

3. APOSTLE, perhaps St. Simon, with a sword of scimitar form in his left hand, stroking his beard with his right hand; on the blade of the sword a pointed quatrefoil ornament. Robe and halo dark green, cloak blue, shoes yellow, background ruby, rose white.

The identification of this figure, which is one of the interpolations, as Simon would involve a duplication with D10, if this is rightly identified as the same Apostle; it is based on the acceptance of the weapon carried as a scimitar, which would accord with the story in the apocryphal *Acts of Simon* of the death of that Apostle by martyrdom in a temple in Persia (see M. R. James, *Norfolk and Suffolk*, London, 1930, p. 217). The figure is obviously from the same cartoon as C10, where, however, the weapon is the two-edged sword normally associated with St. Paul; it is possible that C3 also represents St. Paul, an assumption which would involve location of the two panels originally in two separate windows; but the correspondence in type of the pedestals in the two is in favour of their having belonged originally to one and the same window

---

* See M. R. James, *Norfolk and Suffolk*, London, 1930, p. 132, and G. McN. Rushforth, *Medieval Christian Imagery*, Oxford, 1936, p. 104.

† Reproduced by Rushforth, *op. cit.*, fig. 13.

and therefore depicting two different persons. Against Dr. Mason's identification of C3 as St. Bartholomew is the unlikeness of the weapon to the knife ordinarily carried by that Apostle, as in the lowest range (D9 below) and in the Royal Window (see p. 166). The fact that in the last-named window St. Simon is shown with the saw sometimes accepted (by a variant tradition) as the instrument of his martyrdom need not be taken as arguing against the choice of a scimitar for his emblem in this window, somewhat earlier in date.   Plate 53e

4. PROPHET (unidentified). Hands with palms together as in prayer. Blue robe, murrey mantle (mostly restored), golden-yellow hat similar in form to that of B2, shoes painted in yellow stain on the white glass of the pedestal. Background olive-green, rose white.

5. PROPHET (unidentified). Hands raised in front of him, a book in the right hand, yellow robe ornamented with rosettes and mock black-letter inscription in alternate rows, blue mantle, purple tippet and shoes, cap deep green. Background ruby, rose white.   Colour Plate XIV

6. ST. JAMES THE GREATER, with pilgrim's staff in his right hand, his left hand raised palm outwards. Deep murrey mantle over paler brownish-murrey robe, shoes painted in yellow as in C4; halo blue. His hair is encircled with a fillet on the front of which is a cockle-shell, the emblem of pilgrimage to Compostella. Background olive-green, rose ruby. Originally in the lowest range of tracery lights.   Plate 52d

7. PROPHET (unidentified). Right hand laid on breast, a book in his left hand, yellow robe, blue mantle, olive-green cap, white shoes. Background murrey, rose white.

8. PROPHET (unidentified). Like the figure in B2, which is from the same cartoon reversed, he holds a scroll outstretched in front of him. Cap deep murrey similar to that of B2, robe ruby diapered with a pattern of rosettes and girt with a belt of square links, dark olive-green mantle, shoes in yellow stain as in C4. Background blue, rose white.   Plate 53b

9. PROPHET (unidentified). Right hand laid on breast, left hand at waist. Dark purple pointed cap, robe dark purple diapered with a figure consisting of rosettes in clusters of three, mantle blue with amber tippet, shoes black. Background ruby, rose white.

10. ST. PAUL, carrying a sword in his left hand. His pose is the same as that of C3. Robe dark green, mantle purple, shoes grey, halo grey. Background blue, rose white. The figure is obviously based on the same cartoon as C3 (compare note thereon); the occurrence of a sword instead of a knife is against Dr. Mason's identification of this figure also as St. Bartholomew. This panel is an interpolation.

11. APOSTLE (unidentified), stroking his beard with his left hand. Robe yellow, concealing his feet, blue mantle (much restored), olive-green halo. Background ruby, rose olive-green. An interpolation.

12. Whorl of three dark green leaves about a green central disc, blue ground.
Between ranges C and D on either flank is a small light with two elongated vine-leaves pointing up and down and a bunch of grapes directed inward about a flower (respectively ruby and green, on a purplish and brown ground).   Plate 56b

(a)

(b)

(c)

(a, b) Two Sainted
Archbishops

15th CENTURY
WATER TOWER
Windows II, IV
pp. 138, 139

(c) Arms of Winchelsea
and Guldeford

15th CENTURY
WEST WINDOW

p. 130

58

(a)

(b)

[foot]

[head]

(c)

(d)

(e)

(a) Agnus Dei
(b) Rose
(d) Portcullis
(e) Rebus of Archbishop
Morton

Late 15th or *early* 16th
CENTURY
CRYPT, SOUTH AISLE

p. 176

(c) Tracery Light
14th CENTURY

p. 115

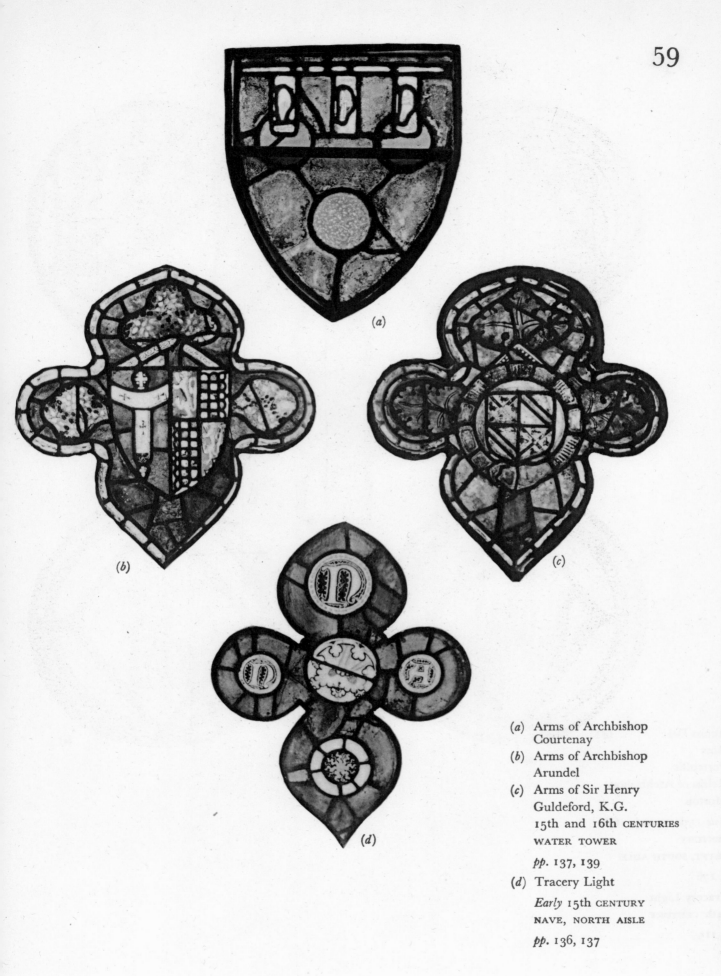

(a) Arms of Archbishop
    Courtenay

(b) Arms of Archbishop
    Arundel

(c) Arms of Sir Henry
    Guldeford, K.G.

    15th and 16th CENTURIES

    WATER TOWER

    pp. 137, 139

(d) Tracery Light

    Early 15th CENTURY

    NAVE, NORTH AISLE

    pp. 136, 137

60

(a)

(b)

(c)

(d)

(e)

(a, c) Two Angels
(b) Christ of Pity
(d) An Apostle
(e) St. Margaret

15th CENTURY
SOUTH TRANSEPT WINDOW

pp. 143, 144

(a, b) Two Seraphs
(c)   Arms of Fitzwilliam
(d)   Arms of Criol

15th CENTURY
SOUTH TRANSEPT WINDOW
pp. 146, 147

62

Sainted Archbishop
First half of 15th CENTURY
WATER TOWER
Window IV

p. 139

63

SOUTH TRANSEPT WINDOW
part, filled with glass of
the 12th, 13th and 15th
CENTURIES

pp. 144–147

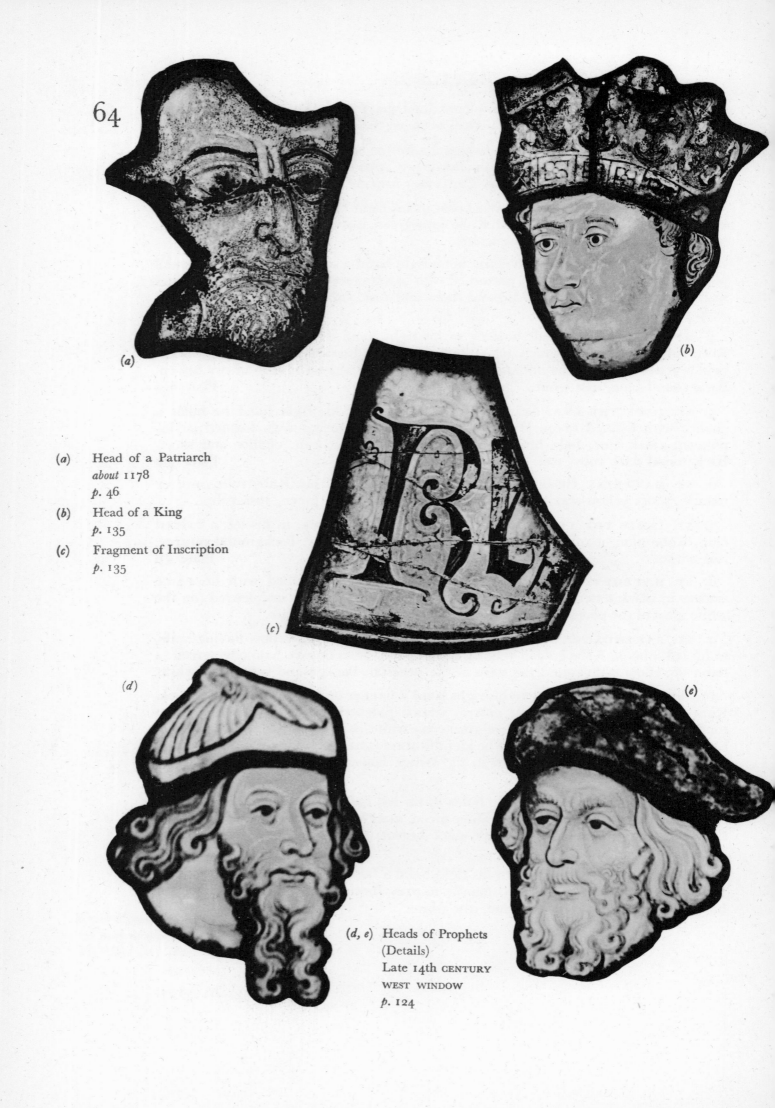

64

(a) Head of a Patriarch
    about 1178
    p. 46

(b) Head of a King
    p. 135

(c) Fragment of Inscription
    p. 135

(d, e) Heads of Prophets
       (Details)
       Late 14th CENTURY
       WEST WINDOW
       p. 124

D1–14. This lowest range originally contained the Twelve Apostles (some of them now transferred to the next range above) between the two angels still in position.

1. ANGEL kneeling on one knee swinging a fretted censer. The hair and amice are painted in yellow stain; wings greyish olive-green, robe largely restored and painted a brownish-grey, background murrey. The censer is in golden-yellow glass. Plate 51a

2. ST. PETER. He is barefoot and holds in his right hand a book, in his left two keys, one white, one yellow-stained. Robe moss-green, mantle murrey (much restored), halo ruby. Background blue, rose white.

3. APOSTLE (unidentified), holding in his right hand a scroll and in his left a small palm-branch. Robe deep green patterned with bands of mock-inscription and rosettes in circles, mantle dark blue; halo and shoes and rose, brownish-green, background deep murrey.

4. APOSTLE (unidentified) holding in his right hand a book, in his left a staff. Robe ruby, mantle olive-green, white shoes with bead border painted in yellow stain (which is also used for the midribs of the leaves in the pedestal); halo tawny brown. Background blue, rose white.   Plate 52c

5. ST. JOHN THE EVANGELIST. He is beardless. In his right hand he holds a chalice with foliated knop. His deep green robe is diapered with foliated trellis-pattern; cloak blue, halo brown, bright golden stain on hair, chalice and shoes. Background dark ruby, rose brownish-green.   Plate 52a

6. ST. MATTHIAS. He holds a spear aslant in front of him. Ruby robe, murrey mantle, shoes yellow-stained, halo blue. Background dark green, rose ruby.

7. ST. JAMES THE LESS, holding in his right hand a book, in his left a twisted club. Robe blue, mantle deep green, shoes ruby, halo tawny. Background murrey, rose white.   Plate 53f

8. ST. MATTHEW, holding with both hands a scroll inscribed with his name *matheus* in black letter. Robe olive-green, mantle murrey, shoes uncoloured (on the white glass of the pedestal), halo ruby. Background blue, rose white.

9. ST. BARTHOLOMEW, holding in his right hand a golden-yellow flaying-knife, in his left a book. Robe golden yellow, mantle blue, shoes brown, halo olive-green; a band of yellow stain round the stem of the pedestal. Background ruby, rose white.

10. ST. SIMON(?), holding in his right hand a banner on a pole, in his left a book. Robe blue, mantle mauve and murrey (much patched with insertions of various tones), halo ruby. Background olive-green, rose white, painted with a smear of brownish enamel, as is also the banner. The identification is based on that of the thirteenth-century figure from the Nave now in the Water Tower, which appears to bear the title S. SIMON (see p. 114).   Plate 53d

11. APOSTLE (unidentified). He holds in his left hand an open scroll at which he is pointing with his right forefinger. Robe green, mantle blue, shoes in yellow stain on the white glass of the pedestal, halo dark brown. Background deep murrey, rose white.

12. APOSTLE (unidentified). In his right hand a book at which he points with his left forefinger. Robe light green, mantle murrey (both much restored), shoes pale blue, halo brown. Background blue, rose white.

13. APOSTLE, perhaps ST. MATTHIAS, holding in his left hand a long-shafted axe or halberd, his right hand being raised toward his chin. Robe and shoes moss-green, mantle blue, halo white with yellow-stain cusping. Background deep ruby, rose green.

14. ANGEL swinging a censer (similar to D1 but reversed). Ruby wings, background blue, censer in amber-coloured glass. Plate 51c

MAIN LIGHTS, UPPER RANGE

These lights retain what are probably the figures that originally occupied them. These figures certainly represent Kings of England, although the titles in black-letter below them, of which, as has been already pointed out, there were a few remnants in the eighteenth century, when Gostling wrote, have now entirely disappeared from the window (a surviving fragment is described on p. 135 below). The second, fourth, and sixth figures face full front, those in the remaining alternate panels being turned slightly towards the second and sixth respectively. Each is enclosed beneath a canopy with elaborate pinnacled top and base of openwork tracery, all enriched with yellow stain; the lateral supporting shafts are depicted as divided into pinnacled niches resting on foliated columns. The lights have lateral borders consisting of a band of colour broken by lozenge-shaped ornaments enclosing quatrefoils; the backgrounds against which the figures are set, within the canopies, consist in every case of a diamond-ways trellis (recalling that of the windows at Warwick, as stated above), with flowers at the points of intersection and whorls of foliage in the interspaces, the colours varying in the several lights. Through the openings in the canopies and bases plain coloured grounds are visible, alternately ruby and blue.

E1. KING (presumably CANUTE). He holds his sceptre (which, like his crown, has yellow stain enrichments) aslant on his right shoulder. He wears a deep green robe, dark purple-brown tippet, and ermine-lined ruby robe with white flowered border. One shoe only, purplish-brown, is visible. The trellis of the background is green, with ruby flowers at the intersections, and blue interspaces. The colour in the flanking borders is blue. The canopy has ruby interspaces; in the middle of it is a small bust.
Colour Plate XV

E2. KING WILLIAM THE CONQUEROR. In his left hand he holds a sword, his right is raised towards his beard. His robe is blue, with a pattern of rosettes on double circles, his mantle green with murrey lining and lozenge-pattern border, his shoes ruby (the 'flash' of which is very thin). The pavement green, with lozenge diaper. The trellis of the background white with blue flowers; the interspaces are of ruby glass with 'flash' so thin as to appear lilac-coloured in places. The colour in the borders murrey. In two niches of the shafts of the canopy on either side are sculptured a sitting hound and a falcon (or eagle) respectively. This figure is the one described by Gostling as being E5 and inscribed . . . *mus Cōquestor Rex*. Interspaces of canopy blue.

E3. KING (presumably HAROLD II). His sceptre is in his left hand. His robe is purplish-black with amber border, his mantle ruby with white border and white-bordered olive-green tippet fastened with a morse in amber-coloured glass (his shoes are not seen). Pavement dark blue. The trellis murrey, with green flowers and blue interspaces. The intervals of the flanking borders blue, of the canopy ruby; a small bust in the middle, as in E1.

E4. KING (presumably EDWARD THE CONFESSOR, originally occupying the place of E2), holding a halberd in his right hand; the position of his left hand, slanting in front of him, is such that it may have appeared mistakenly to Gostling as 'holding a book' (compare p. 119 above); his halberd however remains unexplained if he is to be identified as the Confessor. His robe, diapered with lozenge trellis-pattern, is green, his mantle ruby, white-bordered and blue-lined, and fastened over an ermine tippet by means of a large richly-worked morse in golden-yellow glass (the ornament painted on this has for the most part become effaced); gold shoes. The trellis of the background dark green, with white flowers and deep purple interspaces. The pavement is blue, as are also the intervals in the flanking borders; ruby interspaces in the canopy, which has a bust in the middle. On the shafts of the canopy are sculptured hounds and falcons as in E2. Plate 54d

E5. KING (presumably WILLIAM II). He holds his sceptre erect in his right hand, his left hand being raised with the two first fingers extended. His crown by exception is of deep amber pot-metal, unlike those of most of the remaining Kings, which are in white glass painted with yellow stain. He wears a deep purple robe under an ermine-lined deep-blue mantle with a tippet and borders enriched with a pattern in yellow stain; the ermine lining is turned over to form a wide collar. His shoes are amber-coloured. The trellis of the background white, with amber flowers and ruby interspaces. A sitting hound occupies a niche near the top of each shaft of the canopy. The intervals of the flanking borders blue; the openings of the canopy olive-green. Plate 54a

E6. KING (presumably HENRY I). He holds his sceptre aslant in his left hand. Robe deep purple with white borders, mantle ruby, white-bordered, with olive-green lining and brown tippet fastened with a green morse, shoes golden yellow. The trellis of the background is murrey, with white flowers and deep blue interspaces. The intervals of the flanking border ruby.

E7. KING (presumably STEPHEN). He holds his sceptre in his right hand; his left hand rests on the pommel of a sword. His robe is golden yellow with white border, his mantle blue with purple lining and tippet, his shoes black. The diamond trellis of the background white, with olive-green flowers and ruby interspaces. Flanking border-intervals blue. Plate 54b

MAIN LIGHTS, MIDDLE RANGE

F. Below the upper transoms are the tops of pinnacled canopies, all that remains of the original fillings of the six lights on either side of the middle. The ground seen through the openings of the canopies is alternately blue and ruby (from left to right); the borders which extend downwards to flank the next range of panels (G) have the interspaces between their painted lozenge-ornaments (on white glass, replaced here and there by a crown) in coloured glass as follows: (1) ruby, (2) pale blue, (3) murrey, (4) blue, (5) ruby, (6) blue, (7) ruby.

G1–6. Below the canopy-heads (F) have been inserted, except in the middle light, six panels made up out of fragments of glass chiefly of the fifteenth century surrounding shields of arms, two in each panel; several of the shields bear the personal arms, without the archiepiscopal impalement, of Archbishops of Canterbury, from a commemorative series of which the earliest is Stephen Langton and the latest Thomas

129

Bourchier, showing that these shields date from the second half of the fifteenth century.

1. (*a*) ARMS OF THOMAS OF LANCASTER, Duke of Clarence, second son of Henry IV (who married Lady Margaret Holland and died 1421), France Modern quartering England, over all a label of three points ermine. The field in the 1st and 4th quarters is diapered with rosettes.

(*b*) ARMS OF WHITTLESEY, Or a saltire azure. (William Whittlesey, Archbishop 1368–1374).

The shields are set among fragments of architectural canopy work.

2. (*a*) ARMS OF MEPHAM, Azure three bendlets or. (Simon Mepham, Archbishop 1328–1333).

(*b*) ARMS OF LANGTON, Per pale azure and gules a bend or. The bend is painted with a pattern of stars in circles on a hatched ground. (Stephen Langton, Archbishop 1207–1229).

The setting is composed of architectural fragments (windows, pinnacles, two imbricated turret-roofs).

3. (*a*) ARMS OF WINCHELSEA, Barry of six gules and ermine in chief three cinquefoils or. (Robert Winchelsea, Archbishop, 1294–1313).

(*b*) ARMS OF GULDEFORD, Or a saltire between four martlets sable, quartering Halden, Argent a chief sable over all a bend engrailed gules. The fields of the quarters are diapered with scrolled feathery foliage and cusped edges scratched through grey pigment. (Sir John Guldeford, d. 1493, was Comptroller of the Household to Edward IV; his grandmother Joan was daughter and heiress of John Halden.)

The setting consists almost entirely of architectural fragments (crocketed pinnacles and pendants; also the skirts of a draped figure similar to those in the shafts of I4). Plate 57c

4. (*a*) ARMS OF FRANCE MODERN QUARTERING ENGLAND (as below), over all a label of six points ermine. The fields of the first and fourth quarters painted with a diaper of rosettes. The six points of the label may be a glass-painter's mistake for five points, in which case the shield may be that of John, Duke of Bedford, as borne before 1399.

(*b*) ARMS OF BOKYNGHAM, Gules a cross bottony or. (John Bokyngham, d. 1397, Bishop of Lincoln).

The setting is of architectural fragments (windows, crocketed pinnacles, foliated pendants). Plate 55a

5. (*a*) ROYAL ARMS, Azure three fleurs-de-lis or (France Modern) quartering England (as on p.22).

(*b*) ARMS OF WILLIAM COURTENAY (Archbishop 1381–1396), Or three roundels gules, on a label of three points azure as many mitres argent. Setting of fragments similar to those of G2.

6. (*a*) ARMS OF BRADWARDINE, here emblazoned as Ermine two bars sable ermined argent. (Thomas Bradwardine, Archbishop 1349). Scarlet, in the MS. referred to on p. 21 (Harleian 1366), quotes the arms of Archbishop Bradwardine from the Archbishop's Hall as 'Barrée of six, sable, guttée, argent and ermine (see Willement, *Heraldic Notices*, p. 158).

(*b*) ARMS OF CHICHELE, Or a chevron between three cinquefoils gules. (Henry Chichele, Archbishop 1414–1443).

10′ 0″ × 3′ 9″

Plate XVI

A SAINTED ARCHBISHOP, in mass vest-
ments, with cross in his left hand, his right hand
raised in benediction. Details of the vestments and
canopy are painted in silver-yellow stain. Panel 3 of
Window II of the Water Tower. About 1410. P. 138.

The setting, mainly of architectural fragments, includes also part of a wing, a column twined about with a twisted band, and the legs (in hose, with long-pointed toes) of two men from bracketed niches similar to those in the shafts of I4.

Plate 55b

H1–12. At this level have been inserted a row of twelve small panels with standing figures of Apostles and saints, two side by side in each light, interrupted by the figure of a King of England under a canopy which occupies the middle light. Their original situation is not known, but it is evident from their size and proportions that they were in small tracery lights belonging to a series of windows shown, by the number and diversity of the sets of figures of which they are the remnants, to have been numerous and therefore likely, as Dr. Mason suggests, to have come from the side windows of the Nave. They differ in style alike from the original tracery lights seen above them in the window and from those of the Royal Window, being more advanced, with their pedestals seen in perspective, than the former and less so than the latter; the kidney-shaped leaves diapering the mantle of St. Peter in H3, which seems to be original, suggest a date not later than 1450. The panels may therefore be assigned to the second quarter of the fifteenth century.

1. APOSTLE (unidentified). In profile to left, barefoot, stroking his beard with his left hand. His robe pale green, mantle blue; halo bordered with discs. Ruby background.

2. APOSTLE (unidentified). He holds an open book in his left hand and is barefoot. Robe white, with yellow-stained border, mantle ruby; seeded halo. Background dark blue.

3. ST. PETER, with two keys hanging from his right hand, a book in his left hand, which is swathed in a blue mantle patterned with kidney-shaped foliage; his robe, showing at the skirt only, murrey, with 'seaweed' foliage. Background ruby.

4. ST. PAUL, with sword held erect in his right hand and book in his left. Ruby mantle (the 'flash' almost completely abraded above the waist), dark green robe; halo with bead border. Background blue.

5. A beardless youthful SAINT, unidentified. He carries a cross on a staff in his left hand and raises his right hand in the act of benediction. White alb under a murrey mantle. Cusped halo. Background blue. Plate 56a

6. APOSTLE (unidentified), barefoot. He clasps an open book with both hands to his breast. White robe with tripartite pattern similar to that in C9 above, blue mantle. Cusped halo. Background ruby. Plate 56a

7. APOSTLE (unidentified), holding a staff in his right hand. Robe blue, mantle ruby (the 'flash' much decayed); cusped halo. Background blue.

8. SAINTED ARCHBISHOP (unidentified), in mass vestments, holding his cross erect in his left hand, his right raised in benediction. Blue chasuble, pale murrey dalmatic, tunicle with green fringe, white alb; jewelled mitre and amice painted in yellow stain. Background ruby.

9. APOSTLE (unidentified), barefoot, holding a jewelled book in his right hand which is swathed in his green mantle; blue robe; plain-bordered halo. Background ruby.

10. APOSTLE (unidentified), with right hand extended, left clasping his green mantle. Robe white; halo plain yellow. Background blue.

11. SAINTED ARCHBISHOP (unidentified), in mass vestments, with cross aslant in his left hand, his right raised in benediction. Blue chasuble, deep murrey dalmatic, tunicle with green fringe, white alb; mitre, amice, gloves and shoes enriched with jewelling in yellow stain; halo plain with yellow border. Background deep ruby.

12. SAINTED ARCHBISHOP, corresponding in design with H8 and from the same cartoon, though by a different, more practised hand. Chasuble green, fringed murrey dalmatic with seeded pattern, golden yellow tunicle, white alb with apparel painted in yellow stain with a pattern of rosettes, trellis-patterned shoes. He wears a soft almuce in place of the stiff orphreyed amice. Halo lozenge-diapered. Background deep blue.

I1-7. The places originally presumed to have been occupied by a continuation of the series of Kings of England were assigned in 1797 to figures of the twelfth-century genealogical series brought from the Choir Clerestory; these remained undisturbed until, after the 1914–18 war, Mr. Caldwell reassembled an eighth figure of the series of Kings which was inserted in the middle light of I4. This involved the displacement of a pair of figures of sainted Archbishops and a panel with two shields which had occupied the middle position in ranges G and H and were now transferred to windows in the Water Tower (see p. 139); the figure from the genealogy in the lower part of the light, Jeconias, was removed to the left flanking light (I1) and another figure, probably Salathiel, reconstituted by Mr. Caldwell, was put on the right flank at I7, in place of Juda and Phares, which were put back into the Clerestory, but not in their original positions (see p. 42).

1. JECONIAS(?) (see p. 45).

2. OBED (see p. 37).

3. ROBOAM (see p. 38).

4. KING OF ENGLAND (unidentified), holding the Royal Orb in his right hand, the sceptre in his left. His robe is dark green, diapered with diamond trellis enclosing quatrefoils and bordered at the foot with ermine; his mantle dull murrey, with a narrow border, patterned with ovals round the bottom, and ermine lining, ermine-edged purple tippet, ermine collar and wristbands, amber-coloured shoes. The background is similar to those of E1–7 but the trellis (yellow, with ruby flowers at the intersections) vertical and horizontal instead of diamond-ways; the background, painted with a similar whorl of foliage, is blue. The pavement ruby. In niches at the middle of the canopy shafts, one on each side, are small figures, one kneeling, the other standing, but these have been truncated so that only the heads and legs remain, and it is possible that they may have been made up from figures belonging originally to two different lights. The flanking borders are similar in design to those of the uppermost range and have green intervals; the background of the canopy work is ruby, with a bust in the middle.   Plate 54c

5. ABIA (see p. 38).

6. JESSE (see p. 37).

7. SALATHIEL (?) (see p. 45).

132

West Window

MAIN LIGHTS, LOWEST RANGE

J1–7. At this level the pinnacled tops of the original canopies remain, though perhaps not all in their original respective positions, with the backgrounds alternately blue and ruby (in J5, however, no coloured background is now visible). J1, 2, 3, and 5 are peculiar in having flying buttresses among the pinnacles.

The canopies in this range, unlike those remaining in the two upper ranges have no borders; this seems to show that these lights are not continuous as a series with the others.

K1–7. In each light is a panel similar to those at G1–6, made up of two shields of the fifteenth century in a setting of fragments chiefly of the same period.

1. (*a*) ARMS, Quarterly, 1 and 4 Gules a bend argent, 2 and 3 Checky or and azure (for Warenne). Dr. Mason gives the first quarter as 'apparently Folliot', but according to Willement (*Heraldic Notices*, p. 21) the bend of Folliot, *alias* Foliot, Co. Norfolk, should be or, not argent; Burke and Papworth, however, give it as or.

(*b*) AN UNHERALDIC SHIELD made up of fragments of various colours including a fleur-de-lis, three small lozenges enclosing quatrefoils, a lion's mask, and a band of white glass painted with three mallets in a tray or trough.

Between the shields is a star with serpentine rays; the remainder of the setting consists of small architectural scraps, a fragment with legs in hose similar to those at G6 and I4, another of drapery with a pattern of rosettes, and part of a band with an inscription (. . . *ama* . . .) in black-letter.

2. (*a*) ROYAL ARMS, France Modern quartering England. The field in the 1st and 4th quarters has been of glass diapered with rosettes, but this has for the most part been replaced with plain blue glass; the shield has an unheraldic border of scrollwork scratched through a black band.

(*b*) A CONCOCTED SHIELD in which the first quarter shows a white saltire on a field partly blue, partly ruby, the second and third architectural fragments, the fourth an object in the shape of an inverted mitre patterned with a cross on a hatched ground and provided with a lockplate and keyhole.

The setting is made up of architectural scraps (including one of unusual character with part of a window with curvilinear tracery), part of a fringed vestment, a fragment of the Bourchier shield (compare p. 154), a star, parts of an inscription in black-letter (*S*) and another in the sixteenth-century capitals (UR), and part of a quarry with acorn and oak-leaves.

3. (*a*) ARMS OF THOMAS OF LANCASTER, Duke of Clarence (as in G1 above). The field in the 1st and 4th quarters is diapered with rosettes; the lions in the 2nd and 3rd are obliterated.

(*b*) ARMS OF BOURCHIER, 1st and 4th Argent a cross engrailed gules between four water-budgets sable, for Bourchier; 2nd and 3rd, Gules billety, a fess or, for Louvaine. The billets are rendered by abrasion of the ruby 'flash' and painting with silver-yellow stain. (Thomas Bourchier, Archbishop 1454–1486, Cardinal.)

The surrounding fragments include, besides portions of architecture, two scraps of legs in pointed hose (similar to those of G6) standing on brackets with 'pebble' pavement, fragments of large-scale drapery, two with large toes (in one case accompanied by drapery and a chequer pavement), a large bunch of grapes, a star, links of a large chain, and a fourteenth-century scrap with an ivy-leaf.

133

4. (*a*) SHIELD made up of fragments, Quarterly, with a large star in the 2nd quarter.

(*b*) SHIELD similarly composed, with zigzags in the 1st and 4th quarters and the 2nd and 3rd arranged to give a semblance of France Modern.

Amongst the surrounding fragments, chiefly of architecture, are two legs in pointed hose of a man standing on a chequer pavement, similar to those included in G6 above.

5. (*a*) ROYAL ARMS, France Modern quartering England. The field in the 1st and 4th quarters diapered with dotted spots scratched through black.

(*b*) ARMS OF ARUNDEL, Gules, a lion rampant or, for Fitzalan, quartering Checky or and azure, for Warenne, all within a bordure engrailed argent. The painting on the lions is almost effaced. (Thomas Arundel, Archbishop 1396–1413).

Among the surrounding fragments are part of the large green wing of an angel, a crown, a fragment of inscription (three dots in yellow stain and *C* in black-letter), a four-petalled flower in reserve on a grey ground, half of a large vine-leaf, part of a large cinquefoil, and a scrap of a quarry with an oakleaf.

6. (*a*) SHIELD, probably made up, charged with the Sacred Monogram *ihs* painted in reserve in a golden medallion laid over a processional cross, all on a blue field.

(*b*) ARMS OF ST. LO, Gules a fess between three scallops argent (of which only the two in chief are original). This shield is perhaps to be related to John St. Lo, who married Margaret Courtenay.

The surrounding fragments are mostly architectural, but include also two of drapery (one of these the crested hem of the vestment of a figure standing on a chequered pavement) and part of a large black-letter character.

7 (*a*) ARMS stated by Dr. Mason to be those of Stratford which, according to the manuscript of R. Scarlet (Harleian, 1366) quoted by Willement, *Heraldic Notices*, p. 158, should be 'Per fess, gules and sable, three plates, two and one'. Here the shield shows a fess argent between three plates of pink glass on a ground which is ruby above and patched with murrey below the fess. (John Stratford was Archbishop 1333–1349.)

(*b*) ARMS OF THOMAS OF LANCASTER, Duke of Clarence (as in G1 above). The surrounding fragments are chiefly architectural, but include also part of a crowned initial, a rose and a small piece of drapery.

L1–7. At this level figures from the twelfth-century genealogical series were inserted in 1797 in the positions which they still occupy.

1. ESROM (see p. 36).

2. NAASSON (see p. 36).

3. SEMEI (see pp. 32, 43).

4. ADAM (see p. 31).

5. JOSEPH (see p. 43).

6. AMINADAB (see p. 36).

7. ARAM (see p. 36).

65

St. Christopher
First half of 15th CENTURY

p. 178

66

(a)

(b)

(c)

(a)   Royal Arms
(b)   Arms of Archbishop
       Bourchier
(c, d) Half Figures
(e)   Jeremiah
(f)   Daniel
(g)   Ezra
(h)   St. John the Baptist

about 1470

ROYAL WINDOW

pp. 164, 165

68

(a) (b) (c) (d)

(a) Isaiah
(b) St. Peter
(c) St. Paul
(d) Ezekiel (?)
(e) St. John the Evangelist
(f) St. Bartholomew
(g) St. James the Greater
(h) St. Andrew

(e) (f) (g) (h)

about 1470

ROYAL WINDOW.

pp. 164–166

M1–7. At the bottom, the lights of the lowest range have been filled with seven oblong panels each made up of a shield with the Royal Arms as borne by Richard II and his predecessors (France Ancient quartering England), dating from the latter part of the fourteenth century, set amongst fragments chiefly of fifteenth-century glass. Notes on which the following descriptions are based were made at close quarters when the panels had been taken down for safety during the war; it has not been possible to identify their present sequence except in the cases of Nos. 1, 5 and 7.

1. The Royal Shield is flanked by two roses; the fragments, apart from a few with foliage, are mostly unpainted.

5. The shield is in bad condition. The only noteworthy fragment is one of ruby glass with a cross bottony in white abraded through the 'flash'.

7. The shield is in poor condition. The fragments include one with a cloud and stars scratched through a smear of grey enamel and another, of the fourteenth century, with a vine-leaf and tendrils in reserve on a grey ground.

(*a*). Among surrounding fragments—chiefly architectural—are one of the robe, with a pattern of foliage, of a figure standing on a 'pebble' pavement and another, in ruby glass, with a narrow ornamental border.

(*b*). The Royal Shield is in bad condition. Amongst the setting are fragments of architecture, mostly of the fifteenth century, part of a hand, and foliage in reserve of fourteenth-century type.

(*c*). Among the surrounding fragments are an angel's wing, branching stems with a lily and a small four-petalled rose, and a fragment of sixteenth-century inscription in capitals (H. BI).

(*d*). The fragments include a piece of late fifteenth-century drapery, a monster's head, and a structure with interlaced spokes of uncertain significance painted in yellow stain.

FRAGMENTS OF THE ORIGINAL GLAZING

HEAD OF A KING (perhaps Richard II), beardless, with crown in yellow pot-metal (compare p. 119). Plate 64b

FRAGMENT OF THE HEAD OF A KING, full face; nose, mouth with clean-shaven upper lip, and chin with slight two-forked beard, above a broad collar ornamented with rosettes.

FRAGMENT OF INSCRIPTION, *Re*[*x*], in black-letter, the initial R filled in with yellow stain. Part of the title of one of the kings (see above). Plate 64c

§2 The Music Room

IN a window of this room, which is situated above the Treasury, has lately been placed the panel described below. Nothing is known of its former whereabouts. On stylistic grounds it may be dated in the latter part of the fourteenth century.

THREE BOY MUSICIANS. Half figures, in a building with a column to the right of the centre. One, in the middle, is playing a lute with a plectrum, the other two have harps.

Plate 66c

§3 Aisle Windows of the Nave

'IN the nave, many of the windows contain fragments of fifteenth-century glass* in their heads, sometimes in the original place. Thus on the north side next to the memorial to Dean Stanley'—in the second window from the eastern end—'the letters N and N and S(?) may be an indication of what the window contained. Lower are fragments arranged to make an edging, but two eyes have the old glazing. The third window has the original roses in the top, and two edgings of fragments in the lights below. The fourth has the roses at the top, while four lights have edgings of fragments, and no fewer than all four lights have beautiful canopy work with a ground of blue and red alternately below the transome. The fifth window has the old roses, and, like the rest, the old points of the tabernacle work beneath, and four lights edged with fragments, among which *[Marg]aret* can be read. The sixth has lost its rose at the top, but besides the points of the tabernacles, and four lights of edgings, possesses two nice eyelets and four beautiful tops to the lights under the transome. The south side of the nave has been less fortunate. Only the fourth window from the east has edgings of old glass to five openings at the head; and the sixth to four. The sixth, however, in one opening of the tracery has a quarry with the same kind of pattern as has been seen in St. Michael's Chapel' (M., p. 56). Five of the tracery panels are described below.

1–3. THREE PANELS from tracery lights. Quatrefoil-shaped, the lower lobe of pointed ogee outline. In the middle, a circle of white glass, with cusped border reserved against a yellow-stained ground on which is painted a whorl-motive; in each lobe, a cinquefoil on white glass. The ground of blue glass; in two of the panels it is painted with 'seaweed' diaper, in one it is plain.

4. PANEL from a tracery light. Of the same shape as Nos. 1–3 and similar in design except that the flowers in the lobes are five-petalled roses with yellow-stained centres, and the ground is of plain murrey glass.

5. PANEL from a tracery light. Of the same shape as Nos. 1–3. In the middle, half of a circle similar to that of the other panels, the defective part having been made good with half of a flower with four-cusped petals. In the upper lobes are white

---

* This dating may be questioned: the five panels described below, part of the original glazing of the North Aisle, date almost certainly from the end of the fourteenth century.

circles painted with Lombardic capitals in reserve on a blackground within a seeded border—N in the top and left-hand lobes, A (not S, as suggested by Dr. Mason) in the right-hand lobe; the lowest lobe contains a white circle enclosing a star with wavy rays scratched out of black. The ground plain brownish-crimson glass.   Plate 59d

§4 Water Tower

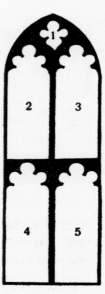

10' 0" × 3' 9"

THE upper part of the twelfth-century Water Tower was rebuilt under Prior Thomas Chillenden (1391–1411) and four of its windows were reconstructed; each was divided by a mullion and transom into four main lights with a small quatrefoil in the head (see diagram). The first window, on the west side, retains its original Norman form. Of the remaining four, described below, No. II retains in its tracery and upper half above the transom, its original early fifteenth-century glazing. In the upper parts of Nos. III and V, thirteenth-century glass with pairs of figures has been inserted (see pp. 67, 114). The upper part of No. IV has been filled with fifteenth-century glass, but from other parts of the Cathedral. In the lower halves of all four windows, fifteenth- and sixteenth-century shields were set among plain glass quarries when the Bishop of Chichester, Dr. Bell, was Dean (1924–1929); at the same time the first window was filled with thirteenth-century glass, and the figures of archbishops in Window IV were brought from the West Window (see p 132) The fifteenth-century and later glass is described below; the panels believed to have belonged originally to their present positions are marked with an asterisk.

WINDOW I (See p. 113.)

WINDOW II

*1. Shield with ARMS OF ARCHBISHOP THOMAS ARUNDEL (1397–1414), See of Canterbury, Azure a cross-staff argent with its cross or over all a pall argent charged with three crosses formy sable, impaling Quarterly, 1 and 4, Gules a lion rampant or (Fitzalan), 2 and 3, Checky or and azure (Warenne), all within a bordure engrailed argent. The shield is slung by its strap on a blue tree with purple bole against a ruby background. The dexter half of the shield is modern; in the sinister the lions have been rendered by abrasion of the 'flash' of the ruby field and subsequent yellow staining; the engrailed border (not seen in the first quarter) is similarly abraded and outlined with painting in black in the fourth quarter, and rendered in white leaded glass in the second and third. The golden head of the Canterbury cross-staff has here four white decorative pearls in its angles; the lower point of the staff has a gold ring encircling it.   Plate 59b

137

*2. A SAINTED ARCHBISHOP, unidentified, in processional vestments—mitre, almuce, ruby cope (of which the 'flash' is largely decayed), white alb with narrow border of trefoils, gloves and yellow-stained shoes; he stands with his cross (with plain yellow-stained head) in his left hand, his right raised in benediction, on a chequer pavement under a canopy which is supported on slender shafts with ribbons twisted round them and two small lions sejant among the pinnacles above. The background is blue behind the figure and pinnacles, ruby outside the shafts. Plate 57a

*3. A SAINTED ARCHBISHOP, unidentified, his face seen in profile, in mass vestments—mitre, amice with pattern of roundels, pallium, light blue chasuble, jewelled gloves, fringed tawny dalmatic with mauve fringe of tunicle showing below, white alb with yellow-stained roundel-patterned apparel, yellow-stained shoes. He stands blessing, cross in hand, as the figure in No. 2, but the head of his cross is elaborately jewelled. The setting is as in No. 2, save that the colours of the background are reversed and one of the lions (on the left) is yellow-stained. Colour Plate XVI

4. Shield with ARMS OF THE PRINCE OF WALES (probably for Henry, afterwards King Henry V), France Modern quartering England (as on p. 130), over all a label of three points argent.

5. Shield with the ROYAL ARMS, France Modern quartering England (as on p. 130).

WINDOW III

1. SHIELD, See of Canterbury (as in II.1 above) impaling a made-up coat, Gules two bends argent. Hung by its strap on a ruby tree with large flower to left and a fragment of seaweed foliage inserted to the right; green ground.

2, 3. FIGURES, two in each light, thirteenth century (see p. 114).

4. SHIELD, Azure a bend argent between two cotices and six lions rampant or (Bohun), impaling Quarterly, 1 and 4 Gules a lion rampant or (Fitzalan), 2 and 3, Checky or and azure (Warenne) (for Humphrey Bohun, Earl of Hereford [d. 1372], who married Joan, daughter of Richard Fitzalan, Earl of Arundel; she died in 1419). The cotices are painted in yellow stain on the white glass of the bend, which is edged with black lines (the intervening ground, which should be blue, has been left white owing to the difficulty of providing such narrow leaded strips of blue glass); the lions are also in yellow stain, in reserve on a black ground, on white glass.
Colour Plate XXb

5. SHIELD, France Modern quartering England (as on p. 130) over all a label of three points argent charged with nine torteaux (for Cambridge), probably, as suggested by Commander Messenger, for Edmund of Langley, Earl of Cambridge (1361–1402) or his eldest son Edward, Duke of York (1373–1415). The torteaux, which should be gules, are rendered as circles painted in black on the white glass.

WINDOW IV

1. Shield with ARMS OF SIR HENRY GULDEFORD, K.G. Quarterly, 1 and 4, Or a saltire between four martlets, sable (Guldeford, *alias* Guildford), 2 and 3, Argent a chief sable surmounted by a bend gules (Halden), the whole encircled by a Garter with the motto: *Honi soit qui mal y pance* (sic). Hung by a strap on a green tree against a ruby background. The surrounding glass is original, of the early fifteenth century, but

the Garter and shield, and the green glass in the intervals between them, are of later date; these may be presumed to date from about 1530.† In the Halden quarters the engrailing of the bend is omitted owing to the exigencies of the small scale, or was perhaps painted in black alongside the leads and has perished. The blue glass of the Garter is interrupted by yellow as a ground for the lettering of the motto. Sir Henry was created K.G. in 1526; he was subsequently Comptroller of the Household to Henry VIII and died in 1532. This armorial medallion was restored to the Cathedral in 1915 by Mr. Ralph Griffin; Dr. Mason in recording this fact (*Guide to the Ancient Glass*, p. 52), mistakenly speaks of the Garter as being inscribed *Dieu et mon droit*.

Plate 59c

2. A SAINTED ARCHBISHOP, unidentified, in processional vestments—mitre, amice, blue cope, blue surplice, and murrey shoes (only one is seen). He stands blessing, with cross in his left hand, on a chequer pavement under a canopy with ruby background between borders of gold crowns interrupting a blue band; between pinnacles above is a shield with the arms of Beaufort (France Modern quartering England within a bordure gobony argent and azure). The arms refer perhaps to Sir John Beaufort, Earl of Somerset, K.G. (d. 1410), first husband of Margaret Holland (compare p. 151).

The glass in this and the next following light was brought from the West Window; it is believed by Mr. Caldwell to belong originally to a side window in the Nave; the panels have been made up to the needful width by the insertion of the late fourteenth-century crown borders.

Plate 57b

3. A SAINTED ARCHBISHOP, unidentified, standing with cross as in No. 2, in mass vestments—mitre, amice, pallium, mauve chasuble, fringed green dalmatic below which is seen the ruby fringe of the tunicle, gloves and white alb, with roundel-patterned apparel. The canopy and border similar to those of No. 2, but the ground is light blue, and ruby in the borders and behind the pinnacles above, between which is a shield with the Royal Arms as borne before 1399 (France Ancient quartering England).

Reproduction *C.C.C.*, No. 2 (April 1929), facing p. 10.

Plate 62

4. Shield with ARMS OF ARCHBISHOP WILLIAM COURTENAY (1381–1396), Or, three torteaux, on a label of three points azure three mitres argent.

Plate 59a

5. Shield with BADGE OF THE PRINCE OF WALES, Sable, three ostrich feathers argent each with quill fixed in a scroll bearing the motto *Ich dien* (painted in black). The sable of the field is rendered in deep purple glass. This shield is sometimes described (as in his Will) as the 'arms for peace' of the Black Prince.

WINDOW V

*1. Shield with ARMS OF ARCHBISHOP THEOBALD (1139–1160), See of Canterbury (as in II. 1) impaling Barry of six or and azure a chief indented gules. Hung by its strap on a green tree with purple bole against a ruby ground.

2, 3. FIGURES, two in each light, thirteenth century (see p. 114).

4. Shield with ARMS OF CAMBRIDGE (as in III 5).

5. Shield with ARMS OF BEAUFORT (as in IV 2).

---

† The Guldeford quarters lack the canton with a pomegranate granted to Sir Henry, according to what the *Dictionary of National Biography* (*s.v.* Guildford, Sir Henry) describes as an 'impossible story,' for his prowess at the capture of Granada from the Moors in 1492.

§5 Chapel of St. Edward the Confessor

IN the middle light of each of the two windows have been placed two small panels with figures of St. Christopher and St. Catherine of Alexandria which originally filled tracery lights in a window or windows perhaps of the Nave. On stylistic grounds and on the evidence of costume they may be dated about the beginning of the fifteenth century.

1. ST. CHRISTOPHER. The saint wades, supporting himself with a tree-trunk and carrying on his shoulders the Child Christ who is grasping a lock of his bearer's hair. The saint is clothed in a white-lined blue cloak, the Child in a white gown patterned with trefoils in yellow stain. The background is ruby.   Plate 66a

2. ST CATHERINE OF ALEXANDRIA. She stands with her right hand resting on a spiked wheel, her left hand supporting a sword, the instruments of her martyrdom. She wears, besides a crown, 'a mantle with two clasps in the form of rosettes linked by a short band. Beneath this, over a dress diapered with flowers in circles, is the cote hardie, which came into fashion at the end of the fourteenth century. This garment, trimmed with ermine, seems to be of the peculiar form, without sleeves and cut away so as to reveal the tight dress beneath it, seen in a French MS. dated 1430 which is reproduced in Viollet-le-Duc's *Dictionnaire du Mobilier Français*. For parallels of somewhat similar style we may turn to the bronze figure of one of the Princesses in the tomb of Edward III in Westminster Abbey, and to the memorial brass of Lady Walsche, at Wanlip, Leicestershire, dated 1393. The latter shows the mantle with its clasps, and the long sleeves with a funnel-like prolongation over the hands, which are a conspicuous feature of the St. Catherine; these sleeves are repeated in brasses at Broughton, Oxon, and Warkworth, Northants, dated respectively 1414 and 1430 . . . The form of the *cote hardi* and the style of painting in general point to the first two or three decades of the fifteenth century as the period in which this lovely painting is likely to have been done.'* The figure is entirely in white glass, with painting in black and silver-yellow stain; the background plain murrey.

Reproduction: *C.C.C.*, No. 40 (October, 1944), pl. facing p. 13.   Plate 66b

§6 South Window of South-West Transept

THIS window was rebuilt in 1792, following the lines on which it was originally designed in the time of Archbishop Chichele (1414–43). Most of its original fifteenth-century glass had probably already disappeared at the time of the reconstruction of the window, and very little of it now remains. The rearrangement in

---

* *C.C.C.*, No. 40 (October, 1944), pp. 13–14, Bernard Rackham, 'Glass-painting of St. Catherine'.

Height 52 feet, width 24 feet

DIAGRAM OF SOUTH WINDOW OF SOUTH-WEST TRANSEPT

1792 was entrusted by Dean Powys and the Chapter to one of the Vesturers, John Simmonds, who selected figures from the genealogical series in the Choir Clerestory (see p. 24) and from other windows to fill the gaps in the three main ranges of lights. On the outside of one of the tracery lights (E8) a record of this reglazing is scratched with a diamond as follows: *William Burgess* 1792 *Thos Pottinger Repaird this Window*; below this has been added a record of still later repairs: *Richd Bowers Jno Egle J. White Surveyer* (sic) *1818*.† Among the panels described below only those marked with an asterisk can be accepted as having originally belonged to the window. The early glass introduced from other windows is described elsewhere. The later heraldic and other glass, approximately contemporary with the window itself, appears to have come chiefly from tracery lights in the windows of the Nave.

TRACERY LIGHTS

*A1, 5. Trefoils of white serrated leaves with midribs in silver-yellow stain, ruby ground.

*A2. SHIELD WITH THE ARMS OF THE PRIORY OF CHRIST CHURCH, CANTERBURY (now the arms of the Dean and Chapter): Azure on a cross argent the letter *x* surmounted by the letter *i* sable. The shield is hung by its strap on a green tree against a murrey background.

*A3. SHIELD WITH THE ARMS OF THE SEE OF CANTERBURY (as on p. 136 above except that the cross-staff is *entirely argent*). Hung on a green tree against a ruby ground.

*A4. SHIELD WITH THE ARMS OF ARCHBISHOP THOMAS BECKET: See of Canterbury (as on p. 136 above), impaling Argent three beckets (or choughs) sable. Tree and ground as in A2.

*B1, 10. Foliage.

B2, 4, 5, 6, 7, 9. Borders from thirteenth-century windows.

*B3. ST. JAMES THE GREATER, with shell reserved in white on hat painted with tawny-yellow stain, a staff in his right hand, his left raised palm to the front. He stands against a ruby background on a pavement of black and white triangles. Below, fragments of black-letter inscription (partly inverted): *ɩdſ S juſt*, in black, partly yellow-stained. Part of the inscription rightly belonging here is now in B8 (see below).

B8. CHRIST DISPLAYING HIS WOUNDS, with hands raised shoulder-high and outspread, an amber-yellow mantle about His shoulders fastened with a square morse; hair and beard yellow-stained. The half-figure, shown against a ruby background painted with battlements (as of the walls of Heaven), is set in a small vesica-shaped panel forming a complete unit of early fourteenth-century date of which the original location cannot be conjectured. Above it, among the remainder of the glass filling the light, is a quatrefoil in reserve on white glass, also of the fourteenth century.

---

† The transcriptions given by Dr. Mason are inaccurate.

Below are fifteenth-century fragments, probably contemporary with the window and in part belonging to it: to left, all but the head of a draped figure kneeling on one knee, holding a yellow-stained chalice in the right hand; to right, upside down, a fragment of canopy work with windows and the top of a cap or turban; below, fragments of black-letter inscription (*Egfridus* and *S. Ja[cobus]*, the latter doubtless belonging to the figure in B3). The name is quoted wrongly as *Egidius* by Dr. Mason, who describes the kneeling figure as 'a deacon or perhaps an angel in tunicle, holding something like a cup'.

Dr. Mason also speaks incorrectly of a 'figure of our Lord with right hand uplifted' (actually both hands are raised), conjecturing that it is 'perhaps from an Ascension scene'; but the subject is rather the 'Christ of Pity', a subject which became common in the fifteenth century.† A fine example, some 50 years later in date, is in a north window of St. Peter's-in-the-East, Oxford; a thirteenth-century French example, in the apse of the choir of Le Mans Cathedral, is cited by Marcel Aubert.‡

As Prof. Claude Jenkins has kindly pointed out in answer to the Author's enquiries, the name Egfridus doubtless refers to Egfrith, King of the Northumbrians, often mentioned in Bede's *History;* Gervase of Canterbury, in his *Gesta Regum* (Rolls Series, Vol. II, p. 37) says that it was at the instigation of Archbishop Theodore of Canterbury that Egfrith promoted St. Cuthbert to the episcopate. Plate 60b

*C1, 2. Lozenge-shaped panels with a ruby disc in the centre of a cross of white leaves on a blue ground.

D1. Fragments, miscellaneous, thirteenth and fifteenth century, largely of blue glass, including also a head swathed in a wimple and two crossed hands (from a different figure).

D2, 3, 6, 9, 12, 13. Thirteenth-century borders with foliage.

*D4. AN ARCHBISHOP, bearded, in the act of benediction, vested in amice, chasuble, pallium, jewelled gloves and maniple, all in white glass with painting in black and yellow stain, and pale murrey dalmatic; of the mitre only the tawny-stained infulae remain, the rest having been replaced by a fragment with yellow volutes. In the point of the light above the figure is a murrey flower on a blue ground.

D5, 10. In each a thirteenth-century rosette and other fragments.

D7, 8. ANGELS (one in each) swinging censers, kneeling on foliated pedestals under canopies, all in white glass with details in yellow stain, with ruby background painted with seaweed foliage. The apparels of the albs in which they are vested are decorated with rosettes in circles. These panels date from the fifteenth century. Their slanting lower edges, below which the remainder of the lights is filled in with fragments, mostly of thirteenth-century glass, show them (as Dr. Mason points out) to have been originally in tracery lights of the Nave windows. Plates 60a, c

*D11. Half-figure wearing a crown (of which only the lower rim remains), amice and alb; he holds in his left hand an open book. The lower part of the light is made up with fragments.

D14. ST. JOHN THE EVANGELIST, holding a small book in his left hand and, in his right, a scroll with the name I OHANNES AO in Lombardic lettering, preceded

---

† See G. McN. Rushforth, *Mediaeval Christian Imagery*, Oxford, 1936, p. 310.

‡ *Le Vitrail en France*, Paris, 1946, p. 29.

by a cross, all scratched in reserve through a black ground. The figure is entirely in white glass, with tawny stain on the hair and cloak; the drapery restored at the left knee with fragments not belonging. This figure is of the fourteenth century.

E1, 16. Ruby discs on blue ground, thirteenth century.

E2, 5, 10, 15. Fragments of thirteenth-century border, with foliage.

*E3. ST. MARGARET, holding in her left hand a cross-staff with a barb at its lower end, with which she is transfixing the head of a dragon. She stands, in white robe and ruby cloak, on a black-and-white chequer pavement. Blue background.

Plate 60e

E4. A MONK, tonsured, with 'pot and cover' (M). In his right hand he holds a circular object and in his left a cylinder of uncertain significance (the 'pot and cover' of Dr. Mason). He is vested in a white habit under a blue cloak; he stands against a ruby background on a pavement with a pattern of quatrefoils in a yellow-stained trellis.

E6, 11. Fragments of trellis diaper, thirteenth century.

*E7. A FEMALE SAINT (?) holding a book, under a canopy (the shafts of which are broken); ruby halo, purple cloak over a white robe patterned with rosettes on a cross-hatched ground; blue background, a white rose with yellow-stained centre and sepals in the head of the light. A technical point of interest is that the hair, painted in yellow stain on the white glass of the head, is continued in tresses in yellow pot-metal on either side of the shoulders.

*E8. A SAINTED ARCHBISHOP, standing under a canopy with a cross in his right hand and, in his left, an unidentified object in the form of a gigantic nail with flat head tapering to a point at its lower extremity. He is vested in mitre, pallium over a blue chasuble, ruby dalmatic with green fringe, yellow-stained fringed tunicle with ends of the stole hanging in front of it, plain white alb (without apparel), gloves and gold shoes (seen against a blue floor). Ruby background. Filling of thirteenth-century fragments below.

Prof. Jenkins has suggested that this may be St. Denis (of France) and that the nail (if such it is) may be due to a confusion with Dionysius, one of the Seven Sleepers of Ephesus, whose traditional emblem was a nail. A possible alternative is that the saint represented may be Archbishop Dunstan, indicated by the golden nail as an attribute of his activities as a goldsmith (instead of his customary emblem, a pair of pincers, in allusion to his encounter with the Devil).

*E9. A SAINTED ARCHBISHOP, standing under a canopy (defective). He is vested like the saint in E8; his chasuble pale blue, yellow dalmatic (pot-metal) with dark green fringe, yellow-stained fringe to tunicle, plain alb. Ruby background.

E10, 11, 15, 16. Fragments of border, thirteenth century.

*E12. AN APOSTLE, bearded, with right hand raised and forefinger pointing up. Yellow-stained book in left hand. White robe, ruby cloak, yellow-diapered shoes. He stands on a diamond-pattern chequer pavement; blue background.

Plate 60d.

*E13. A FEMALE SAINT, standing holding a book in her right hand, against a ruby background. Halo and circlet (jewelled with rosettes) stained in deep brownish-yellow; blue cloak over a white robe with star-patterned apparel at the skirt.

Plate 63

E14. A MARTYR SAINT, bearded, standing on a chequer pavement, with palm-branch in his left hand, his right hand raised palm to the front. Blue halo, green cloak over a murrey robe. Filling of thirteenth-century fragments below.   Plate 63

MAIN LIGHTS

F. *The original cusped heads of the uppermost range of main lights remain, with pinnacles set against grounds of various colours as follows:—

F1, 8, blue; F2, 3, 5, 7, ruby; F4, ruby and purple; F6, purple.

G. At this level are eight panels consisting of fifteenth- or early sixteenth-century† quatrefoil tracery-lights from elsewhere, each in a square flanked by lengths of thirteenth-century foliage border to fill up the rectangle of the panel, and enclosed by a narrow outer edging of miscellaneous later fragments, as follows:—

G1. ARMS OF GAGE, Party per saltire argent and azure a saltire gules. The edging is composed mostly of fifteenth-century canopy fragments but includes also a white bell-flower reserved on a black ground, which may be compared with the 'Canterbury Bells' on a continuous stem in the borders of fourteenth-century windows at St. Nicholas, Harbledown.

G2. ARMS OF WYKEHAM, Argent two chevrons sable between three roses gules. The centres of the roses are abraded white. The background ruby with feathery diaper. The outer edging is made up of fragments of architectural canopies. The arms are familiar as those of William of Wykeham's foundations, New College, Oxford, and Winchester College.

G3. ARMS OF WILLIAM WARHAM (Archbishop 1504–32), See of Canterbury (as on p. 136 above, except that the cross-staff is *entirely or*) impaling Gules a fess or in chief a goat's head couped argent in base three escallops argent.

G4. ARMS OF QUEEN MARY BOHUN, first wife of Henry IV (m. 1381, d. 1394), France Modern quartering England, impaling Azure a bend argent cotized or between six lions rampant or (Bohun). The lions of England are painted in silver-yellow stain on a white glass field (instead of gules). The edging of fifteenth- and sixteenth-century glass includes fragments of architecture, inscriptions in Roman capitals (on the left side: U R . . USH; OF A; THE; on the right: IS . . RDO; LL; NI), a quarry with the sacred initials *ihs* in black-letter, and quatrefoils in amber-yellow stain.
          Plate 63

G5. ARMS OF THOMAS ARUNDEL, Quarterly 1 and 4, Gules a lion rampant or (Fitzalan, 2, and 3, Checky or and azure (Warenne) within a bordure engrailed argent. Thomas Arundel was Archbishop of Canterbury (1396–1413); the shield shows his personal arms without the impalement of the See. Outer edging of fifteenth- and sixteenth-century fragments, including the head of a youth, part of a seraph with hands clasped in prayer, a horned head (perhaps of a bull) with wings; also pieces of fourteenth-century quarries with four-petalled flowers.   Plate 63

G6. ARMS OF ARCHBISHOP THOMAS BECKET, See of Canterbury (as on p. 136 above) impaling Argent three choughs sable (partly effaced). Fragments, mostly of architecture, compose the outer edging.   Plate 63

---

† They include the arms of Archbishop Warham, 1504–32.

G7. An unidentified shield, Party fesswise battled of one embrazure sable and argent a griffin's head couped or between three rowels of six points argent in chief and three annulets sable in base. Outer edging as in G6.　　　　　Plate 63

G8. A shield, Quarterly, 1 and 4, Checky gules and sable, 2 and 3, Gules a saltire argent (Nevill of Raby). The 1st and 4th quarters, in which the field is partly of blue and partly of ruby glass, have been made up in modern glass and were perhaps originally Azure fretty argent (Etchingham). Outer edging as in G6.

H. At this level eight twelfth-century figures from the Choir Clerestory have been inserted as follows:

H1. Joanna (see p. 42); H2. Er (see p. 41); H3. Joseph (see p. 40); H4. David (see p. 37); H5. Nathan (see p. 38); H6. Jonan (see p. 40); H7. Jose (see p. 41); H8. Juda (see p. 43).

I. Panels made up of fifteenth-century quatrefoil lights from the traceries of the Nave, surrounded by fragments of thirteenth-century foliage within a narrow edging of contemporary glass fragments, as follows:

I1. A SERAPH, with scarf round the neck, six wings, hands upraised with palms to the front, standing on a wheel of which only part is in view. The figure is flanked by two suns with alternate white and gold rays. The spandrels of the panel are filled with thirteenth-century foliage; in the outer edging are fifteenth- and sixteenth-century fragments including canopy and pavement details, large-scale drapery, part of a sixteenth-century console inscribed [I]VSTITI[A], *mo* and parts of other inscriptions in black-letter, and fleurs-de-lis in reserve, stained yellow, on a black ground.

　　The seraph may be compared with one in a window dating from the second half of the fifteenth century at Great Malvern Priory (reproduced by G. McN. Rushforth, *op. cit.*, Fig. 98).　　　　　Plate 61b

I2. ARMS OF THE PRIORY OF CHRIST CHURCH (as in A2). The shield has been partly restored (the lettering is modern); it hangs by a white strap on an olive-green tree against a murrey background. The spandrels are filled as in I1; in the edging are fifteenth-century fragments including part of a quarry with a large bird, the hindquarters of an animal (hare or rabbit), part of an open book, and a fragment (two hands and feathers with peacock's eyes) of an angel apparently playing a viol.

I3. AN ANGEL standing between two rayed suns, clothed in an amice and an alb, with quatrefoil-patterned apparel, holding a shield with the arms of Criol, Or two chevrons and a quarter gules. Spandrels as in I1. Among the fifteenth-century fragments in the edging are *pr, n,* and other scraps of black-letter inscriptions, canopy work, and a finial, perhaps of a bedstead or seat, in front of a cloth with a pattern of cinquefoils.

　　'The Criols had held, at various periods, important offices in connection with the county of Kent' (Willement, *Heraldic Notices*, p. 18).　　　　　Plate 61d

I4. ARMS OF UFFORD, Sable a cross engrailed or. Shield hung by a white strap on an olive-green tree, background ruby. Spandrels as in I1; the fragments in the edging include part of a fourteenth-century quarry with a small quatrefoil in the middle, another quarry fragment with a fleur-de-lis, fragments of drapery (one of them shows a pattern of flowers in yellow stain, another the end of a scroll and a fringed border hanging over a pavement of oblong tiles), part of an angel's wing.　　　　　Plate 63

Plate XVII

(a) ARMS OF THE SALT FISHMONGERS'
COMPANY.

(b) ARMS OF BARNEWELL. Two tracery
lights of a west window in the North-West
Transept, which was probably the gift of John
Barnewell in memory of Thomas Barnewell,
Alderman of London (d. 1446). About 1450.
P. 153.

I5. ARMS OF CHICHELE, Or a chevron between three cinquefoils gules. The shield is hung by a white strap on a blue tree against a pale murrey background. Spandrels as in I4; the fifteenth-century fragments in the edging, mostly of canopies, include also foliage, part of a scroll (illegible) and an eight-petalled flower.   Plate 63

I6. AN ANGEL, similar to that of I3, and between two suns, holding a shield with the arms of Fitzwilliam, Lozengy argent and gules. Spandrels as in I1; the fragments in the edging, mostly of fifteenth-century canopies, include also a crown, part of the Bourchier slip-knot badge (see p. 154), part of a fish, and fragments dating from the second or third decade of the sixteenth century, painted in reserve on a black ground, with volutes, and two griffin's heads in Renaissance style.   Plate 61c

I7. ARMS OF ST. AUGUSTINE'S ABBEY, CANTERBURY, Sable a cross argent. The shield hangs by a white strap from a blue tree; ruby background. Spandrels as in I3; the fragments in the edging include chequer pavement and other fragments of architecture, and a fragment dating from the fourteenth century, with maple-leaf foliage in yellow stain on a stem.   Plate 63

I8. A SERAPH between two suns, similar to that in I1 (the feet missing and one hand replaced by a fragment of wing). Spandrels as in I1; the fifteenth-century fragments in the edging include a variety of architectural details and part of a large-scale ermine cloak.   Plate 61a

K. * Original cusped heads with pinnacles of canopies against varied grounds, as follows:

K1, 3, 6, 8, blue; K2, 7, purple; K4, 5, ruby.

L. Panels made up as in I, with fifteenth-century shields, in some cases hung on trees, surrounded by fragments of thirteenth-century foliage, as follows:

L1. ROYAL ARMS (late fourteenth century), France Ancient quartering England. In the edging are the pointed head of a fourteenth-century canopy, a thirteenth-century fragment of a man in armour (probably from the Trinity Chapel), and fifteenth-century fragments including the coiled end of a large scroll and parts of the slip-knot badge of Bourchier, and of the shield with white billets abraded out of ruby 'flash' of Louvaine (compare p. 154).

L2. A shield, Quarterly, 1 and 4, Gules a fess between four crosslets or with a crescent sable on the fess for difference (Beauchamp of Bergavenny); 2 and 3, Quarterly, 1 and 4, Or three chevrons gules (Clare), 2 and 3, Quarterly argent and gules fretty or a bendlet sable (Despenser). The crosslets in the first quarter should correctly be six, not four. The arms are probably those of Richard Beauchamp, Earl of Worcester, Second Baron Bergavenny. The edging is made up of fifteenth-century fragments, including a scrap of a face in armour (an eye and part of a raised visor), and inscription (*osit* in black black-letter on a yellow-stained band), as well as the letters HO (sixteenth century), probably from the Garter motto, *Honi soit*, etc.

L3. ROYAL ARMS (as in L1). The edging of fifteenth-century fragments includes details of architecture, a quarry with a quatrefoil ornament, a bare foot among herbage, and *Sp*, also *er* and *n*, in yellow-stained black-letter.

L4. ARMS OF COCKFIELD, Azure a cross checky argent and gules. The blue field is diapered with feather-pattern scratched through a grey wash; the chequers are painted each with a cogged circle inscribed in a cross. The shield is hung on a tree, as in I2, set in a quatrefoil from a tracery light, the spandrels being filled with thirteenth-century foliage. The strap of the shield yellow, the tree green, the background ruby, with seaweed diaper in reserve. Among the surrounding fragments are part of the left hand of Christ and a nail (from a Crucifixion), part of a leg (apparently also from a Crucifixion, but another, on a smaller scale), and part of a griffin. This shield has been inserted recently in place of a made-up shield.

L5. An unidentified shield, Or a chevron between three fusils sable. The field has a feathery scroll diaper scratched through grey pigment. The setting is as in L4; the strap ruby, tree green, background blue. In the edging are part of a thirteenth-century face, part of a tonsured head (fifteenth century), small fragments of two faces (a fifteenth-century eye and a sixteenth-century nose, respectively), a right hand holding a staff or sceptre. The arms are perhaps those of Parker, in which the fusils are correctly *azure;* this tincture may have been rendered in black pigment owing to the difficulty of inserting fusils in blue glass.

L6. The ROYAL ARMS (as in L1). The edging includes thirteenth-century *grisaille* foliage and fifteenth-century architectural details.

L7. ARMS OF BARNEWELL, as in the West Window of the North-West Transept (see p. 153). The edging, mostly fifteenth century, includes fragments of canopies, part of a quarry with the Bourchier slip-knot (as in L1), part of the Sacred Initials *ihs,* and part of a falcon (probably from the Bourchier crest, see p. 154).

L8. The ROYAL ARMS as in L1. The fragments in the edging include fifteenth-century architectural details and wings.

M. Figures from the Choir Clerestory and elsewhere, as follows:

M1. Abraham (see p. 35); M2. Unidentified (see p. 44); M3. Ezekias (see p. 39); M4. David (see p. 68); M5. Unidentified (see p. 68); M6. Ozias (see p. 39); M7. Unidentified (see p. 44); M8. Zorobabel (see p. 42).

N. Quatrefoil tracery lights of the fifteenth century, each containing a shield hung by its strap from a tree, as at I2; the spandrels of the panels are, in each case, filled with thirteenth-century foliage, and the whole is enclosed by a narrow edging made up of fragments, mostly of the fifteenth century.

N1. ARMS OF JOHN HAUTE of Surrenden Manor (Or a cross engrailed gules with a crescent argent on the cross for difference), impaling an unidentified blazon (Dancetty argent and azure on a chief ermine an indecipherable charge). The crescent is done by abrasion of the ruby 'flash' of the cross; in the impaled coat the charge on the chief is also in ruby glass, partly abraded. The shield hangs by a strap of ruby glass (on which the 'flash' has now almost disappeared) on a green tree against a murrey background. The edging consists of fifteenth-century canopy fragments. The shield did not belong originally in its present position, being too small, a crescent-shaped green piece having been inserted below its base.

N2. ARMS OF HEVER, Gules a cross argent. The shield is surrounded by a bordure azure, which is, however, perhaps a non-heraldic accretion. The strap is white, the tree green, the background murrey and blue. Among the fifteenth-century fragments in the edging are crowns and foliage, and part of the base of a column. Dr. Mason suggests that the shield may be 'that of Cobham, unless indeed, it is here intended to represent St. George'; the Cobham arms, however, show a cross ermine, not argent, on a field of gules, and in the shield of St. George the tinctures are reversed, gules on argent. Gules a cross *or* within a bordure azure is given by Papworth as the blazon of Rockelton.

N3. ARMS OF ARCHBISHOP WILLIAM WARHAM (as in G3 above). The strap white, the tree green, the background ruby. The fifteenth-century fragments in the edging include small architectural details and crowns from borders.

N4. ARMS OF HOLLAND, Gules three lions passant gardant or within a bordure argent. The bordure is diapered with small flowers. Strap amber-yellow, tree murrey, background olive-green with 'seaweed' diaper. The fragments in the edging include fifteenth-century canopy-work, foliage, the toes and tips of the feathers on the leg of a seraph (as on I1), black-letter inscription (*rd* and the upper half of large-scale letters *Scūs*, the initial being yellow-stained); also a fragment of a fourteenth-century quarry with a yellow-stained maple-leaf. The fragment of lettering may be for *Sanctus*, or possibly *Secundus*, from the name-label of one of the Kings of England in the West Window (see p. 118). Commander Messenger suggests the arms may be for Thomas Holland, K.G. (d. 1400), or Edmund Holland, K.G. (d. 1407), father of Lady Margaret Holland (see p. 151), 1st and 2nd Earls of Kent.

N5. ARMS OF ETCHINGHAM, Azure fretty argent. The strap orange, the tree pale murrey, the background yellowish-green. The edging fragments include three pieces of maple-leaf quarries, as in N4, as well as part of a border with an ivy stem and leaf (also of the fourteenth century), part of a door with ring knocker, and a scrap painted with billets in yellow stain on a grey ground (perhaps part of the shield of Louvaine, see p. 154), all of the fifteenth century. This shield may perhaps relate to William Etchingham, whose daughter Joan married Sir Arnold Savage, the Speaker (see Messenger, *Heraldry of Canterbury Cathedral*, p. 86).

N6. ARMS OF STRABOLGI, Paly of six or and sable (the sable pales are rendered in dark purple glass). Strap white, tree green, background ruby. In the edging are several crowns and lozenge-motives from borders, together with fragments of canopies, all of the fifteenth century.

'David de Strabolgi, Earl of Athol, by marriage with Isabel, co-heir of Richard de Chilham, obtained considerable lands in the county of Kent. His wife died at Chilham Castle, in 1292, and was buried in the Cathedral' (Willement, *Heraldic Notices*, p. 81).

N7. ARMS OF HARDRES, Gules a lion rampant ermine over all a chevron or. The chevron is diapered with pinnate foliage. Strap ruby, tree green, background purple. The fifteenth-century fragments in the edging include one with part of a right hand, and another (perhaps from a figure of St. John the Evangelist) showing human toes and the legs of an eagle standing on an angular platform; there is also an ivy-stem, stained yellow, with white leaves in reserve on a black ground, probably of the fourteenth century. The arms are to be seen also in windows at Upper Hardres Church.

N8. ARMS OF WIKE (*alias* Wyke), of Somerset, Argent a chevron gules between three crosses moline sable. Strap yellow, tree pale murrey, background pale blue. In the edging are fifteenth-century fragments of battlements and pinnacles, and part of a quarry with an oak-leaf.

O. Original cusped heads as at K, with varied grounds as follows:

O1, 3, 6, 8, blue; O2, ruby; O4, 5, 7, purple.

P. All eight panels at this level contain shields with the Royal Arms. They occupy each a middle strip flanked by thirteenth-century borders and hang on a stem which divides above the shield into three branches with terminal flowers (except in P6, where the shield hangs on a tree, as in I2). The shields are not all of the same period. In P3 and P7, the first and fourth quarters show France Ancient (Azure, semy of fleurs-de-lis or); in the remainder the charge is France Modern (Azure, three fleurs-de-lis or). The accessories and details vary as follows (in most cases architectural fragments are comprised in the surround):

P1. Strap blue, stem green, flowers white, background murrey.

P2. In the third and fourth quarters of the shield, the lions are missing. Strap white, stem and flowers murrey, background olive-green.

P3. Strap white, stem green, flowers white, background ruby.

P4. Strap yellow, stem green, flowers white, background murrey. Part of a quarry, with a quadrifoliate ornament, is included among the fragments in the edging.

P5. Similar to P4, except as regards the edging.

P6. Strap white, tree green, background ruby.

P7. Strap, stem, and flowers white, background purple. The surrounding fragments include part of a large Tudor rose, also a small fleur-de-lis in reserve on a black ground.

P8. Strap blue, stem green, flowers white, background purple. The fragments in the edging include, besides canopy work, part of the head of a horse with bit in its mouth.

Q. Figures from the Choir Clerestory as follows:

Q1. Lamech (see p. 33); Q2. Noe (see p. 33); Q3. Thara (see p. 35); Q4. Jared (see p. 32); Q5. Mathusala (see p. 32); Q6. Phalec (see p. 34); Q7. Ragau (see p. 34); Q8. Enoch (see p. 32).

R. The panels at the foot of the window are entirely made up of thirteenth-century glass within a narrow edging of fifteenth-century architectural fragments. They are thus described by Dr. Mason (p. 14).

'Beneath the great figures are squares containing green rosettes in quatrefoils. The corners of the squares are filled with demi-semi-circles. These demi-semi-circles came from one of the windows of the North-East Transept, where they formed eight complete circles. The rosettes in quatrefoils come from the south side of St. Thomas's Chapel' (the Trinity Chapel).

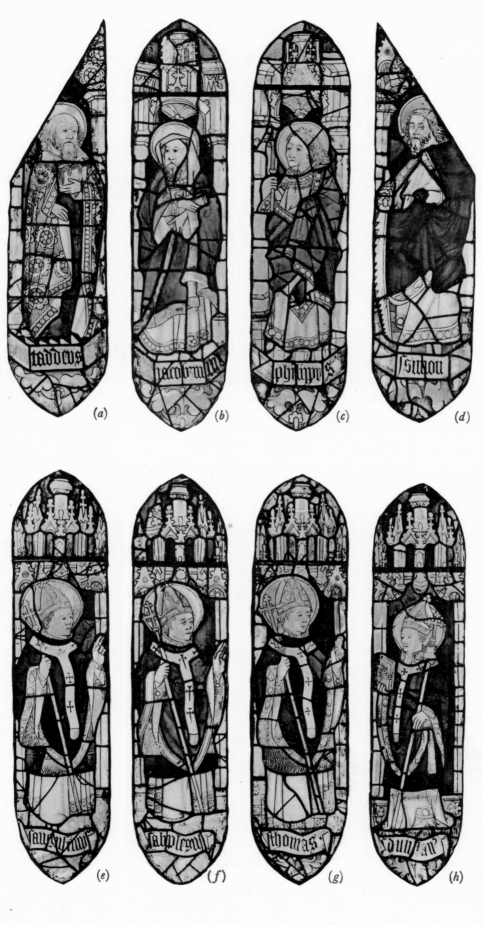

(a) taddeus

(b) iacobominu

(c) philippus

(d) ſſimon

(e) auguſtini

(f) alfegus

(g) thomas

(h) dunſtan

(a) St. Thaddaeus
(b) St. James the Less
(c) St. Philip
(d) St. Simon
(e) St. Augustine of
    Canterbury
(f) St. Alphege
(g) St. Thomas of Canterbury
(h) St. Dunstan

about 1470

ROYAL WINDOW

pp. 165–169

70

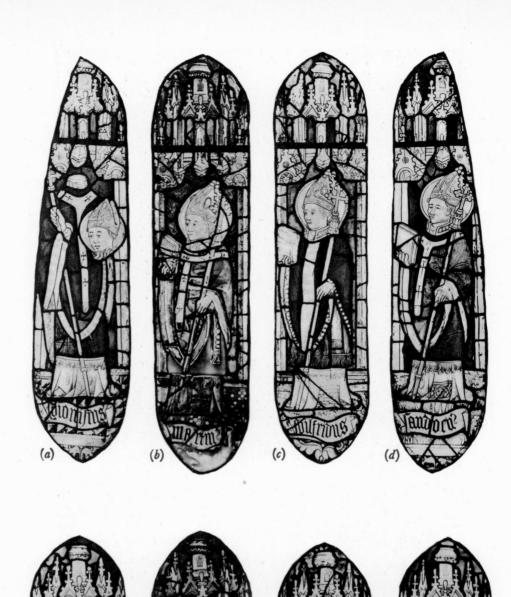

(a) St. Denis
(b) St. Martin
(c) St. Wilfred
(d) St. Audoen
(e) St. Augustine of Hippo
(f) St. Jerome
(g) St. Nicholas
(h) St. Gregory

about 1470

ROYAL WINDOW

pp. 167–169

71

Edwardus dei gracia Rex Anglie
et ffrancie et dominus hibernie

King Edward IV
ROYAL WINDOW
about 1482
p. 174

72

(a)

(c)

(a) Arms of St. George   (c) Richard, Duke of York
(b) Arms of Guldeford   (d) Edward, Prince of Wales

about 1482 ROYAL WINDOW   *pp.* 170, 173, 174

§7 West Window of South-West Transept

FRAGMENTS of fifteenth-century glass have been retained in the tracery lights of the modern window designed by the late Christopher Whall. They consist almost entirely of architectural canopy work, but include also part of a figure with hand laid on the folds of a garment, a hand holding a scroll, and a third hand (of St. Philip) holding two yellow loaves similar to those in a tracery light (C2) of the West Window (see p. 125.)

§8 St. Michael's Chapel

THE ancient glass belonging to St. Michael's Chapel, some of which was removed from its East Window to make room for the Crimean War Memorial, has recently been gathered into the easternmost window on the south side of the Chapel. The window is divided by mullions into four main lights and two rows of tracery lights, four in the upper and eight in the lower row. Newly made copies of old medallions and quarries have been inserted to make good the inadequate supply of ancient glass. The old medallions belong to two distinct periods. Some of them display badges relating to Lady Margaret Holland, whose effigy between those of her two husbands, Sir John Beaufort, Earl of Somerset, and Thomas of Lancaster, Duke of Clarence, lies on the tomb in the middle of the Chapel. The glass with these badges, a greyhound with collar and leash, for the Duke of Clarence, and a hind couchant, the badge of Lady Margaret's grandmother, the Fair Maid of Kent,* may be presumed to date from the time of the building of the Chapel, which was dedicated in 1437, eleven days before the death of the Duchess. The rest of the old medallions, like those of the Lady Chapel (p. 154), where it is probable they originally belonged, show one of the Bourchier badges—a falcon or eagle with wounded wing; the quarries which form the background of the window display, like those of the Lady Chapel, the stem of oak 'leaved and fructed', for Thomas of Woodstock (see p. 154). These Bourchier panes may be dated about 1455.

---

* The drawings of R. Scarlet (see p. 21 above) include on p. 4 one of the Beaufort shield flanked by a greyhound and hind, with the legend 'Therle of Somersett' as being 'in the first syde Wyndowe in the sayde Chappell on the South Syde'. For the hind see also p. 124 above.

The medallions and quarries are all in white glass, with painting in black and silver-yellow stain; the background in most cases is coated with a smear of grey enamel through which the various diapers and certain details of the figures are scratched out. The falcons and hounds are set in pairs facing one another. The birds stand on mounds; their feathers are rendered in some cases by painting in black, in others by scratching through the smear; they are surrounded by a border with trefoil cusping. The greyhounds are couched among herbage, with a leash attached to their collars and wound up in a tight coil; the background behind them is diapered with scratched-out 'seaweed' foliage. The hinds are similarly couched, and gorged with a coronet; by a cord attached to this they are tethered to a ring fixed among herbage on the ground. In the main lights there are four rows of medallions (A–D), the uppermost immediately below the cusped heads of the lights, and, at the foot of the window, a row of shields (E).

Of the medallions, the following are ancient:

    Falcons: A1, A4, C2.

    Greyhounds: B3, C1, C4.

    Hinds: D3.

The shields of the three upper rows are modern. Of the shields in the lowest row, two are ancient.

E1. ARMS OF ISABEL, wife of Henry Bourchier, Earl of Essex (as on p. 154).

E2. ARMS OF CLARENCE, Quarterly, 1 and 4, France Modern, 2 and 3, England, over all a label of three points ermine. (Partly restored.)   Plate 76a–e

§9 West Window of North-West Transept

THE northernmost upper window on the west side of the transept is shown by the heraldry of its tracery lights to have been the gift of a freeman of the Salt Fishmongers' Company, of the Barnewell family. Willement, *Heraldic Notices*, p. 36, quotes a manuscript in the British Museum (Add. No. 5479, fol. 253) as giving 'the following inscriptions which were formerly perfect in this window. "*Orate pro anima Thomae Barnewell Piscenarii ac Aldermani London Orate pro Bono Statu Johñis Barnewell, Civis et Piscenarii London et Emmae Uxoris ejus*" '.* He further states that according to 'a curious MS. by Smith, Rouge Dragon', in his possession 'Thomas Bernwell was Sherif, an. 1435, and was buried at St. Mildred's, in Fryday St. an.

---

* The inscription, inaccurately transcribed by Willement, has been corrected by the Author from the original MS.

1446'. The window was doubtless the gift of John Barnewell in memory of Thomas, presumed to be his father. An interesting account of the dealings of the Prior and monks of Christ Church with John Barnewell for the supply of fish and wine for the Priory is given in *F.C.C. Nineteenth Annual Report* (1946), pp. 33, 34; it is there shown that John Barnewell probably died in 1478 or 1479. The date of this window would thus be between 1446 and 1479, a period to which the glass is attributable on stylistic grounds; as suggested on p. 11 above, it is possible that payments made to the London glaziers, Richard Sawyer and John Pyle, in 1447–1449 may relate to this window. All three lights have four cusps; the shields in each case are surrounded by four white gambolling dolphins on a blue ground.

Reproduction: *F.C.C. Nineteenth Annual Report* (1946), pl. facing p. 33.

1. ARMS OF THE CITY OF LONDON, Argent a cross in dexter chief a sword erect gules. The blue ground of the light is diapered with rosettes in circles.

2. ARMS OF THE SALT FISHMONGERS' COMPANY, Gules three pair of keys in saltire two and one or; on a chief azure three dolphins embowed argent. The ground of the field within the bows of the keys is done by grinding holes through the yellow glass and inserting leaded discs of blue.   Colour Plate XVIIa

3. ARMS OF BARNEWELL, Per pale argent and gules three beavers in pale counterchanged. The white eyes and tusks are rendered by abrasion of the ruby glass.
Colour Plate XVIIb

§10 Lady Chapel

THE Lady Chapel (also known as the Dean's Chapel) was built by Prior Thomas Goldstone I and completed about 1455, when Thomas Bourchier was Archbishop, to replace the earlier Lady Chapel in the Crypt (see p. 16). The old glass with which its East Window is filled dates from that period,* but was probably originally in the North Window, from which it was removed to its present position some time after the erection of the baroque monument of Dean Turner, who died in 1672; this, as Mr. Caldwell has pointed out, accounts for the position in the lights of the window of the five shields, in a chevron arrangement designed to keep them clear of the pediment of the monument with an urn on its finial. It may be taken as certain that this window originally contained a figure of the Virgin (or scenes from her life) which would have been sacrificed to Puritan iconoclasm. The small uppermost tracery lights are filled with suns in golden stain 'pulled out into the shapes of

---

* It is possible that the payments made to two London glaziers in 1447–1449, mentioned on p. 11 above, may relate to the glazing of this chapel, or to the Barnewell window described above.

the openings—except four, which have blue glass' (M). Of the ten lights in the next row, Nos. 1 and 10 (from left to right) contain each a rose in a circle; Nos. 2 and 9, the slip-knot badge of the Bourchier family in golden stain on a diapered white ground; Nos. 5 and 6, the same badge but on a cusped ground golden-stained all over; Nos. 3, 4, 7, and 8, each a falcon or eagle with wings expanded and wounded in the upper edge (from the Bourchier crest), in stain, varying in their treatment and standing in pairs *vis-à-vis* on mounds, also differing in treatment; No. 7 has a crocketed border in stain. All these badges are in roundels set among quarries painted mostly with four trefoils of oak-leaves springing from a circular twig; some have a rosette with spiky rays. In the lowest row of tracery lights, Nos. 1, 2, 5, 6, 9, and 10 have the same falcon badges, some on a plain ground, some on a ground of feathery diaper, and one against a solid black ground through which small hooks have been scratched away; here again the badges are in roundels among quarries like those of the row above. The five main lights of the window have similar borders of oak-leaf ribbons in stain twined about a 'ragged staff', rising to rich finials in yellow stain. They contain shields, one in each, set at varying levels near the foot of the light against a ground of quarries which are painted in stain alternately with the Bourchier slip-knot badge and a stem of oak, 'leaved and fructed' (*i.e.*, with two acorns), the badge of Thomas of Woodstock, Duke of Gloucester, from whom Archbishop Bourchier was descended through his mother. The five shields are described below.

When Scarlet wrote his MS. description of 'Our Ladie Chapell, called sometyme Jesus Chapel' (compare p. 21 above), there were still several other shields relating to the Bourchier family, as well as that of John de Mowbray, Duke of Norfolk, in the windows of the Chapel; at that time also it seems that the shield of Archbishop Bourchier and one of the other Bourchier shields bore inscriptions (now lost), respectively: *Dn̄s Archip̄s Cantuariensis* and *Mon̄s de Bourchier*.

1. ARMS OF ISABEL, daughter of Richard of Coningsborough (second son of Edmund of Langley, Earl of Cambridge), WIFE OF HENRY BOURCHIER, EARL OF ESSEX, brother of Archbishop Bourchier (compare p. 138). Quarterly, 1 and 4, Argent a cross engrailed gules between four water-budgets sable (Bourchier), 2 and 3, Gules billety or a fess argent (Louvaine), impaling Cambridge (as on p. 138). It will be noted that the engrailing of the Bourchier cross is here *cut in the glass*, not painted (as in the shield of the Royal Window, see p. 164). The billets of Louvaine are done by abrasion of the ruby 'flash' and painting with silver-yellow stain. The lilies of France in the Cambridge coat are of leaded yellow glass inserted in openings ground out of the blue field. Owing to technical difficulties in dealing with so small a shield, the torteaux, which should be gules, are painted in black outline. (It will be noted that the arms of Isabel are here without the bordure argent with ten lions passant purpure thereon adopted by her father, as seen in the Great Cloister (see A. W. B. Messenger, *The Heraldry of Canterbury Cathedral, The Great Cloister Vault*, Canterbury, 1944, p. 80.) Plate 75a

2. ARMS OF BOURCHIER (as in the dexter impalement of No. 1) within a narrow white bordure which is probably not intended to be heraldic.

52′ 0″ × 24′ 0″

Plate XVIII

ANGEL WITH THE SHIELD OF KING
EDWARD IV. Panel (F.3) in one of the main
lights of the North (Royal) Window of the North-
West Transept. About 1482. P. 172.

3. ARMS OF BOURCHIER treated as in No. 2.   Plate 75c

4. ARMS OF FULKE BOURCHIER, LORD FITZWARINE (d. 1478), Quarterly, 1 and
4, Bourchier (as in No. 2) over all a label of three points azure charged with nine
fleurs-de-lis or, 2 and 3, Quarterly 1 and 4, Quarterly per fesse indented argent and
gules (Fitzwarine), 2 and 3, Argent two bendlets wavy sable (Hankford). The tiny
fleurs-de-lis on the labels are painted in reserve in black on transverse strips of yellow—
or possibly yellow-stained—glass. Lord Fitzwarine derived his affinity to the earlier
Lords Fitzwarine through the Hankford family.*   Plate 75b

5. ARMS OF HUMPHREY STAFFORD, DUKE OF BUCKINGHAM, Quarterly, 1 and
4, France Modern, 2 and 3 England, within a bordure argent (Buckingham), impaling
Gules a saltire argent (Nevill). This shield is so interpreted by Willement in his footnote (*Heraldic Notices*, p. 161) to Scarlet; he explains it as 'Humphrey Stafford Duke
of Buckingham, impaling Nevill, having married Anne, daughter of Ralph Earl of
Westmoreland.' On p. 38 of the same work, however, Willement gives the arms as
those of York impaling Nevill, commenting that 'Sandford mentions other instances
of the arms borne by the father of King Edward, being without the label, intimating
that by right he was king.'

    Reproductions: *F.C.C. Eighteenth Annual Report* (1945), pl. facing p. 36 (parts of first
and third main lights), accompanying an article on Archbishop Bourchier, his family
connections and career, by Prof. Claude Jenkins.

§11 The North (Royal) Window of
North-West Transept

THE great Perpendicular window filling the north wall of the North-West
Transept or Martyrdom is as regards its masonry part of the building begun
under Prior Thomas Goldstone the Elder in 1448, of which the vaulting was
not completed until after 1468. 'This goodly and glorious window, a piece in its kind
beyond compare' to quote the words of Somner in the earliest published reference
to it,† is traditionally recorded to have been given by King Edward IV, in memory
of the wedding in the transept itself of Edward I and Margaret of France by
Archbishop Robert Winchelsea in 1299‡. That it was the gift of this King is borne out
by the internal evidence of his portrait as donor introduced with those of his wife and
children; the surmise of Dr. Mason however that one of the half-figures in the topmost range (below the shields) of the tracery is also a portrait of King Edward,

---

  * See Willement, *Heraldic Notices* p. 38.

  † *Antiquities,* 2nd edition, Part I, p. 91.

  ‡ "Somner . . . says no such thing" is Dr. Mason's comment on Miss Williams's statement of
this tradition.

cannot readily be accepted (see p. 165). J. D. Le Couteur, who wrote a detailed examination of the window in *Archæologia Cantiana*, Vol. XXIX, states that the contract for it may have been placed with the glaziers in 1465 (when Edward IV visited Canterbury). He suggests 1477 at the earliest as the date of completion; but the presence in the window of the arms of Viscount Wells, to whom Princess Cicely was married after the annulment in 1482 of her first marriage (by proxy) to King James III of Scotland, proves that the window cannot have been finished before this later date. The death in the same year (1482) of Princess Mary, whose portrait also is included, warrants the assumption that the date of completion was not later than that year.

For what is known of the original character and composition of the window we are indebted to Richard Culmer, the fanatic responsible for its partial destruction, on December 13, 1643. We learn from him that it contained 'the picture of God the Father, and of Christ, besides a large Crucifixe, and the picture of the Holy Ghost, in the form of a Dove, and of the twelve Apostles'; also 'seven large pictures of the Virgin Marie, in seven several glorious appearances, as of the Angells lifting her into heaven, and the Sun, Moon and Stars under her feet, and every picture had an inscription under it, beginning with gaude Maria: as *gaude Maria sponsa dei*, that is Rejoyce Mary thou Spouse of God. There were in this window, many other pictures of Popish Saints, as of St. George &c. But their prime Cathedrall Saint—Arch-Bishop Thomas Becket was most rarely pictured in that window, in full proportion, with Cope, Rochet, miter, Crosier, and all his Pontificalibus, And in the foot of that huge window, was a title, intimating that window to be dedicated to the Virgin Mary. *In laudem &c. honorem beatissime Virginis Maria* [sic] *matris dei, &c. . . . .*' This description is followed by the famous account of the defacement of the window by 'a Minister . . . on the top of the citie ladder, near 60 steps high, with a whole pike in his hand ratling down proud Becket's glassy bones'. Mention may here be made of Culmer's statement that 'Out-landish Papists' offered for the window 'many thousand pounds'; Gostling, giving no authority, says the offer was of £10,000 and from 'a Spanish Ambassador'. From this description it may be inferred that St. George and other saints, including Becket, with the Holy Trinity in the midmost light, occupied the upper range of main lights, together with, in their heads, shields held by half-figures of angels which have either been replaced there in recent times or were never removed. The middle main range was devoted to the 'glorious appearances' of the Virgin, whilst the lowest contained the figures of the royal donor and his family, with angels holding their shields, one at the foot of each light.

At some time after it had been—in the words of Somner's second edition—'shattered to pieces in the Storm of our Civil Wars', the parts of the window were rearranged, mostly in the order in which they are now to be seen.

The North (Royal) Window of the North-West Transept

When Gostling wrote (1774), the figures of the donor and his family had already been given even greater conspicuousness by being raised to the place of honour, in the middle range of lights, than when, in accordance with the custom of their time, they were prominently displayed in the lowest range, whilst the angels holding their shields, formerly beneath them at the foot of the window, were set across the uppermost row of main lights. The middle place between the King and Queen in Gostling's time was occupied by 'a very large arched crown over the arms of the prior irradiated' (described by Burnby, 1783, as 'the arms of the church under a canopy'), and below this by a panel still in the same position. The arms, presumably those of the Priory, now borne by the Dean and Chapter (see p. 142), were at some later date, but before Westlake wrote his 3rd volume (1886), removed, and in their place was put the panel still remaining with the royal shield and supporters as used by Henry VII and Henry VIII. The presence of the extraneous lower panel now between the royal figures has led to some strange surmises. The right-hand figure in this panel, with hair falling in curls over plate armour, was taken by Gostling for 'a lady, not young, and full bosom'd'; he conjectured that she might be Margaret of Anjou, 'martial Queen' of the companion figure, Henry VI, an assumption which, he admits, involves regarding as irrelevant the mutilated legends below each figure. It is true that in a footnote he prints the presumption of 'a learned friend' that the figures were 'a part of the original window in the chapel of the martyrdom' and therefore 'a compliment to the memory of the donor's ancestors,' Edward III and his Consort, rather than 'persons so obnoxious to Edward IV as Henry VI and his Queen must have been'; the 'learned friend' supports this conjecture by reference to 'the large beard and an aspect rather ferocious' displayed by Vertue's engraving of an ancient painting of Edward III at Windsor Castle; there follow ingenious arguments too long to be quoted here, which will entertain those who have time to read them in the pages of Gostling.

It will perhaps never be known how or when this panel, which will be shown (p. 180) to be of Rhenish origin, came to be introduced into the window; it was, however, probably brought from St. Augustine's Abbey. Westlake noticed that the figures in the panel are set 'in niches of German-looking work', but makes no further comment. Le Couteur speaks of the 'female figure' and suggests that the panel is perhaps the work of 'the same artist who was employed upon the inscriptions in the tracery; . . . . it would appear that this interesting piece of work once formed part of the shrine containing the large crucifix to which the Royal Family knelt in prayer'. As will be seen when the panel is fully discussed, its style would make this surmise untenable on chronological grounds.

Even an untrained observer must be conscious of a great difference in style between the upper part of the window (the tracery lights) and what remains of the original glass belonging to the three tiers of main lights. Whilst the tracery lights are low in tone and linear in drawing, with only a moderate use of grey enamel for shading or 'matting', the royal portraits and the angels and shields relating to them are executed in glass of strong colour, with heavy shading carefully stippled to give an effect of chiaroscuro in which the influence of panel-painting in tempera is unmistakably apparent. This striking difference can only be explained on one of two assumptions: either (1) there is an interval in date, the tracery lights having presumably been inserted when the masonry of the window was completed, that is, about 1465-70, and the remainder added subsequently, at a date which, as we have seen, cannot on internal evidence have been earlier than 1482, or (2) the whole of the glazing was done at the same time (1482) but from the designs of different artists.

On examination of the two portions of the window we find the tracery lights to have much in common with traditional English work of the fifteenth century—the normal style which developed with the evolution of the distinctively English Perpendicular style of Gothic architecture; whilst some of the figures show vitality in conception and competence in drawing, there are some in which the level of achievement is lower, owing perhaps to their having been carried out by inferior painters, though perhaps from cartoons by the same designer as the remainder. There is one curious circumstance which has been the subject of remark by earlier writers: whereas the rest of the names attached to the figures are in Latin, the name below the 'Prince of the Apostles', to whom the senior station is allotted, in the dexter light of the middle pair, is written *Pieter*. Gostling in a footnote writes: 'Query: If this spelling is not German; and may show the artist was of that country?'. Dr. Mason comments: 'The name "Pieter" seems to betray a German or Dutch hand, as Gostling observed'. It is true that this form of the name is Netherlandish (Dutch or Flemish—the two were indistinguishable in the fifteenth century), not German however; but what little remains to us of fifteenth-century windows in the Low Countries shows no stylistic resemblance whatever to these paintings, whilst the architectural accessories—the canopies under which most of the figures are depicted as standing—are quite definitely English in character. Le Couteur seems to have been misled partly by this vagary of spelling and partly by the presence in the midst of the royal portraits of the 'two figures in niches of German looking work' (he quotes Westlake's phrase), into conjecturing that the firms responsible for the window had one or two German workmen, and that these executed the inscriptions and some other details, the more important part being entrusted to Englishmen. Substituting 'Netherlandish' for 'German', we may perhaps accept a foreigner among the painters (but not a foreign designer) of the tracery lights as the most plausible explanation of the mystery.

Arguing doubtless from the style of the main lights Westlake* came to the

---

* Vol. III, p. 54.

conclusion that 'if done in England' the window 'probably came from some *atelier* in Westminster'. In an unpublished paper read by the Author before the Royal Archaeological Institute in 1926 this window was mentioned in relation to others of approximately the same period showing certain features in common. There is firstly the glass in the Beauchamp Chapel of St. Mary's Church, Warwick (already referred to, on p. 120 above), the covenants for which have been preserved and show the windows to be the work of John Prudde, who was in 1433 appointed by Henry VI to be the glazier of the royal works at Westminster, a post which, on the evidence of the Westminster Abbey records, he appears to have vacated before 1484; in the same records there is mention in 1470 of a certain 'Thomas the Glazier' who may have been Prudde's assistant or successor. There is a strong presumption of a workshop in Westminster or its neighbourhood producing windows continuously throughout the second half of the fifteenth century for the royal chapels and palaces (its location in 1505, when Barnard Flower was appointed King's Glazier, may have been in Southwark, where Flower and many of his assistants are known to have been domiciled).

It is reasonable to suppose that the Canterbury glass with royal portraits, a gift from the King, was furnished from this same workshop. It is interesting to compare it with the fragmentary East Window at Little Malvern Priory church, inserted about 1481 by Bishop Alcock of Worcester (later of Ely), tutor of Edward IV; like the Canterbury window this originally contained kneeling portrait figures of the Royal Family, though there now remain only Edward, Prince of Wales, and the lower parts of the Queen and her daughters (see Plate B(*f*)). The Little Malvern window, though similar in the general arrangement of the figures kneeling with hangings behind them under canopies, differs widely in style from that at Canterbury; like the glass in the neighbouring priory church at Great Malvern, it seems likely to have been painted in a workshop somewhere in that region. This relationship of the Royal Window to others of its period, and its kindred origin, were discussed by the Author in an article in the *Sixth Annual Report* of the Friends (1933, p. 34) from which the following is quoted (with emendations which later research has prompted):—

'In comparing the window with others of its time we may take first the great window in St. Mary's Hall, Coventry, with figures of nine kings (or reputed kings) of England—they include the Emperor Constantine. This window is credibly conjectured to have been set up early in the reign of King Henry VII to celebrate the visit of that monarch to Coventry and was probably the gift of the king. Here again, as at Canterbury, we find the figures set against curtains hanging from a crested board; those behind some of the figures are decorated with monograms relating to the Coventry guilds enclosed in circles in the same manner as the various badges which enrich the hangings in the Canterbury window. At Great Malvern Priory we find kneeling figures under canopies, including Arthur, Prince of Wales, brother of Henry VIII; there is good reason to think that this figure dates from the year 1501.* Here again we see a crested board with a fringe below it and curtains hanging behind the figure. There are somewhat similar royal figures of which the identity is not established with certainty† in the chapel of Christ's College, Cambridge; they are older than most of the present building itself and were doubtless brought from the mother foundation, God's-house, from which Christ's College was descended.‡ Lastly may be mentioned the apse windows of Westminster Abbey; they also may date from the early years of Henry VII's reign, and, though much mutilated, they present several features in common with the Canterbury window. The curtains in the Westminster windows are treated in a somewhat more realistic manner; they hang in loose folds and are attached to the crested beam by means of a curtain-rod and rings. In the painting of the faces at Westminster—or of those amongst them which are not later substitutions for the originals—there is a decided similarity of style to those of our Edward IV and Elizabeth Woodville.

'The similarities in general layout to be found in all these windows may in my opinion be accounted for by the assumption that all except those at the Malverns, which are markedly different in style, came from the same workshop, and this was the royal workshop at Westminster. We know that this workshop supplied glass for Windsor, Winchester College and Eton College, and it is natural to suppose that the windows at Canterbury and Coventry, which were gifts from the Sovereign, were also painted there. In these great windows we have in fact the last monument of English Gothic glass-painting, before fashions were completely changed, as we may see in such places as Fairford or King's College, Cambridge, by the introduction, under Henry VII and Henry VIII, of artists from Germany and the Netherlands.'

In glass-painting it was the appointment by Henry VII, in 1505, of Barnard Flower and, after his death in 1517, of his successor Galyon Hone (both aliens from Flanders or Germany) as King's Glazier, that brought about a change of style; this change, which can be seen not only at Fairford and King's College but also in the Chapel of The Vyne in Hampshire, in the windows at Basingstoke Parish Church formerly in the Chapel of the Holy Ghost (built like the Vyne by Sir Reginald Bray,

---

* Or 1502, between his marriage in November 1501, and the death of his mother, also portrayed in the window, three months later; see Rushforth, *op. cit.*, p. 369.

† Two are almost certainly Henry VII and his Queen, Elizabeth of York, the Princess Elizabeth of the Canterbury window (not Henry's mother, Lady Margaret Beaufort foundress of the College, as generally supposed); another is probably Henry VI, who gave the first charter to the parent society of God's-house.

‡ Entries in the building account of Christ's College give reason for believing that the chapel is substantially that of God's-house, refounded by Henry VI on the present site of Christ's College when the original building was pulled down to make room for the building of King's College Chapel on its site; the structure was modified in 1508 and later, to adapt it for the new college. One entry (1510) provides for 'the setting up of all the old glasse in the chapell' (A. H. Lloyd, *Early History of Christ's College*, Cambridge, 1934, p. 315).

for many years Governor of Calais and thus in touch with Netherlandish artists), in the scanty remnants surviving until recently of the original glass of King Henry VII's Chapel at Westminster Abbey, and in the small church of Withcote, Leicestershire. Here we have windows of distinctly Flemish character, markedly different from the style, of English parentage, previously followed in the royal workshop and exemplified in the Canterbury window.

To sum up, it may be pointed out that the difference of character between the tracery lights and the main lights of the Royal Window is due to the fact that the former, whether executed some years earlier (probably when the window was first commissioned) or contemporaneously with the latter, are the work of a designer and painters, probably local, following an obsolescent provincial manner and out of touch with the latest developments of the style, whilst the latter exhibit the ideas current in the leading school of glass-painting, that of the King's Glazier in the Capital. This school, though advanced, and not unaffected by the developments of panel painting in tempera, was still English and Gothic in its traditions and distinct from contemporary Continental schools, in spite of certain parallelisms that can be observed; it had not yet given place to the new Renaissance fashions which only become perceptible in glass-painting as in the other arts in England after the introduction of artists from abroad in the reigns of Henry VII and Henry VIII.

TRACERY LIGHTS

The tracery lights display a uniformity of style and colouring which show them to be the work of a single artist so far as their design is concerned, but an unevenness of execution due probably to the fact that more than one hand was employed, either in making the cartoons or in transferring them to glass; an indication of this is that some of the figures are noticeably better drawn than others, whilst the use of yellow stain for the eyebrows in a single instance only (St. Simon) points to the same probability. Their range of colours is restrained—limited, with the exception of two lights on the extreme left of the window, to ruby, murrey (deepening here and there to purple), blue, and white glass with yellow stain; the colours vary a little in tone, but are mostly pale. The two exceptional lights, showing green in their background, are unaccountable and must be regarded as instances of that waywardness of medieval artistic practice, which was not over-careful about a rigidly balanced symmetry. There are several instances of the custom of glass-painters in the Middle Ages already discussed (p. 13) of using a single cartoon repeatedly, perhaps with slight variations or in reverse, for different figures; thus one cartoon has served for the flanking half-figures in the second tier (B1, B10), another for Daniel (B3) and Amos (B7), a third for Ezra (B4), Micah (B8) and St. James the Great (C5). Isaiah (B2) does duty in reverse, with adjustments, as Ezekiel (B9); St. Bartholomew (C2) and St. John the Evangelist (C3) provide a similar case. Other correspondences among the Apostles are those of Paul with Philip and of Thomas with Matthew. This economy of means is exhibited especially in the figures of sainted ecclesiastics in the lowest tier (D); here a single cartoon can be recognised in Nos. 2, 4, 6, 8, 10, 12 and 14 and again, reversed and varied, in Nos. 3, 7, 9, 11 and 13.

161

Height 52 feet, width 22 feet

DIAGRAM OF NORTH (ROYAL) WINDOW OF NORTH-WEST TRANSEPT

The North (Royal) Window of the North-West Transept

A feature of these lights which has not been mentioned in earlier publications*
and seems indeed to be without recorded parallel is the presence in many of them of
painters' marks. These occur chiefly in the lowest range (D), where they are painted
in black and consist of various combinations of small crosses and strokes; they differ
from light to light—no two lights show the same mark—and in some instances appear
on many of the panes, both white and coloured, in the light. This circumstance
seems to prove that they are intended not as 'signatures' of the painter but as aids
to the glazier charged with the work of assembling and leading-up the several parts;
moreover different marks are seen on lights which are obviously the work of one hand.
The only mark observed elsewhere than in range D is that on St. Thaddaeus (C1),
which is not painted but wiped out of the smear of grey enamel (see p. 165).

The uppermost range (B) below the two shields which occupy the summit of the
window is devoted, apart from two half-figures on the flanks, to Prophets, including
St. John the Baptist, who foretold the coming of Our Lord. Next below (C) come the
Twelve Apostles; in the lowest tier of tracery lights (D) are fourteen sainted church-
men of whom several have some connection with Canterbury and Becket, either
directly as Archbishops (Augustine, Dunstan, Alphege, Anselm, and St. Thomas
Becket himself) or indirectly, such as St. Gregory, the Pope who sent St. Augustine
on his mission, or St. Denis, to whom with St. Alphege Becket commended his
cause at the moment of his death, or St. Martin of Tours, to whom it was surmised
that Queen Bertha of Kent re-dedicated the little church on Roman foundations in
which her husband Ethelbert was baptised. It may be mentioned here that scenes
from the life of St. Gregory were amongst those now lost in the 12th of the early
'Theological Windows.'† Wilfred and Audoen find places as saints whose bodies
were brought as gifts to Canterbury from Ripon and Normandy respectively, when
Odo was Archbishop.‡

The setting of these figures shows a general uniformity; all except B2, B9, C1 and
C12 are under architectural canopies and have, with one exception, their names
written on a tablet (in rows B, C) or a scroll (row D) below the pavement or sward
on which they stand; the pointed base of the light, with few exceptions, is filled with
a pair of large branching leaves. The canopies of the Prophets have ogee-arched
vaulted tops, varied in B7 and B8 by a second vaulted opening above. Those of the
Apostles have lateral turrets and pinnacles above their vaulted arch; exceptions are
C6 and C7, which have a vaulted upper stage like B7 and B8. The canopies of the
lowest tier (D) are more elaborate, with crocketed pinnacles, lateral vaults, four
openings in their lower range and latticed windows in a middle turret above.

The figures of ecclesiastics form an admirable illustration of the canonical vestments of the fifteenth century. All but St. Jerome and St. Gregory, in their cardinal's
hat and papal tiara respectively, wear the jewelled episcopal mitre with, behind it, a
plain bordered halo (in the case of Jerome the halo has gold rays); they are vested
in white amice with pattern of discs, chasuble (wrongly described by Gostling as a
cope), dalmatic and alb; in some cases the stole and tunic are also visible. The alb
differs from what is usual in displaying round its hem a wide ornamental border or
orphrey with a plain interruption in front, instead of the customary patterned
square or 'apparel' in the middle. Most of the figures have episcopal tasselled gloves,

---

* Mr. Caldwell had already observed it when the Author drew his attention to it.

† See Somner (ed. Battely 1703), part I, Appendix pp. 30, 31; see also p. 51 above.

‡ See Willis, *Architectural History*, pp. 4, 5.

but SS. Denis, Wilfred, Dunstan and Audoen show a bare right hand. Dr. Mason points out that, of the bishops, only St. Nicholas carries a pastoral staff or crosier; the others—SS. Wilfred, Augustine of Hippo, Martin and Blaze—have the same archiepiscopal cross as the archbishops. Likewise all the figures except SS. Wilfred and Jerome have the pall, the crosses on which in the cases of all but SS. Blaze, Alphege and Audoen are merely formy instead of the usual formy fitchy.

The small openings in the intervals between the larger tracery lights are filled with various designs. In five 'eyes' at the summit of the window are stars or suns with rays in yellow stain; on the narrow slit at each end of range C are oak-leaves painted in yellow.

A1. SHIELD with Royal arms as borne from 1405 (France Modern quartering England as at 5(*a*), p. 130). The fleurs-de-lis and lions are in golden glass leaded in the blue and ruby grounds respectively. The triangle above the shield filled with purple glass within white borders; below the point, stem-and-berry pattern wiped out of grey matt and yellow-stained on white glass. Plate 67a

A2. SHIELD with the arms of Archbishop Thomas Bourchier (1454–1486), Azure, a cross-staff or with its cross argent and over all a pall argent charged with four crosses formy sable (See of Canterbury), impaling Quarterly, 1 and 4, Argent a cross engrailed gules and four water-budgets sable, for Bourchier, 2 and 3 Gules billety a fess argent, for Louvaine. The blue ground of Canterbury is diapered with discs scratched through a matting; the pall is curved at the top, not Y-shaped as in most of the shields of the See. The engrailing is rendered by painting in black, mostly concealed by the leads. The triangle above and pattern below as in A1.

There is a contemporary shield with the arms of Bourchier as Archbishop in a window at Tawstock Church, Devon. Plate 67b

B1. HALF-FIGURE OF A YOUNG MAN wearing a white hat with broad brim turned up in front and decorated with a rosette-like jewel, and purple gown or tunic, with fur collar in golden glass; he holds in one hand a book, in the other a folded sheet of paper. Background blue with white border; amber stain on the book. See B10. Plate 67c

B2. ISAIAH. Standing figure, bearded, in pale grey-blue turban and deep purple cloak with border of rosettes on white, over a white robe with large rosettes in reserve on yellow-stain ground. At either side herbage partly painted in black, partly scratched through a grey smear. He holds a book in his left hand, in his right a scroll inscribed *Isayas* (missing when Gostling wrote and since retrieved). Background white painted with rosettes. Plate 68a

B3. DANIEL. He wears a white soft cap and white cloak with a border of discs over a murrey robe; he stands on a chequered pavement with his name: *daniel* and branching foliage below, under a canopy with blue background. In his right hand a coiled scroll. Plate 67f

B4. EZRA. Blue hat, white cloak with border of discs and lozenges in stain over a deep murrey robe; in his left hand a crumpled sheet. Chequered pavement with name: *esdras;* canopy with ruby background. Plate 67g

B5. ST. JOHN THE BAPTIST. He is bareheaded and barefoot and wears a ruby mantle with border of discs on white over his camel-hair coat, in which the head of the camel is seen hanging down; in his left hand he supports his emblem, the Agnus Dei, on a book; his right hand is raised in blessing. Chequered pavement, name: *Iohes;* blue background to canopy.　　　　　　　　　　　Plate 67h

This figure and B9 (Micah) are described as 'lost' in Gostling's list and have since been recovered.

B6. JEREMIAH. He is haloed, bareheaded and bald and wears a white robe, patterned with large rosettes reserved on yellow stain, under a ruby cloak bordered with discs; in his left hand a book, in his right a paper. Below, pavement of black and white triangles and the name: . . . *emias;* blue background to canopy. The beginning of the name is defective and illegible, the part above an oblique repairing lead being modern and the lower (old) portion probably introduced from elsewhere to fill the blank.　　　　　　　　　　　Plate 67e

B7. AMOS. Blue hat, ermine-lined white cloak with border of foliage on wavy stem in yellow stain, robe purple. In his right hand a coiled scroll; his left hand swathed in the folds of his cloak. Pavement as in B6, with name: *amos* below; the canopy, with ruby background, has two tiers of ribbed vaulting.

B8. MICAH. Ruby cap, pale blue robe under white cloak with border in yellow stain of 'seaweed' leaves on alternate sides of a wavy band; in his left hand a book, in his right a folded paper. Pavement plain, with name: *micas;* two-tiered canopy as in B7, with blue background. Compare note on B5.

B9. EZEKIEL. He wears a ruby turban and robe and an ermine-lined cloak with a pattern of large 'slipped' trefoils on yellow-stain ground. In his left hand a book with chain clasp, in his right a crumpled paper. Blue background with white border. This prophet has no name-tablet but may plausibly be assumed to be Ezekiel.

　　　　　　　　　　　Plate 68d

B10. HALF-FIGURE OF A YOUNG MAN similar to B1 (from the same cartoon, reversed) and similarly coloured, but with a jewel of different design in his hat, which is more definitely painted to resemble felt.　　　　　　　　　　　Plate 67d

Dr. Mason comments that 'there can be little doubt' that this bust 'is a portrait of King Edward IV . . . It can only be conjectured who occupied the corresponding place on the left'. He gives no reason or authority for this assumption, which can hardly be accepted; the difficulty of a satisfactory identification for the companion figure, which Dr. Mason himself notices, points to the probability that both are conventional representations of a young scholar or lawyer.

C1. ST. THADDAEUS. Unlike all the other Apostles, he is bald, with plain-bordered halo. He wears a white cloak, richly patterned with large rosettes on hatched ground, amber stained, over a ruby robe; in his left hand a book with two clasps. Dark green background with column to the right and, above, a filling of rosettes like those on the robe; pavement of black and white triangles with name: *taddeus* and branching foliage below. The pane bearing the name is entire and modern; when Gostling wrote only . . . *deus* could be read—he expands in a footnote: 'I suppose Thaddeus'. On the fold of the mantle a painter's mark (a circle traversed by a bar, resembling the badge of London Transport) has been wiped out of the smear of thin grey pigment with which the glass is 'matted'.　　　　　　　　　　　Plate 69a

C2. ST. BARTHOLOMEW. His head, in profile, has a moustache in amber stain and a plain-bordered halo. His cloak is white with border of 'seaweed' foliage on a wavy stem, in yellow stain; in his left hand he holds a knife, instrument of his martyrdom, with a mark like the letter S, perhaps a painter's mark, on its curved blade. Background blue, pavement plain, with the name: *tholom* below; the name seems always to have been thus curtailed, since the slanting bands by which it is flanked have a pattern in yellow stain analogous to that filling the similar bands in all the companion lights in this row.   Plate 68f

C3. ST. JOHN THE EVANGELIST. He is seen in profile, beardless, with long wavy hair and a plain-bordered halo. Cloak murrey with border of yellow-stained discs over a white robe brocaded with a pattern of large rosettes and trefoils on a striped ground, similarly stained. He holds in his swathed left hand his emblem, a dragon in a chalice; he alone amongst the Apostle figures shows a bare foot appearing amongst herbage below his robe. Inscribed: *Iohes̄*. Background blue.   Plate 68e

C4. ST. ANDREW. Crocket-bordered halo, ruby robe with blue belt, white mantle with disc and cross-hatch in stain; below his beard are seen three small discs painted, on the same sheet of glass as his head and halo, in a deep tawny stain darker than that of the halo, produced by two applications and firings of the pigment. He stands with his saltire cross (heavily mottled with amber stain) in front of him on a pavement with a pattern of plain and cross-hatched stripes; below, the name: *andreas*. Murrey background.   Plate 68h

C5. ST. JAMES THE GREATER. He stands, holding in his left hand his pilgrim staff with a shell attached to it, among herbage with his name: *Iacob'* below. Halo stained solid in amber. Murrey robe, white mantle with border of discs and half-rosettes. Background blue. A painter's mark of a saltire cross is wiped out of the grey shading on the fold of his cloak hanging over his left arm.   Plate 68g

C6. ST. PETER. Halo with crocketed border in yellow stain, robe murrey (with buttons in front), cloak ruby with plain border stained to a deep amber, as is also his emblem, a key, held in his right hand. Blue background, pavement of cross-hatched and plain chequers with the name: *pieter* below. (For possible implications of the spelling of the name see above, p. 158.)   Plate 68b

C7. ST. PAUL. Halo similar to that of C6, white cloak with yellow-stained quatrefoils in the border, blue robe. He holds in his right hand the sword of his martyrdom, in his left, which is swathed in the folds of his cloak, a book. Background ruby, pavement as in C6, with the name: *paulus*.   Plate 68c

C8. ST. THOMAS. Plain halo, deep mazarine-blue cloak with plain yellow-stain border over white robe. He holds in his right hand the spear of his martyrdom, which has a yellow-stained shaft and a rivet securing the head; his left hand rests on his right wrist. The saint stands on grass rendered by wiping-out on a thin smear of enamel. Below, the name: *Thomas*.

C9. ST. PHILIP. A beardless figure with plain-bordered halo, murrey cloak with border (alternate white and yellow-stain discs) the same as on his white robe; he holds a yellow-stained cross-staff. Background behind the figure blue, above the canopy murrey. Pavement of plain and hatched chequers; name: *philippus*. Plate 69c

C10. ST. MATTHEW. Plain halo, white cloak with border of discs and half-rosettes over a blue robe. In his right hand he holds a halberd. Pavement of plain and cross-hatched chequers; name: *matheus*. The back of the head is a modern restoration.

(a) Arms of Archbishop
Becket
(b) Arms of the Prince of
Wales
about 1482
ROYAL WINDOW
pp. 170, 171

(a)

(c)

(a) Arms of Edward the
Confessor

(b) Arms of Viscount Wells

(c) Arms of Queen Elizabeth
Woodville

(d) Arms of Castile and Leon

about 1482

ROYAL WINDOW

pp. 171, 172

(b)

(c)

(a) Arms of Bourchier
   impaling Cambridge
(b) Arms of Bourchier
   impaling Fitzwarine
(c) Arms of Bourchier

about 1455

LADY CHAPEL

pp. 154, 155

76

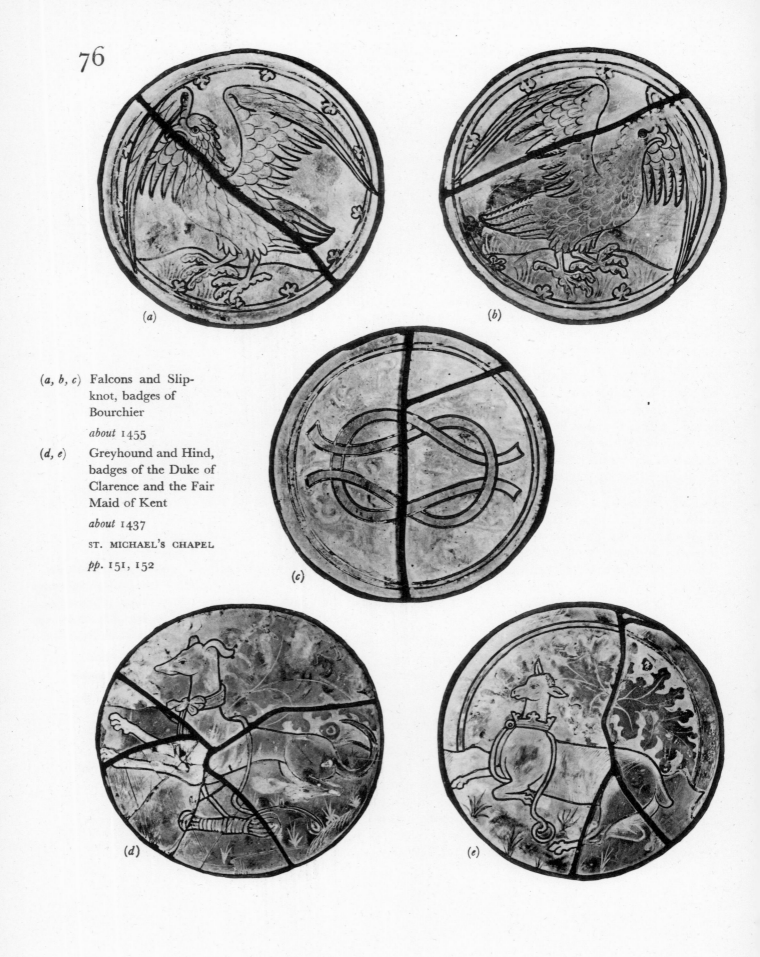

(*a*) (*b*)

(*a, b, c*) Falcons and Slip-
knot, badges of
Bourchier

about 1455

(*d, e*) Greyhound and Hind,
badges of the Duke of
Clarence and the Fair
Maid of Kent

about 1437

ST. MICHAEL'S CHAPEL

pp. 151, 152

(*c*)

(*d*) (*e*)

As Dr. Mason points out, there has here been a confusion between St. Matthew and St. Matthias; instead of a halberd, by which the latter suffered martyrdom, the emblem of St. Matthew should be a sword.

C11. ST. JAMES THE LESS. Halo with plain yellow-stained border. He wears his murrey yellow-bordered cloak thrown as a hood over his head, showing the white lining; white robe with border of discs partly changed at the bottom to a pattern of quatrefoils which is, however, not an extraneous insertion. He holds in his right hand a rolled parchment, in his left the fuller's club of his martyrdom. Background blue behind the figure, ruby above the canopy; pavement plain with name: *iacob' mini* below; the last three letters are an insertion from an inscription on a larger scale.

Plate 69b

C12. ST. SIMON. Yellow-stained halo with white border; deep mazarine-blue cloak with border of large flower-buds over a white robe, which has a border of circles shaded to look like large pearls. Pavement of white and cross-hatched chequers. His left hand clasps a fold of his cloak; in his right is the saw of his martyrdom. The apex of the light has been filled with a jumble of canopy fragments. The name, *S simon* (presumably for '*Sanctus Simon*') is a modern insertion made since Dr. Mason wrote his book (1925).

Plate 69d

D1. ST. DENIS. He stands on a pavement of black and white triangles, holding in his right hand his cross, in his left his mitred and haloed head, in reference to his decapitation; he is vested in a blue chasuble with orphrey of yellow-stained discs, white pall, and fringed ruby dalmatic below which is seen the white fringe of the tunic, over an alb with an apparel patterned with quatrefoils; an amice with pattern of discs encircles his headless neck. On a scroll below, his name: *S dionisius* and branching foliage. Background blue behind the canopy, green behind the figure. Plate 70a

D2. ST. WILFRED. He walks on grass (scratched through a smear of enamel and yellow stained), in his bare right hand a book, in his gloved left hand his episcopal cross. Amice with rosette-pattern, chasuble dark blue with orphrey of discs, fringed murrey dalmatic over which the end of his jewelled stole is seen, fringed white tunic, alb with orphrey painted with an oak-leaf in yellow stain. Background ruby of cherry-red tone. Name: *S Wilfridus* on scroll. This figure has been replaced here in recent times after having been removed to a window in the Water Tower (see p. 137).

Plate 70c

D3. ST. AUGUSTINE OF HIPPO. He holds his cross in his right hand, a book in his left. Chasuble ruby with orphrey of pearls, yellow-stained fringed dalmatic, fringed murrey tunic, alb with border of rosettes and foliage. Background blue. He stands among flowers reserved on a matt enamel. Name on scroll: *S augusein'* [sic], which is read erroneously by Dr. Mason as 'Augus: eps' (Gostling in his list gives 'S. Augus episc'.). Painter's mark on several panes: ∓.

Plate 70e

D4. ST. MARTIN. Cross in left hand, book in right. Amice with pattern of circles, chasuble ruby with plain orphrey, dalmatic blue with fringe, stole visible below his right arm, yellow-stained fringe of tunic showing over alb, which has an apparel of quatrefoil and cinquefoil pattern. Background murrey, pavement of chequers (cross-hatched with a white spot and yellow-stained with five spots in reserve), name: *martin'* (all but the first two letters modern) on scroll. Like D2, this figure has in recent times been brought back from the Water Tower.

Plate 70b

D5. ST. JEROME. He has a gold-rayed halo, and is vested as a Cardinal, in deep ruby hat, ruby mantle of lighter tone with amice having a pattern of discs, over a white robe with border of large discs and crowns in yellow stain. In his left hand he holds a book, in his right a fold of his mantle. Blue background (partly missing and replaced with a fragment of ruby drapery), pavement of plain-stained and hatched triangles. Name on scroll: *Hieronymus*. A painter's mark (т, sometimes reversed) appears on several of the panes forming the pavement. Plate 70f

D6. ST. DUNSTAN. In his right hand a book, in his left his cross; tasselled gloves. Amice with design of discs, white pall, murrey chasuble with jewelled orphrey, disc-embroidered stole, fringed blue dalmatic, fringed tunic over alb with apparel of discs. Ruby background. He stands among herbage and flowers rendered as in D3; name: *S dunstan'* on scroll (Gostling unaccountably gives the inscription as '. . . us'). Painter's mark on several panes: ∓ or ⊥. Plate 69h

D7. ST. THOMAS OF CANTERBURY. His vestments are similar to those of St. Dunstan (D6) except that his chasuble is blue and his dalmatic murrey, and no tunic is visible. He holds his cross in his right hand and in his left a scroll. Background murrey behind the canopy, ruby behind the figure. He stands on a pavement of tiles decorated alternately with sexfoils and with five spots reserved and yellow-stained on a grey matt ground. Name: *S thomas* on scroll. Painter's mark: ∓ on many of the panes, both white and coloured.

Dr. Mason comments: 'The place of honour in the middle under St. Peter and St. Paul is given to 7, Thomas, and 8, Gregorius. Thus, in spite of Culmer, St. Thomas still looks down on the place of his martyrdom.'

Reproduction: *C.C.C.*, No. 42 (October 1947), pl. facing p. 24. Plate 69g

D8. ST. GREGORY THE GREAT. He is vested in the papal triple crown, amice with disc-pattern, ruby chasuble with spotted orphrey, pall, tasselled gloves, stole, fringed blue dalmatic over fringed tunic, alb with quatrefoil-patterned apparel. He holds a book in his right hand, his cross in his left. Background ruby behind canopy, murrey behind figure. The pavement on which he stands has alternately five spots and a fleur-de-lis reserved and yellow-stained on grey matt ground. Scroll inscribed *S gregorius*; the pavement continued below it in place of foliage. Painter's mark on several panes: ∓. Plate 70h

D9. ST. AUGUSTINE OF CANTERBURY. Cross in right hand, left raised in blessing. Chasuble ruby with orphrey of pearls, white fringed dalmatic, fringed murrey tunic, alb with border of discs. He stands among flowers like St. Dunstan (D5). Background blue. Name on scroll: *S augustinus*. Painter's mark: ≡ on lining of chasuble and on tunic. Plate 69e

D10. ST. ANSELM. Cross in left hand, right hand raised in blessing. Chasuble pale murrey without orphreys, disc-patterned amice, pall, fringed ruby dalmatic (no tunic visible), alb with apparel decorated with quatrefoils and crowns in yellow stain. He stands among flowers similar to those of D5. Background above the pinnacles murrey, between them blue, behind the figure blue (the ruby glass to the left of the head, coming next to the dalmatic of the same colour, is doubtless a restorer's insertion). Name on scroll: *S ancelm'*. Painter's mark on several panes (white and coloured): ±.

D11. ST. NICHOLAS. Amice with disc-pattern, chasuble ruby with orphrey set with pearls, fringed white dalmatic with cinquefoil pattern, below which shows the fringe of the tunic, alb with wide border of disc-pattern. In his right hand he holds a pastoral staff with foliated crook, in his left a book. Background murrey. He stands on a pavement of chequers, cross-hatched, and yellow-stained with a rosette scratched in reserve on matt enamel. Name on scroll: *S nicholaus*. Painter's mark at end of pall: ⚏.

Plate 70g

D12. ST. BLAZE. Cross in left hand, book in right. Amice with disc-pattern. Chasuble murrey with plain white border, fringed ruby dalmatic with white fringe of tunic below, and alb with plain apparel interrupting a border of cinquefoils. Background ruby. He stands among flowers and herbage scratched through matt enamel. Name on label: *S blasius*. On nearly every pane in this panel except in the canopy and head is a painter's mark (a small cross, +).

D13. ST. ALPHEGE. Cross in right hand, left hand raised with all fingers extended as if in exposition. Amice with disc-pattern, chasuble murrey with plain white border, pall, fringed white dalmatic over ruby fringe of tunic, alb with double border of discs interrupted by a plain apparel. Background behind canopy blue, behind figure ruby. He stands among flowers, like those of St. Blaze (D12), but continued below the scroll with the name (*S abplegus*) in place of the usual branching leaves. A painter's mark: ⚏ on several panes.

Plate 69f

D14. ST. AUDOEN*. Book in right hand (apparently gloveless—the fingernails are clearly shown), cross in left. Amice with disc-pattern, chasuble murrey with plain white border, pall, fringed ruby dalmatic, tunic with yellow-stained fringe, alb with apparel of cinquefoil-pattern. The glove on his left hand shows a round bob instead of the usual tassel. Background ruby. He stands among flowers and herbage, as in D12. Name on scroll: *S audoen'*. A painter's mark: ⚏ (on the ruby ground as well as on white glass).

Plate 70d

MAIN LIGHTS

The main lights are divided by transoms into three ranges, with seven lights in each. They have been bordered, probably when the glass was rearranged after the mutilation of the window, with narrow coloured strips composed of a great variety of fragments some of which probably came from the destroyed panels, others being introduced from various other windows. Among the former are many fragments of the *rose en soleil* badge of Edward IV, particularly in the middle light of the upper range. Le Couteur comments: 'These suns are chiefly set in blue glass, diapered in like manner to the blue half-curtain behind Prince Edward. Judging by this it would seem that some of the figures in the top row were set against backgrounds powdered with Edward IV's badge'. A few of the other fragments are interesting enough for special mention as follows:

Upper range. 1st light. A piece (set sideways) with, apparently, the leg of a man in a landscape (all in black).
Fragments of battlements and pinnacles, fifteenth century.
Fleurs-de-lis.

---

* Sir Harold Idris Bell has pointed out to the Author that this saint (Ouen, of Rouen) is sometimes confused with the Welsh Owen (Eugenius).

Parts of two lions abraded from ruby glass and yellow-stained, probably from the Royal arms, and several similar pieces.

Middle range. 5th light (above portraits). A bunch of grapes some of which are white, others yellow-stained, late fifteenth century.

2nd light (below portraits). A piece of traceried window from a canopy.

3rd light (below portraits). Part of a support for an angel like those still remaining with shields.

Fragments of pavements of black and white triangles.

6th light. Part of a fifteenth-century quarry with a primrose plant.

A fragment inscribed *quarto* in black between two yellow-stained bands.

A small piece inscribed in black *de xt* (probably for *de Christ*[*o*]).

The cusped heads of the upper range of lights are filled with half-figures of angels holding in front of them various shields of arms (of which only some have the 'field' diapered with patterns painted in black or scratched through a thin wash of matt grey enamel). All the angels have amber-stained hair and wings, the latter painted with 'peacock's eyes'; only E3 and E6 have original heads, with 'needle-point' work in the hair, the remainder being later restorations of inferior execution. It is note-worthy that these panels of glass are not cusped, but in the shape of a plain ogee-pointed arch; the cusps in the masonry are carved only on the inner surface of the tracery and not on the outside, partly concealing the glass, which thus also appears to be of cusped outline when seen from the inside. The backgrounds have clouds and stars wiped out of the matt enamel with which the coloured glass is coated.

E1. ANGEL with arms of St. George (Argent a cross gules); field of the shield dia-pered with scratched circles. Ruby background much patched. This shield has been replaced as it was when Gostling wrote, in substitution for the arms of the Dean and Chapter. Plate 72a

E2. ANGEL with arms of Guldeford, *alias* Guildford (Argent—incorrectly, for or—a saltire and four martlets sable) quartering Halden (Argent a chief sable over all a bend engrailed gules); field of the shield diapered with scratched feathery scrollwork. Murrey background. Probably in reference to Sir Henry Guldeford, K.G. (see p. 138).

It will be noticed that this panel has been cut down, the shield being larger than the others and lacking its point; it must have belonged originally to the head of a light in the middle or lower ranges. Dr. Mason comments: 'Gostling, in whose time it was already here, says that it had taken the place of one which was, vert, three crowns, or. I cannot find whose coat this was. The Needlemakers have the same blazon but the crowns are argent.' Plate 72b

E3. ANGEL with the arms of Thomas Becket as Archbishop: The See of Canterbury, as in A2, except that the cross-staff is entirely gold, impaling Becket (Argent three beckets or choughs sable); field of the dexter half diapered with scratched circles, of the sinister with rosettes on a hatched ground painted in black outline. Background ruby. When Dr. Mason wrote, the personal arms were 'on the wrong side'; the shield has since been reversed. Gostling comments: 'As this was the bearing of Becket, here was probably his effigies' (*i.e.,* in the same light, below). Plate 73a

E4. ANGEL with the shield of the Holy Trinity, Gules an orle and pall argent con-joined and surmounted of four plates occupying the dexter and sinister chief and the

52' 0" × 24' 0"

Plate XIX

QUEEN ELIZABETH WOODVILLE. Panel
(H.5) in one of the main lights of the North (Royal)
Window of the North-West Transept. About 1482.
P. 174.

base and fess points respectively, the first inscribed 'Pater', the second 'Filius', and the third 'Spiritus Sanctus', the centre 'Deus', the connecting portions of the orle between them having the words 'non est', and those of the pall 'est'. Background ruby.

Gostling describes the shield as having 'the monkish device of the Trinity'; he is undoubtedly right in supposing that beneath it, in the middle light of the upper range, was 'the representation of God the Father, and of Christ, besides a large crucifix and the picture of the Holy Ghost in the form of a Dove, mentioned by Culmer, p. 2'.

E5. ANGEL with the arms of St. Edward the Confessor (as patron of the donor, Edward IV), Azure a cross paty and five marlets or. Background ruby. Owing to difficulties in leading, the cross has the appearance of being botonny rather than paty; Gostling erroneously describes the field as 'gules'.   Plate 74a

E6. ANGEL with the arms of Lord (afterwards Viscount) Wells, husband of Princess Cicely, Azure the framework over a well or. Background murrey. The well-head is painted in yellow stain of various tones on white glass; the field of the shield is in notably pale blue glass.   Plate 74b

E7. ANGEL with the arms of the Priory of Christ Church, Canterbury (as on p. 142). The shield is a modern insertion, in place of the broken shield described by Gostling* as having still remaining on it 'the foot of the T, or St. Anthony's cross with which the field was charged'; this had already disappeared when the window was overhauled in 1879.† Dr. Mason speaks mistakenly of the modern shield as that of the See of Canterbury.

Halfway down this tier of lights is now the row of complete figures of angels kneeling which originally occupied the foot of the lowest range of lights, below the portraits of the royal persons whose shields they support in front of them. The angels have yellow-stained hair; their pinion-feathers are white, painted in yellow or amber stain and black with 'peacock's eyes', the under side of the wings being in variously coloured 'potmetal'; the heads are original, with fine 'needle-point' work in the curls, only in F1, F2 and F3, the remainder being later restorations with painting of inferior quality. They kneel on pavements of various designs. The backgrounds are variously coloured and painted with a large brocade-pattern of rosettes surrounded by rays and crossed lozenges, either in outline or reserved on a grey matt ground.

F1. ANGEL with the arms of the Duke of York, France modern quartering England with a label of three pieces argent. Wings ruby underneath, plain alb, background green; the pavement shows a pattern of Ss in circles inscribed within squares. The nine torteaux with which the label is normally charged in the Duke of York's blazon are here omitted.

F2. ANGEL with the arms of the Prince of Wales (identical with those of the Duke of York, F1); he is vested in an alb under a cape with gold-stained orphreys showing a pattern of rosettes in circles; wings blue underneath. Pavement with pattern of quatrefoils in squares, background violet.   Plate 73b

F3. ANGEL with the Royal arms, France Modern quartering England. His vestments are similar to those of F2, but with a lozenge-shaped morse for the cope instead of a

* In the 2nd (1777) edition.
† Information of Mr. Samuel Caldwell.

strap; wings blue underneath, pavement in squares painted with mock lettering, background murrey. No trace remains of the 'fleur-de-lis irradiated' which, according to Gostling, was embroidered on the bottom of the angel's garment on the right side; it has presumably been removed in subsequent restorations, and it is questionable whether it rightly belonged in this position and may not have been introduced from elsewhere.   Colour Plate XVIII

Reproduction: *F.C.C. Seventh Annual Report*, January 1934, pl. facing p. 36.

F4. ANGEL with a shield of arms, Gules three crowns in pale or. Over his robe is a stole, amber-stained and painted with crosslets in black, crossed over his breast; wings ruby underneath, pavement with pattern of bordered squares, background blue. Dr. Mason quotes Willement as the authority for the ascription of the arms to King Ethelred, but comments that they 'might be intended for King Arthur (see Papworth's *Ordinary*, p. 593)'.

F5. ANGEL with the arms of Queen Elizabeth Woodville, France Modern quartering England, impaling Quarterly of six pieces three in chief and three in base, 1 Argent a lion rampant queue forchée gules (Luxemburg), 2 Quarterly, 1 and 4 Gules a star argent, 2 and 3 Azure semy of fleurs-de-lis or (Baux), 3 Barry of ten argent and azure over all a lion rampant gules (Lusignan Kings of Cyprus), 4 Gules three bendlets argent, a chief party per fess argent, charged with a rose gules, and or (Orsini), 5 Gules three pallets vair, on a chief or a label of five points azure (St. Paul), 6 Argent a fess and a canton gules (Woodville). The angel's robe is plain, wings ruby underneath, pavement with indistinct geometrical pattern, background green. Gostling quotes Sandford in explanation of the Queen's blazon: Peter Earl of St. Paul surnamed of Luxemburg, was her mother's father, her grandmother was Margaret, daughter of Francis de Baux, Duke of Andree,* her great grandmother was Susan, daughter of Count Orsini and wife of Guy of Luxemburg, the Queen's great-grandfather. 'Thus, says he, were these several coats marshalled for the honour of this Queen, to show the illustrious nobility of her maternal descent (and impaled in the royal escutcheon with those of King Edward IV, who first of all our Kings married his subject)'. When Gostling wrote, this shield had changed places with that of F6.   Plate 74c

F6. ANGEL with the arms of Castile and Leon, Quarterly, 1 and 4 Gules, a castle or, 2 and 3 Argent a lion rampant purpure. Plain robe, wings ruby underneath, pavement similar to that of E4, background blue. 'These arms were borne in right of Edmund of Langley Duke of York, greatgrandfather of Edward IV, whose first wife was Isabel, the younger daughter and coheir of Peter King of Castile and Leon' (Gostling). Murrey 'potmetal' is employed for the lions in the shield. Plate 74d

F7. ANGEL with arms of Mortimer quartering De Burgh, Quarterly, 1 and 4 Barry of eight or and azure and a chief or with two pales and two girons azure thereon and an inescutcheon argent over all (Mortimer), 2 and 3, Or a cross gules (De Burgh). Over the white robe a long crossed stole decorated with crosslets as on E4; wings ruby underneath, pattern of pavement indistinct, background green.

Unlike the upper range of main lights the two lower have lost the original filling of their heads, doubtless half-figures of angels with shields like those at E. In place

---

* *Sic*, Andria in Apulia.

of them have been inserted, within the cusping, detached shields brought from other parts of the building and having no direct relevance to the window.

G1. SHIELD of white glass painted in black and yellow stain with a mitre (with *infulae*) with a crozier behind it and a stone below (in the base of the shield) and, on either side, in Gothic lettering, G (or T) *pⁱ*. This appears to be the rebus of Thomas Goldstone I, Prior of Christ Church 1449–1468; a similar rebus, but with *three* gilt stones (seen on Bell Harry Tower and on Christ Church Gateway), was used by his namesake who was Prior from 1495 to 1517. The shield is at present set inside out.

G2. SHIELD with the arms of Archbishop Becket (See of Canterbury impaling Becket (as in E3, except that the cross-staff is argent, with cross or)).

G3. SHIELD with the arms of Bourchier quartering Louvaine (as in A2).

G4. SHIELD with the Royal arms (as in A1).

G5. SHIELD (modern) with the arms of the Priory of Christ Church (as in E7).

G6. SHIELD with the arms of Henry Despenser, Bishop of Norwich (1370–1406), Quarterly, Argent and gules fretty or over all a baton sable within a bordure azure charged with mitres or. Commander Messenger has pointed out that the same arms are carved on a ceiling-boss of the North Aisle of the Nave.

G7. SHIELD with the arms of Molleins (Paly wavy of six or and gules). Katherine, daughter of Lord Molleins, married Sir John Howard, 1st Duke of Norfolk.

The royal portraits show a general uniformity of arrangement with differences in detail. All the figures are kneeling at prayer-desks, the King and his sons facing right, the Queen and Princesses facing left; behind them, hung from a board with carved Gothic cresting, are curtains divided vertically, half with a brocade pattern of King Edward's badge of the *rose en soleil,* painted in black enamel, half (except in H6 and H7) with the badges of the respective persons. Only the figures of the King and Queen retain the original heads, which after having been removed to the Deanery, were restored to their proper places with the consent of Dean Wace.

H1. RICHARD DUKE OF YORK, second son of Edward IV. The place of the face, which is modern, was in Gostling's time occupied by a mitred head. The Duke's patterned mantle is murrey-coloured with ermine cape and border over a white robe with brocade-pattern in amber stain. He kneels on a blue cushion. The desk is carved with Gothic tracery. The curtain behind him is divided vertically, half ruby with a pattern of rosettes in reserve, half diapered with the Duke's badge of 'a Falcon rising on the wing within a fetterlock somewhat open' (Gostling) in yellow stain on white glass. Inscription: *Ricardus dux Eboraci secundus filius Edwardi quarti.*

Gostling comments: 'Sandford says that on St. George's day 1466, the King determined that his second son should bear . . . for his badge a falcon volant silver membred with two sewels gold with a fetterlock unlocked and somewhat open gold; but the falcons here were gold. This device Camden (in his remains page 215) tells us he gave in memory of his great grandfather Edmund Langley, the 5th son of King Edward III, who gave for his device a falcon in a fetterlock closed, having then no near hope of the crown, but his descendant, Edward IV, having obtained the crown, gave now the fetterlock open.'   Plate 72c

H2. EDWARD PRINCE OF WALES (afterwards King Edward V). His face (modern) was formerly replaced by 'the fair face of a mitred saint' (Gostling). He is robed similarly to the Duke of York; his desk also has somewhat similar carving. Blue cushion. The curtain is divided, half blue with the rose brocade-pattern, half again divided vertically white and green, with the Prince's badge of a single ostrich feather and a scroll inscribed with the motto *Ic dien*, either painted in black on the white glass or inset in white leaded glass on the green ground. Inscribed: *Edwardus princeps Wallie primus filius Edwardi quarti.*

Reproduction: *F.C.C., Sixth Annual Report,* 1933, pl. facing p. 27.   Plate 72d

H3. KING EDWARD IV. His white robe has a pattern in yellow stain; over it the mantle is ruby, with ermine cape and border. He holds in his clasped hands a sceptre with jewelled head. Blue cushion. On the side of his prayer-desk is a standing figure of St. George killing the dragon. The curtain is half ruby, half murrey, set with the *rose en soleil* badge, white, with amber-stained rays. Inscribed: *Edwardus dei gracia Rex anglie et francie et dominus hibernie.*

The head, unlike those of the King's family at Little Malvern, has every appearance of faithful portraiture; it may be compared with the panel portrait of the King, apparently at an earlier age and fuller in the cheeks, belonging to the Society of Antiquaries.

Reproductions: Westlake, Vol. III pl. XL*a*; Read, pl. 54; *F.C.C., Sixth Annual Report* (1933), pl. facing p. 34.   Plate 71

H4*a, b.* In the presumed place of the original Crucifix are now the panels described on pp. 178 183.

H5. ELIZABETH WOODVILLE, Queen Consort of Edward IV. She wears a crown of crosses (incorrectly described by Gostling as 'patée') and fleurs-de-lis, a chain necklace, a white dress with embroidered or brocade pattern in yellow stain, and a ruby mantle with borders of ermine; a cross hangs by a chain from her girdle. She kneels on a blue cushion. The desk is carved with Gothic panelling. The curtain is half diapered ruby, half blue, set with green sprigs (described by Gostling as broomstalks) each with an open ruby flower between two buds tipped with ruby (the badge of Margaret of Anjou taken on from her by the Queen, who had been her Maid of Honour); Canon Crum suggests that this flower is 'some crimson dianthus on a green calyx'. Inscribed: *Regina Elizabetha consors Edwardi dei gracia Regis.*

The face was already cracked in Gostling's time; he states further: 'The desk has been broken and ill patched up, as has the Queen's neck and hair, which have been ridiculously filled up with an arm and up-lifted hand placed so as to touch her left cheek'.

Reproduction: Read, pl. 54.   Colour Plate XIX

H6. PRINCESSES ELIZABETH (afterwards Queen of Henry VII), CICELY (married about fourteen to John, Lord (afterwards Viscount) Wells), AND ANNE (who married Thomas Howard, second Duke of Norfolk). They wear coronets set with pearls, close-fitting ermine-trimmed diapered purple dresses, and chain girdles. Green cushion, carved desk, curtain half ruby, half blue. Inscribed: *Dn̄a Elizabeth prima filia Edwardi quarti Dn̄a Cecilia scda filio Edwardi quarti Dn̄a Anna tertia filia Edwardi quarti.*

Reproduction (in colours): *F.C.C., Sixth Annual Report* (1933), frontispiece.

(a)

(b)

(a) Arms of Bishop Warham

WATER TOWER CORRIDOR

Early 16th CENTURY

p. 177

(b) Arms of Archbishop Grindal

about 1576

p. 183

(a)

(b)

(a) Royal Arms of England
Early 16th CENTURY
WATER TOWER CORRIDOR
p. 177

(b) Rebus of Prior Thomas
Goldwell
about 1517
pp. 178, 179

(a)

(b)

(a) Arms of Archbishop
     Abbot
(b) Arms of Damaris Kingsley
     about 1620
     LIBRARY CORRIDOR
     p. 184

80

St. Maurice and St. Henry
(or Charlemagne), with
the arms of St. Augustine's
Abbey, Canterbury.

Rhenish, *early* 16th
CENTURY
ROYAL WINDOW

pp. 179–182

H7. PRINCESSES KATHERINE (who married William Courtenay, Earl of Devonshire) AND MARY ('promised to the King of Denmark but never married, for she died 1482'—Gostling). Their costume and the curtain are similar to those of their sisters (in H6). The cushion is blue; the Gothic panelling of the desk is in relief against a seeded ground. Inscribed: *Dña Katherina septima filia Edwardi quarti Dña Maria quinta filia Edwardi quarti.*

The figures in H6 and H7 have been extensively restored since Gostling wrote. He comments: 'Her face [that of Princess Elizabeth] is gone, but supplied by one of a smaller-sized person . . . The second has on her neck a white head-kerchief bordered with an open gold lace falling over the shoulders. The third has no pearls in her coronet. The fourth has lost her head, which has been supplied by a man's head and neck, with light hair and an ermined collar close up to the chin, below which the princess's golden locks flow over her shoulders. The man's head seems of the same workmanship with the other figures here. The coronet over this lady's head is lost.' The original head of one of the princesses was at one time exhibited on loan from the late A. L. Radford in the Victoria and Albert Museum. Dr. Mason comments: 'It is perhaps merely a mistake made when the figures were shifted, or later, that the two ladies should be in this order'.

The lowest range of lights retains none of its original glass. Shields have been inserted in the cusped heads as at G, and also, in isolation, in the middle of the three midmost lights (the arrangement in both cases was altered since Dr. Mason wrote his account of the window).

I1. SHIELD with the arms of Archbishop Becket (as in G2).

I2. SHIELD with the personal arms of Archbishop Thomas Arundel (d. 1413), Quarterly within a bordure engrailed argent, 1 and 4, Gules a lion rampant or (Fitzalan), 2 and 3, Checky or and azure (Warenne).

I3. SHIELD with the arms presumably of Archbishop John Stafford (1443–1452), Or a chevron gules with a mitre argent thereon. Archbishop Stafford's shield usually has a bordure engrailed sable, but the omission may be compared with a similar case in a shield of Archbishop Arundel on a boss of the Great Cloister (Messenger, p. 76, No. 9/21).

I4. SHIELD with the arms of Fitzalan quartering Warenne (as in I2).

I5. SHIELD with arms unidentified, Or a pile indented and voided gules.

I6. SHIELD with the arms perhaps of Sherley or Solers, Paly of six or and azure, over all a bend gules.

I7. SHIELD with arms unidentified, Paly argent and azure over all three escutcheons of pretence or. (The blazoning of this shield is indistinct.)

K1, K3. ANGELS with shields, probably from Archbishop Warham's Chantry (see p. 176).

K2. SHIELD with the arms of Scott of Scot's Hall, Argent three Catherine wheels sable within a bordure gules. When Miss Williams and Dr. Mason wrote, this shield, shown by its shape and style to be of the sixteenth century, occupied the position of I5.

§21 Crypt, South Aisle

IN a window of the South Aisle of the Crypt beneath the Choir have been inserted four small panels of white painted glass dating from the late fifteenth century; each originally consisted of a medallion enclosed within a large lozenge with cusped foliage filling the points.

1. HERALDIC FIVE-PETALLED ROSE, with sepals painted in yellow stain. Medallion set in a lozenge made up of fragments with stems.　　　　　　Plate 58b

2. QUARRY, with yellow-stained portcullis, one of the badges of the Tudors introduced by King Henry VII in 1485. Set in a medallion with a circle in yellow stain on a ground of scroll foliage wiped out of a thin 'smear' of grey, the medallion itself enclosed within a large lozenge with foliage in the points.　　　　Plate 58d

3. QUARRY with yellow-stained rebus of Archbishop John Morton (1486–1501): an eagle (the emblem of St. John the Evangelist) wearing an archiepiscopal pallium, standing on a barrel ('ton') inscribed in black-letter *mor*. Setting as in No. 2 above.　　　　　　Plate 58e

4. THE *Agnus Dei* holding a cross, couched among trefoils and grass against a background of rectangular diaper. Medallion set in a lozenge with foliage.　　Plate 58a

§13 Glass formerly in
Archbishop Warham's Chantry

IN 1507 Archbishop Warham built for himself a small chantry chapel outside the north wall of the North-West Transept, behind the tomb in which he was buried when he died in 1533. This chantry was pulled down at some date before the printing of the edition published in London in 1729 of Archbishop Matthew Parker's *De Antiquitate Britannicae Ecclesiae;* a plate facing p. 488 of that book shows a blocked-up doorway at the back of the tomb. It may be taken as certain that two panels now at K1 and K3 in the Royal Window (see p. 175), with figures of angels holding shields, were originally in the windows of this chantry; their style is entirely in conformity with the date of its erection. Both angels have blue wings with murrey

176

undersides and stand on a pavement in white and yellow stain. The shield, later in date, now in the corridor to the Water Tower (see below) may have been a later addition to the glazing of this chantry.

1. ANGEL with the arms of William Warham as Archbishop, See of Canterbury (as in II1, p. 137), impaling Warham, Gules a fess or in chief a goat's head couped argent horned or in base three cockle-shells argent.

2. ANGEL with the arms of Thomas Arundel as Archbishop (See of Canterbury, as in II1, p. 137, impaling Arundel, as in I2, p. 175).

§14 West Window of Corridor to Water Tower

IN this window have been inserted two heraldic panels described below, given to the Cathedral in 1946 by Miss Catherine Athill, to whose grandfather, the Ven. Archdeacon B. F. Smith, they were given by Dean Farrar. They date from the first half of the sixteenth century. They were originally in the Chapter House, whence they were removed to make room for Dean Farrar's arms.

1. ROYAL ARMS, France Modern quartering England. Shield surmounted by a royal crown painted in silver-yellow stain of amber tone on white glass and enclosed within rose-branches in green glass with ruby roses. The lilies in the first and fourth quarters are in yellow glass leaded into holes ground out of the blue glass field; in the second and third quarters the lions are abraded in the ruby 'flash' and painted with silver-yellow stain. The panel is of early-sixteenth century date.   Plate 78a

2. ARMS OF ARCHBISHOP WILLIAM WARHAM (1503–1533), (as above, except that the entire head of the cross in the arms of the See is of amber-coloured glass without the white pearls in its angles, and its lower extremity is of the same piece of white glass as the pall, which is charged with *three*, not two, crosses). The Warham charges are abraded out of the ruby glass of the field, the horns of the goat being painted in silver-yellow stain. The fields and the fesse are diapered with leafy scrolls. The shield is flanked by monsters and scrollwork painted in yellow stain on white, of early Renaissance character, indicating a date about 1520; the whole is enclosed by a border of green glass. Above the shield is a scroll with the inscription: *Auxilium me̅u̅ a d̅n̅o̅* ('My help [cometh] from the Lord', *Psalm* CXXI, 2).   Plate 77a

§15 Tudor Glass

ROYAL ARMS as borne by Henry VII and Henry VIII: Quarterly, France Modern and England (as at 5(*a*), p. 130), supported by a dragon gules and a greyhound argent collared or, with motto *Dieu et Mon Droit* in black-letter on a white ribbon below and royal crown of four arches above. The heraldic shield is set on a scalloped and fluted shield of the type that became common with the introduction of the fluted armour first made by Conrad Seusenhofer, the armourer of the Emperor Maximilian I; it is in golden-brown 'potmetal', serving (as Mr. Caldwell has pointed out) to detach the blue of the heraldic quarterings from the blue background of the panel which, like the blue quarters, is diapered with feathery scrollwork scratched through a coating of grey enamel. The eyes and fangs of the dragon are shown in white by abrasion of the 'flash' of the ruby glass. The panel has a border of white roses at intervals on a ruby band at the top, of gold crowns and ruby at the sides. An interesting point of technique is the use of a few slight smears of grey enamel on the reverse (outer) side to temper the colour, especially on the greyhound.

This panel (or at least the lower part of it) was placed in its present position, at H4*b* in the Royal window (see p. 174), after the publication of Gostling's 2nd edition (1777); its former location is unrecorded. It appears that the upper part of it, with the crown, may be the 'very large crown' over 'the arms of the prior [*i.e.* the Dean and Chapter] irradiated' which Gostling describes as filling this position. The date of the panel is probably about 1500; the dragon and the greyhound supporters were used by both Henry VII and Henry VIII, but the style is rather that of the first King's reign. Colour Plate XXa

§16 Miscellaneous Late Gothic Glass

ST. CHRISTOPHER. Part of a panel of the first half of the fifteenth century or slightly earlier, painted in black and yellow stain, the figure in reserve against a solid black background. The saint, wearing a cloak thrown as a hood over his head, is wading barefoot with a staff in his left hand and the Child Christ supported on his right shoulder. The Child, with nimbus divided by a foliated cross and close-fitting sleeved gown, stretches out His left hand in benediction above the head of the saint; His gown is ornamented with small black discs on which a quatrefoil is scratched with a needle point. Plate 65

REBUS OF PRIOR THOMAS GOLDWELL. Roundel painted in black and yellow stain of amber tone with the monogram *T G* above two octagonal well-heads. On a scroll above is the inscription in black-letter: *Q̄ue pictura Docet rigidos hic ex pu . . . euros.* Sir Ellis Minns has kindly supplied a brilliant solution, and surely the right one, of a puzzle caused by the flaking of the glass which had defeated other authorities; to fill the lacuna he reads *expulit euros* ('It is he who is meant by the picture that has

178

(a)

52′ 0″ × 24′ 0″

Plate XX

(a) ROYAL ARMS OF ENGLAND, as borne
by the Tudor sovereigns. Panel (H.4*b*) inserted
in the North (Royal) Window of the North-
West Transept (its original location is unknown). About 1500. Pp. 174, 178.

(b) ARMS OF HUMPHREY BOHUN, EARL
OF HEREFORD (d. 1372), who married
Joan (d. 1419), daughter of Richard Fitzalan,
Earl of Arundel. Shield inserted in Window III
of the Water Tower. About 1410. P. 138.